To Mamaw and Papaw
from Billy and Barbara

Christmas 1996

EightySomething

EightySomething

*Interviews With Octogenarians
Who Stay Involved*

by Louis Mucciolo

A Birch Lane Press Book
Published by Carol Publishing Group

A Birch Lane Press Book
Published by Carol Publishing Group
Birch Lane is a registered trademark of Carol Communications, Inc.
Editorial Offices: 600 Madison Avenue, New York, N.Y. 10022
Sales and Distribution Offices: 120 Enterprise Avenue, Secaucus, N.J. 07094
In Canada: Canadian Manda Group, P.O. Box 920, Station U, Toronto,
    Ontario M8Z 5P9
Queries regarding rights and permissions should be addressed to Carol
Publishing Group, 600 Madison Avenue, New York, N.Y. 10022

Carol Publishing Group books are available at special discounts for bulk
purchases, for sales promotions, fund-raising, or educational purposes.
Special editions can be created to specifications. For details, contact Special
Sales Department, Carol Publishing Group, 120 Enterprise Avenue,
Secaucus, N.J. 07094

Manufactured in the United States of America
10 9 8 7 6 5 4 3 2 1

Library of Congress Cataloging-in-Publication Data

Mucciolo, Louis.
    EightySomething : interviews with octogenarians who stay
involved / by Louis Mucciolo.
        p.   cm.
    ISBN 1-55972-149-9
        1. Aged—United States—Interviews. 2. Self-realization in old
age—United States. I. Title.
[HQ1064.U5MB   1992]
305.26'0973—dc20   92-28224
                                                                 CIP

This one is for the grandkids—
Aaron, Danielle, Michael, Adam, and Theodore.

May they never lose their curiosity and interest
in all that surrounds them.

My heartfelt thanks to all those who
shared their memories and their active
todays. They were gracious, patient, and
generous with their time. I enjoyed every
moment of my visits with them. And
there was an additional bonus—their
vitality was indeed inspirational.
LM

CONTENTS

PREFACE

THOSE demographic studies that shouted the end of the baby boom, the rapidly increasing number of seniors, the upcoming shortage of youthful workers, and the need to welcome immigrants with special skills—they didn't send me flying, one way or another.

But there was one statistic, not long ago, that proclaimed the fastest-growing population segment in the United States today was that of eighty-five-year-olds. In 1900, there were only 100,000 people in that age group—today, over three million! Fantastic, was my first thought. Then, maybe not, as visions of wheelchairs, canes, crutches, nursing homes, and sparkling white angels of mercy crowded out that initial wonder.

Soon, other thoughts intruded. Statistics were just numbers; who were the *people* behind those figures? Why the elongation of the life span? Was it medical advances, changed lifestyles, health technology, or just happenstance? Octogenarians—what had their lives been all about? Were any of them still active?

That's when I thought about my remarkable mother, who had made it to her ninetieth year before leaving us. In her eighties, she was *still* active. Then her meals for family gatherings were both memorable and gustatory delights. Her absorption with the afternoon "soaps" and her retention of each character's convoluted trials and tribulations left us constantly amazed. The interest in family activities and her immediate surroundings never flagged, and sage advice, if welcomed, was always available. Later, sad to say, the sparks were dimmed and then extinguished.

All this reminded me that a relative had visited her (at eighty-seven), and tape-recorded some of her early memories. It had been fun for Mother, but for some unknown reason no one had asked to hear a playback at the time. Not long ago, I called that relative and asked for the tape. "Oh," she apologized, "I wouldn't know where to dig it out, it's been put away with *all those yesterdays.*"

In retrospect, I guess that's when it all started. The tape finally came, and it was an absolute delight and awesome wonder to hear Mother's voice again. The flow of my own memories that it stimulated was remarkable. All readers should record their elders now, before the opportunity vanishes. You won't regret it.

The taped interview alternated between her native Italian and her acquired English—depending upon the degree of excitement and sorrow. Anecdotal capsules recaptured her confusion at arriving in America, her teenage impressions, the wonder of an unusual courtship. A man she had never met, who nonetheless insisted he was going to marry her, because his first sight of her had created an infatuation. Then their actual marriage and the raising of a family—all the hard times and the good ones. Her voice was youthful and excited as she relived the early days, sober and mature as she recounted some of the other indelible events in later days.

These were fascinating memories for a son, but also, perhaps, somewhat interesting and insightful for those from another era. The interview with Mother did, as a matter of fact, become the final impetus for this book. My original curiosity about people—not numbers—resurfaced. Would their memories be distinct ones, or blurred outlines of recollections no longer retained? And, finally, what of the present? Should my interviews relate only to those who have remained active?

After a while, the last question resolved itself and those who remained active, mentally and often physically, took precedence. As such, there is no intention on their part or mine to attribute their longevity and health to any magic potions or faddish lifestyles. Those who study the complexities of aging will be the ones to offer conjectures and conclusions in this area.

The book's interviews, however, do give a great many plus marks to remaining active throughout one's life. Not only physically, but also intellectually—truly enjoying one's work, having other interests, changing careers if necessary, maintaining positive outlooks, and exercising a healthy curiosity about the people and events around you.

Traveling across country and meeting each person that I interviewed was a revelation in itself, for it gave me the opportunity to note the vitality each of them exhibited. Of course, age may have taken its toll in the areas of physical strength, muscular activity, less strenuous exercises, having to take one-mile walks instead of five-mile ones, a few new aches and pains, and so on. But the vigor remained, and whether the interviewees voiced it or not, it was quite evident from their lifestyles that retaining a definite interest and active participation in areas they enjoyed was a meaningful key to their longevity.

There were a few surprises. In my initial test interviews of three octogenarians, two had been married *four* times. The third one, however, was celebrating his sixty-fifth anniversary—much more the norm for what I had perceived of that generation. Additionally, I met two interviewees in their mid-eighties, each happily celebrating their *third* wedding anniversary—a real pleasure! Then there were a number whose lack of formal education didn't stand in the way of ambition or making one's own opportunity. The determination to keep going forward was an integral part of their lives. And almost all of those interviewed had no problems at all with lucidity, whether dealing with past or present.

In all those yesterdays the work ethic was a thriving force—that certainly was no surprise. They all seemed to have been go-getters throughout their lives, and apparently that drive still continues.

- Joe Flieger, ex-cowboy, rodeo rider, and rancher, shrugs off the now-recurring aches and pains of a hundred or so earlier falls and, at eighty-eight, has just about completed an autobiography.

- Lillie Harrington, at eighty-two, is still running a small hotel in the Southwest and enjoying every minute of it. No recipient of a silver spoon, she has worked hard all her life and epitomizes the image of the strong, rugged, pioneering woman.
- Hardy Howard, Sr., retired from his job as a truck driver for a wholesale food distributor—this after sixty years on the job. Now, at eighty-six, he fishes, volunteers, and works a few selected accounts in his landscaping business.

My wife, Mary, joined me in the cross-country trip, which, when completed, totaled seven thousand miles— from Tucson to New York and return. The mileage resulted from stopping and doubling back for scheduled meetings, and traveling in a zigzag fashion rather than the shortest straight-ahead route. The reward, however, was worth it—personally visiting everyone I interviewed. Although we are in a technological age, where phone interviews are the accepted mode, the in-person approach enabled me to see and feel the interests of these octogenarians.

Arizona to Oklahoma, then down to Texas, up to Illinois, across to Virginia, back to West Virginia, up to Maryland, up and back to Ohio, and then on to New York. Having Mary with me provided another driver and a great companion for those never-ending miles. She sat in on a few of the interviews, and they were pleased she was there. We missed Senator Strom Thurmond twice when passing through Washington, D.C. Once he was attending the David Souter hearings, and the other occasion was the famous—or should it be the infamous—budget hearings. That was a true disappointment, but federal concerns come first. Our return trip included one stop in Maryland for an interview with a glass sculptor, Herman Perlman, and then a straight drive home. By that time, we wanted no additional side trips, for we had been away almost a month.

Transcribing the interview tapes was a lengthy job, but I preferred doing it myself. As the tape played, I could see the person, and that often helped when the voice wasn't clear or there was a drop in the sound level. What many of them hadn't realized was that the final printed interview would consist of their own words. Yes, there would be some editing and a deletion of repetition, but the final form I was seeking was their recollections and feelings—in *their* words. Author Phyllis Whitney wrote me, "the spoken word is not the written word, and I might have a problem with that format." I agreed with her, but since that concept had always been my intention, I guessed I had to carry it through.

Another intention related to celebrities. Although I did want to include some of them—for their lives are always interesting—I preferred the majority of interviews to be with those not always in the limelight. Perhaps I thought there would be more surprises with those whom you knew very little about. Nevertheless, to find those who are not constantly in the news is not an easy task. Fortunately, a few did have a paragraph or two in the print media, and I was able to follow up those leads.

- Mary Peyton Meyer noted that was exactly how the Johnny Carson show coordinator contacted her—by reading a short piece in a Chicago paper about her sixty-nine years as a local gossip columnist. Her TV appearance was then picked up by a columnist in my local paper, and I went on from there.
- William Schumacher being ordained as a Catholic priest at the age of seventy-nine and a half also caught my attention. At the end of our interview, we talked about his parish duties. I couldn't believe the work load—at eighty-two!

- Barbara Barondess MacLean had a few paragraphs in a long article about the Ellis Island opening, which noted that she was the only American ever detained there. However, our interview encompassed a remarkable life, in which Ellis Island was only one dramatic incident among many.
- Zaka and Milton Slawsky—their write-up in a feature story caught and entranced me, because I kept thinking, one hundred and sixty years old! They are eighty-year-old twins and energetic as all get-out, with their teaching chores at the University of Maryland.

The follow-ups to those and other media stories were not too difficult—a little sleuthing effort, plus phone calls and letters, made it all work. When it came to asking people to recommend active eighty-year-olds, I ran across something interesting. Thinking it made sense, I asked people in their seventies if they could steer me to one or two. Invariably, the answer was, "Gee, I don't know anyone *that* old—in their eighties." In the long run it was the mid-lifers who gave me the leads, and I now thank them for their help.

Getting back to well-known personalities. Those whom I interviewed were wonderful—cooperative in taking time out of a busy schedule to spend an hour or two with me. They all seemed to be on the go, but none tried to shorten the session in any way. And the areas they covered were interesting—film, television, theater, music, writing, business, and communications. In my own experience, there have always been great difficulties in trying to schedule interviews and sessions with celebrities. They get much too many requests for interviews, photos, autographs, and appearances—combine that with the other demands of their profession and the time problems are overwhelming. Because I was aware of this, I contacted many to be able to get an affirmative from a few.

- Katharine Hepburn sent a short, personal note: "I'm sorry but I'm so busy writing my own book that I honestly don't have time to talk to you."
- Henrietta Wyeth wrote—she finds that the interview process takes a great deal of energy, which she prefers to reserve for her painting.
- Gene Autry noted he has myriads of interview requests coming in daily. Given his age and ongoing business commitments, he just cannot honor all of them.
- Artie Shaw sent an intriguing preprinted postcard containing a number of thoughts. Among them: "I decided for the sake of my sanity to get out of the 'Artie Shaw' business"; "If I were to deal with all the requests I get, I wouldn't have time for anything else"; "If you happen to respect, admire, or simply enjoy anything I've ever recorded or written, please buy it and tell your friends to, too"; "I trust you'll understand. And thanks for reading this."
- Greer Garson indicated that her schedule and commitments did not allow her to participate, but she wished me success with what is obviously an intriguing and very positive endeavor.

With Cesar Romero, it was another story. One night while randomly selecting television programs, I tuned into a new pilot featuring Romero and Connie Sellecca, called "Mulberry Street." Apparently it didn't make the grade. Seeing Cesar Romero, however, reminded me of his octogenarian status, and I immediately sent off an interview request. The next day, while reviewing my letters, I noticed an inexcusable error. In a postscript to Romero's letter, I had written, "From 'Dallas' to 'Mulberry Street,' that's quite a change."

I really winced at the error. What would he think? He'd been featured in numerous episodes of "Falcon Crest," not "Dallas." Would that kill the interview? I immediately sent off a letter of apology, with the first paragraph stating, "If you have received my letter of August 9th, you may have already noticed a mispelling in the postscript. 'Falcon Crest' is incorrectly spelled 'D-A-L-L-A-S.'"

Within a few days, I received a handwritten note approving an interview. He graciously did not mention my faux pas.

There were many more responses, with most in the vein of "too many requests, not enough time." My research turned up a surprising number of personalities from the entertainment world who had drifted into octogenarian status. We all know about Bob Hope, George Burns, Milton Berle, Helen Hayes, Jessica Tandy, and Jimmy Stewart, because they are often featured in current productions. Some of the others who brought back wonderful memories are Burl Ives, Buddy Ebsen, Greer Garson, Imogene Coca, Victor Borge, Cab Calloway, Robert Young, Sylvia Sidney, E. G. Marshall, Don Ameche, Burgess Meredith, Joseph Cotten, and Henny Youngman.

Yes, time does march on—even the first of the baby boomers will soon hit the fifty mark. Along that line, the research into life expectancy doesn't seem to project any rapid increase in the present figures—age seventy-nine for women, seventy-four for men. Although some researchers disagree, there are many who believe that after the age of eighty-five, our organs tend to wear out. At the same time, all is not lost. They also predict that the present number of eighty-five-year-olds, now more than three million, will double in the next twenty years. And there will also be hundreds of thousands of centenarians at that time. Most likely, as is the case today, only a minority will be free of chronic disabling diseases. Perhaps, then, the researchers should concentrate their efforts on how to *enhance* life for the elders, rather than simply prolonging it.

All those I interviewed seemed to have their interests

centered in the areas that relate to the *quality* of life and the enjoyment that goes with it. They've expressed it in many ways:

"Never give up, just hang in there."
"I've been curious about a lot of things all my life."
"We keep busy."
"It's a *new challenge* that gets me going."
"Retire? I'd be bored stiff."
"What you get out of life is what you put in."
"If you lose interest, you yourself are lost!"
"You have to have something to retire to."
"[You're] never too old to start something new."
"I used positive thinking in all my life."
"[Getting] older doesn't hurt . . . you start to think better."
"Be interested, get excited."
"It's better to wear out than to rust out."

Contrast those thoughts with this passage from Robin Marantz Heinig's *The Myth of Senility:* "Either consciously or subconsciously, some old people will bend to the subtle social pressures to become crotchety, withdrawn, asexual, passive, dependent, depressed—not only because they're supposed to, but because it's easier than fighting."

Add that to my own many-months' experience of visiting a nursing home, where almost all sat around watching television and anticipating what the next meal would be. Although there were some activities available—simple aerobics, lectures, craft activities, and so on—attendance usually resulted from the coordinator's physical determination to round up some participants. Without doubt, many of the older men and women in nursing homes may have quit on life and given up the struggle. But struggle is what life is all about.

Those I interviewed, however, have all kept up their vitality, even though their strength may have ebbed. Some did it by continuing careers they thoroughly enjoy, others by being involved in a variety of interests. Career changes, instead of pure retirement, was another road to follow. Service to others was an important part of their lives for many interviewees. Curiosity about people, and new things to look into and investigate, also played a role in their lives.

As noted earlier, it was curiosity that got me actively involved in writing this book, and it was, as I suspected, tremendously interesting. Now, what to do with it? John Steinbeck once wrote, in a letter to a student, about critics daring him to be great. "You didn't want to be great," he noted. "You just wanted to write a book and have people read it." I agree.

EightySomething

RALPH BELLAMY

When you hear his voice on the phone, the visual image immediately materializes—just as you remember him from any one of his over one hundred films. He was visiting relatives in Tucson, and our meeting later, at the Arizona Inn, was most convenient. I noticed a group of the latest best-sellers on the coffee table, indicating a constant lookout for good parts. His most recent film opened last year, and he's looking forward to the next script. He loves his profession and wants to keep active.

Bellamy enjoys a good anecdote and chuckles about many of them from the early days of Hollywood. His easy-going, gracious manner made the interview an enjoyable one. Halliwell's Filmgoer's Companion *lists all his films and adds one of its scarce rosette symbols, which represents its own Hall of Fame. "For solid service and the occasional gleam of brilliance" is Bellamy's salute.*

* * *

I WAS BORN in the South Side of Chicago near the old Midway—that was the Fairgrounds in the 1890s—and it's still there, preserved as a park. We moved to Wilmette when I was quite young.

When I was about six, my parents brought me out of the house, all wrapped up in blankets, at three or four in the morning, and put me on a stump which was used when you stepped out of a carriage. They wanted me to see Halley's Comet flash across the sky. Well, I didn't see it then, and last year, when it was to appear again, I still didn't see it. The sky was overcast and it wasn't visible in California.

I went to public school in Wilmette, no big problems there. Gangs didn't exist then . . . most likely the word wasn't even improvised yet. There was one thing, though. I was raised a Baptist and on the way to school we passed a parochial school and we stopped long enough for us to call

1

them "catlickers" and for them to call us "doglickers." Then we went on our way.

Incidentally, I was almost drowned when I was being baptized. The Baptists practiced complete immersion, as you know, and when the minister let me down, he neglected to say, watch your feet. Well, the body went down, my feet came up, and he couldn't get me back out until I finally came up sputtering and spitting, gasping for breath. So, of course, I later married a Catholic.

In high school I was president of the dramatic club and, as such, I had keys to the auditorium. So, on one dismal, overcast, typical Midwest noon, I wanted to smoke a cigarette after lunch. My folks knew I smoked, but we were *never* allowed to smoke on campus. Well, I went over to the auditorium, let myself in, and went down to the basement. I walked down a long corridor and at the end was a room with a window at ground level and in the room was an enormous wheel, about ten feet in diameter, encased in a protective ironwork cage.

I lit a cigarette and blew a puff into the spinning wheel, then another, then another, watching them get caught up and disappearing. Soon, standing in the doorway, was the professor who had caught me at everything in the past four years. This was my senior year and it was almost graduation time. He said, "You know the rules, so should I go and tell the principal, or will you?" I said I would. I had been there many times before for other [*chuckle*] indiscretions. I went up through the auditorium, which was now reeking of cigarette smoke. Then it dawned on me, that was the auditorium ventilator I had been smoking through. The school superintendent was furious, "This is one too many—take your books and get out!" So I was kicked out of school in my fourth year for smoking.

About two weeks later, I signed for a job with the Chautauqua tent performers, playing in Harold Bell Wright's *A Shepherd of the Hills*. I played the leading man's father. There were about sixty-eight one-night stands, and I turned eighteen on that tour. I wore more makeup in that show than in the next sixty-eight years of acting. I wore a full beard and makeup, and then I doubled as the heavy in the third act of this four-act play. At the end of the second act, I had to peel off the beard, which was put on with spirit gum and removed with acetone. I had to apply the other makeup for the third act and then replace the beard for the last act. Finally, after the show, the beard had to be taken off again—it's a wonder I had any skin left.

On road trips like that with lots of one-night stands, there were no hotels, motels, or anything else in the towns we played. We depended on rooming houses, and that didn't always work out. Sometimes there was the sign ROOMS, but beneath it there would also be added NO DOGS OR ACTORS. We didn't have a very good reputation then, but I think we've since built up on that one.

But that was the beginning of my professional career, and acting was what I had been determined to do when I was in high school. In school, one of my best buddies was in a school play about a shipwreck. I had been forbidden to be in it because of some other [*chuckle*] earlier indiscretion. He was the butler and was to guide all the wet survivors to the beach, gather up some kindling, start a fire by striking two stones together, get them all set, and, finally, lean back and rest himself. Well, I wanted him to make a good appearance, so I mentioned that all the cast were English and all Englishmen smoke pipes. I warned, don't do it in rehearsal because you're not allowed to smoke on campus, but in the performance when it's your turn to rest, pull out a pipe and smoke it.

On play night, he guided the wet survivors to shore, gathered the kindling, struck two stones for sparks to light the fire, leaned back on a boulder, filled his pipe, and then took out a large *kitchen match* and lit up. The audience roared, and I think they're still laughing.

After the tent tour, I got into a sort of stock company which was half amateur, half professional. They did charge, but it was only fifty cents. A couple of us, including Melvyn Douglas, who started out about the same time I did, acted out scenes from Shakespeare. I don't recall ever doing a total Shakespeare play at that time. From there I got a job in a real stock company. In those days, every city of fifty thousand or over in the United States had one resident stock company. The company consisted of a leading man and woman, a second-business man and woman, a juvenile, an ingenue, a character man and woman, a comedian, a stage manager, a director, and scenic artists. There were three to five sets for each production, and we did a different play *each week.* While we were performing one play at night, all day long we had been rehearsing *next* week's play, which opened Sunday afternoon. Ten performances a week, seven nights and three matinees—no days off! It was great training.

Most people don't know what a stock company is—they confuse it with summer stock. It has nothing remotely to do with summer stock. A lot of people, with my background and age, came from the stock companies . . . Fredric March, Robert Montgomery, Clark Gable, Jimmy Cagney, all about the same era. Acting really meant the stage in those days, although the silent movies were just getting started. The movie theaters were called nickel shows, because it only cost a nickel to see the silent pictures. If there was a big one—like a DeMille—it cost twenty-five cents and was called a road show.

Well, I went from one stock company to another, through the Middle West and part of the East. In one of the towns on Long Island, I was broke and worked for fifty dollars a week as a leading man. I did two O'Neill plays . . . fifty dollars a week!

At the height of the depression, I hit New York. Having been in stock companies and played all kinds of parts, I considered myself trained and ready for Broadway. But there was nothing doing—not even a walk-on. I remember at one point living in a hall bedroom and not having eaten for some time. I went out that morning and was about to lift a bottle of milk from a doorstep near the street. I had actually leaned over to pick it up when I saw a cop coming down the sidewalk. Well, he smiled, and I smiled, and I left the bottle there. So much for that breakfast!

I went back to the stock companies. I even had my own company in Des Moines for two seasons and Nashville for two seasons. I acted and sometimes directed during those seasons. After that I went back to New York and did a play, *Roadside*. This got me out to Hollywood with an offer from practically every film company. I was practically broke when I went out there.

Films were obviously a different technique than the stage. On the stage, you're playing way out to a gallery and a gesture is bigger and broader—in films, it is much lighter and restrained, sometimes even accomplished by a facial expression. Your voice on the screen is not loud, it's projected. In my first film, *The Secret Six*, the cast also included Clark Gable, Wallace Beery, Marjorie Rambeau, Lewis Stone, and others. I remember coming on the set for the first day to do a four-page scene and everybody had their scripts, but I didn't. Someone shouted, *"He* knows his script, *he* knows his lines!"

Later, I was in Charlie Chaplin's restaurant on Hollywood Boulevard when Clark Gable came in and offered to join me. He sat down and asked, "What do *you* think of this place [Hollywood]?" I replied I didn't know, for I had just arrived here. He said, "I just got fifteen thousand dollars for playing a heavy in a Bill Boyd western. *Fifteen thousand* dollars—no actor's worth that!" He continued, "I got myself a secondhand Ford, I live in a rooming house at the head of Vine Street, and I'm not buying anything I can't put on the Chief [the Santa Fe train going back East] . . . because all this *isn't going to last!"*

In those days a bunch of us came out at the same time because the silent-picture actors were having trouble learning and speaking their lines. So they went to the nearest source—the theater—for people. Most of us came from the stock companies, had known each other in New York—broke—and were all out here earning money. It was fun working together. It wasn't exactly a challenge, but we were all playing parts—the way in a stock company you created a part. There, we only had a week, so we were used to working fast and drawing on all our memories and impressions of people and friends to make a character. Some pretty good pictures were made—even some of the B pictures weren't so bad. There were a group of us, maybe fifty or so, who had known each other. So we worked together, socialized together—it was that kind of life, almost like a small town.

Oh, there were moments, of course. I remember one of the early movies on location, at sea. John Gilbert, the great silent star, hadn't worked much lately, and this was an opportunity. Well, after working awhile, he got hold of a case of booze and locked himself in one of the staterooms, refusing to come out. Bert Lahr said he knew him very well and he would get in and get him out. Bert did go in, but he stayed and never came out. Naturally, along the way, production time was being lost and one day Lewis Milestone, the director, gets a cable from Harry Cohn: "Hurry it along, the production costs are staggering." Milestone cabled back, "So is the cast!"

I should tell you I've always had a space separation between my two front teeth. In fact, a number of us did . . . Clark Gable, Barbara Stanwyck, and quite a few others. Well, there was a dentist in Hollywood who specialized in making a very thin facsimile of two teeth in one piece, and this would cover the space. You put it on over the others with a bit of adhesive, and we were told to just be careful with those words starting with *f*'s or *s*'s. Well, I was working on a film with Ruth Chatterton and sure enough, in one of our scenes, it happened—the dental piece came off. Although I was playing a blind man, I and the rest of the cast went down on hands and knees searching for those teeth. At one point, I looked up at Ruth, who was bent over and looking down. I practically flipped—the teeth were stuck on *her forehead*!

In another time, we were making the film *Boy Meets Girl*, in '38 I believe. The cast included Jimmy Cagney, Pat O'Brien, Marie Wilson, Ronald Reagan, and myself. We had already shot a couple of days when word came down from the producer. He said, "Make it over, make it louder, faster, and funnier!" So we started the whole thing over.

I never went to the rushes, and Cagney, who was my oldest friend, never did either. I learned quickly not to go to those screenings for fear of finding something I liked and repeating it, or hating myself and wishing I could do it again. But after a few days of shooting it louder, faster, and funnier, Cagney decided to go and see what it was like. He showed up when I was taking off my makeup. "Ralph," he said, "you know I'm a fast talker, don't you?" I nodded. "Well," he continued, "I couldn't even understand *myself!*" So much for louder, faster, and funnier.

But seriously, I'll tell you one thing about those old moguls—the Harry Cohns, the Louis B. Mayers, the David Selznicks, and the others, they had a finger on the pulse of what the moviegoing public liked and wanted, and would buy. And, of course, that was the time when the studios also owned the theaters. Each production company had its own staff of writers, directors, musicians, and a large publicity organization. Everyone was given a halo individually and collectively. In those days you couldn't get on a lot unless you belonged there. Today, of course, they're begging you to come—for a fee.

Those old producers knew what they were doing, and they had good reasons for it. In my opinion, too many of today's producers are not qualified. They are lawyers, accountants, crapshooters, and in some cases don't care if they win or lose. If it's a loss, write it off. If it's a winner, do *another* one . . . just keep going. There isn't the knowledge, the entertainment-world-business knowledge that those old fellows had. Whatever you want to say about them, and *everything you ever heard about them is true,* they did know the picture business, and they had pride about it.

I think when the theaters were separated from the studios, our troubles began. For instance, in the later thirties, we were making about six hundred pictures a year in Hollywood. Today, I doubt if we make one hundred, although we make them everywhere else—all over the world. Hollywood was the center of the movie industry then, and *it* had a halo around it. People still come here today and there's still a fascination, but not the way it was then.

There were a couple of films I was in that sort of became minor classics—*The Awful Truth* and *His Girl Friday. The Awful Truth* was the craziest movie story I ever had anything to do with. I was under contract to Harry Cohn, at Columbia, where it was made. The studio manager called me one day and said he was sending over the script, with so-and-so's part, but don't pay any attention to it. When I said that was the most idiotic direction I had ever received and *why* should I read it, he replied, "That's what Harry Cohn said."

The part was an Englishman, previously played on Broadway by Roland Young, a very good friend of mine. Well, I went to see Harry Cohn and told him I wouldn't even attempt to play an Englishman, and for another thing, Roland Young played it beautifully and he's right here—all you have to do is call him. Cohn said, "Never mind, just mind your own business. You'll see later."

Time passed, and a writer friend called and said he was working on my part in *The Awful Truth,* trying to make a westerner out of an Englishman—could I come over and help out? I did, but we got nowhere. Time again passed, and Dorothy Parker called and said she was working on the script; nothing happened. Another writer called later, but nothing happened.

Finally, the studio manager called and asked me to report Monday to play in *The Awful Truth.* I said, to *play*

Life Begins at 80

Author Unknown

I have good news for you. The first 80 years are the hardest. The second 80 are a succession of birthday parties.

Once you reach 80, everyone wants to carry your baggage and help you up the steps. If you forget your name or somebody else's name, or an appointment, or your own telephone number, or promise to be three places at the same time, or can't remember how many grandchildren you have, you need only explain that you are 80.

Being 80 is a lot better than being 70. At 70 people are mad at you for everything. At 80 you have the perfect excuse no matter what you do. If you act foolishly, it's your second childhood. Everybody is looking for symptoms of softening of the brain.

Being 70 is no fun at all. At that age they expect you to retire to a house in Florida and complain about your arthritis (they used to call it lumbago), and you ask everybody to stop mumbling because you can't understand them. (Actually your hearing is about 50 percent gone.)

If you survive until you are 80, everybody is surprised that you are still alive. They treat you with respect just for having lived so long. Actually they seem surprised that you can walk and talk sensibly.

So please, folks, try to make it to 80. It's the best time of life. People forgive you for anything. If you ask me, life begins at 80.

what? He didn't know, but Mr. Cohn said something about a westerner. Since those were the days we all used our own clothes, I asked, what kind of clothes? Again, he said he didn't know, but to bring lots of them. So, Monday morning, with no real idea of what the script was, I reported to the stage with armfuls of clothes, all kinds.

Leo McCarey was the director. He was a wonderfully weird sort of a fellow. His eyes danced, and he was smiling as he greeted me. I told him I didn't know what I was supposed to be doing and brought a lot of clothes—what do you want me to wear? As I plopped all the clothes down, he looked at the odd jacket and trousers I was wearing and said that's just what he wanted. He went over to Irene Dunne, sitting at the piano looking at sheet music. She looked at McCarey. "Leo, you know I don't read music." She groaned. "I'll never get this in time to shoot it." Leo waved his hand, "Don't worry about it."

Well, the camera was already lined up, and Leo asked if I knew "Home on the Range." I said sure, but I can't sing, I can't get from one note to another. "Oh, that's just what I wanted," he said gleefully. He then told Irene to do the best she could with the song and motioned to me. "Ralph, you sing it, belt it out and don't care how it sounds." So I belted it out right to the end and nobody said "Cut." I finally looked up, and McCarey was literally on his hands and knees, under the camera, dying from laughter. He gasped out, "Cut it!" And that's what's in the final picture.

I went to see Harry Cohn to get out of it because I still didn't know what the hell we were playing. Irene Dunne was in tears, and Cary Grant said to Cohn, "Let me out of this and I'll do another one for you, *for nothing!* I don't know what I'm doing here." Cary continued, "Or let me play Ralph's part as an Englishman and let him play my part. I *am* English, you know."

Cohn practically snarled, "Get out of my office, all of you, get out!" He turned it all over to Leo McCarey, and we never did get a script. Leo would come into the stage every morning, sometimes literally with his notes on a piece of brown wrapping paper, and start to give us his directions. And that's the way it went. Do this, maybe do that—say this and see how it plays, and so on. One day when we were shooting, Harold Lloyd came over to visit Leo on the set. In those days, there was a guard at the door, but he naturally let Lloyd in. Between shots, Leo used to fiddle with an old upright piano to release excess energy. Well, he was playing and Harold Lloyd was talking to him and Cohn stormed onto the set. Apparently someone had reported an intruder. He fired the guard on the spot and kicked Lloyd off the lot. McCarey was so furious he tore up his contract for four or five more pictures, right in front of Cohn. But . . . with all that topsy-turvy going on, *The Awful Truth* was a big hit.

A few years later, I did another one of those "I never get the girl" pictures—*His Girl Friday,* which was a remake of *The Front Page.* I was visiting the set on one of my off days, and Harry Cohn invited me up to see rushes from the day before, a day I hadn't been working. After a reel or so, we were watching a scene where Cary Grant is on the phone and he's saying, "Well, I don't know, what does he look like . . . like that fellow in pictures—what's his name . . . Ralph Bellamy?" No way was that in the script, and Cohn screamed, "What are they doing down there on the set?" He got up and ran down to the stage. It took everybody, Howard Hawks, Cary Grant, and Rosalind Russell, to calm him down. It was just an ad lib, but it stayed in the picture.

Around that time, I was in the film *The Wolf Man* with Lon Chaney, Jr., Evelyn Ankers, Claude Rains, Bela Lugosi, and others. The director [George Waggner] was a little fellow who dressed the part. He wore a Norfolk jacket, riding britches, boots, and a scarf. A huge megaphone was part of it, as well as a tall, lanky woman secretary with a hat, who followed him—fifteen feet behind—wherever he went.

One day, on the set, Waggner said to visitor Sir Cedric Hardwicke and myself, "You fellows take it easy, we're going to the back lot for a silent shot with Evelyn Ankers, be back in no time at all." After a few hours, we decided to go over and see what was taking so long. The set was the standing Notre Dame staircase, very impressive and ornate. On the set they're yelling lighting directions and camera angles, and the assistant director finally told the director it's ready. Although he was fairly close to the foot of the staircase, Waggner picked up his huge megaphone and shouted to Evelyn Ankers.

"Now, Evelyn, your mother's been carried away by the Frankenstein monster; your father's been killed by the Wolf Man; your lover is being chased over the moors by the dogs; it's four o'clock in the morning and you're all alone in this slimy, ancient castle; the servants have all fled . . . and I want to get the feeling from you that *you're fed up with it all.* Okay?"

And, for years, whenever Sir Cedric and I saw each other—and we did a few times in France and England— we'd yell across the room, "Are you fed up with it all yet?"

By the way, there's another Cagney story. He and I were in a scene in which I was to hit and knock him out. I had never hit anybody, but I did know how the stuntmen handled it. They choose a camera angle, over the shoulder, and your fist is to just graze the other guy's chin. But Jimmy Cagney, who used to be a boxer, said we shouldn't worry about it. He said, "You guys pick the best camera angle to make it even more dramatic, and Ralph, you aim right here and I'll get out of the way." I said I was scared to death and didn't want to hurt him. Jimmy just laughed. "Look, even if you do it, it won't be your fault. It'll be my fault— don't worry." Well, we went ahead. I hit him—right on the chin, knocked his tooth out, and we had a three-hour delay until he was fixed up. And [*chuckle*] I haven't hit anybody since.

So for over twenty years, I played all kinds of roles in films . . . villains, detectives, Ellery Queen, lawyers, psychiatrists, the guy who never gets the girl, and a bunch of others. Finally, I went back to Broadway, where I had a terrific run in some excellent plays. There was *Tomorrow the World; State of the Union,* which got the Pulitzer Prize; *Detective Story;* and *Sunrise at Campobello,* for which I received a Tony award. I also returned to Hollywood to do the film of *Sunrise at Campobello.*

While I was onstage in New York, they had been experimenting and producing television programs upstairs in Grand Central Station on Forty-second Street. There were two studios at that location, and in one they were doing the "I Remember Mama" series and the "Ford Theatre." In the other studio, we began my program, "Man Against Crime," which ran for three or four years. It went on every Friday from 8:30 to 9:00 P.M. But at the same time I was starring on the Broadway stage in *Detective Story.* In those days, curtain time for all theaters was 8:40 P.M., and my audience had to wait every Friday for twenty or so minutes while I raced from Grand Central to the Hudson Theatre. I guess there may have been many in the audience who were a bit impatient.

At the end of each TV episode I would announce that the makers of Camels would donate gift cigarettes to hospitalized servicemen and women, and veterans. As I named the specific hospitals, I would light up a Camel (which I did smoke), take a deep puff, and continue the list of recipients. One night a piece of tobacco lodged in my throat. I *had* to continue—this was live TV—so I hoarsely sputtered along, tears rolling down my cheeks, and croaked out the message to the bitter end. That was live TV for you—and I do have a kinescope of it.

Incidentally, because there was no delayed transmission, or whatever they called it, we had to ship a kinescope of "Man Against Crime" to California for their showing. Others, like the "Theatre Guild of the Air" did it a different way—they had to do two shows, one at 8:00 P.M. in New York and an identical second show at 11:00 P.M. to accommodate the three-hour time difference on the West Coast.

I did a lot of TV after that—top dramatic shows, series, guest appearances, both live and on film. Did a half dozen with Helen Hayes and half dozen with Gertrude Lawrence. She came before the curtain one night to do a warm-up and announced, "It's my great pleasure to announce that tonight, once again, I have as my leading man—Mr. *Cyril* Bellamy." With that I came out and said, "It's always a great pleasure to be on the *Sarah* Lawrence Show." And the audience roared, they all loved it—including Gertie.

By this time I was back in Hollywood and stayed there for the rest of my career, doing films, films for TV, and TV series. Some good, some not so good—the latter, I guess, we just call "flops." By the way, as long as you're featuring eighty-year-olds, let me tell you about the time we were filming *Oh God,* with George Burns. That particular day was his eighty-eighth birthday, I think, and they had given him a later call—about 10:00 A.M. He was coming in for a long sequence he had to do in the witness box in court. It was a really long speaking scene and he had to handle a lot of props while he was emoting. The crew had everything set up—both the cue cards and the prompting system. Well, George did it all in *one* take, without using the cue cards or teleprompter. He did another take, the same way, and then went home *before noon.* At eighty-eight, wow!

As far as films go, I've done 107 so far. The last one was *Pretty Woman,* with Richard Gere and Julia Roberts. She's delightful and so young—I think you're going to hear a lot more about her. It was an excellent company, and I had a great time with all of them. It's a cute picture, and I think the last reports show it making more money than the other new ones—way over $150 million so far, and it's only been out a short time.

While on that film I banged myself up pretty good, at home. The Achilles tendon in my heel was severed and I had a full cast, up to my thigh, for about four months. It's been off a few months now, but they say I'll still feel it for quite a while. But anyway, I'm looking forward to the next film, whatever it may be. Just turned down two scripts, but maybe the next one will be the right one.

I love the business of acting. It's too bad the young people don't have the opportunities that we had—people my age—like working in the stock companies, the road companies, and vaudeville. That's where we had to learn our business, where one of the main things was discipline. For instance, in the stock companies you rehearsed every morning at 10:00 A.M. and you got there at ten even if you had to crawl, because everybody else did.

Today there isn't that urge, there isn't that force at work. I don't blame the young, it's not their fault—it just isn't a part of the business any longer. They have not had the luck that we had, to have that kind of a beginning. I wish that something could make them realize the depth of the responsibility of being an actor. I think you owe it to the business you're in and to the people's concept of you . . . as a person and as an actor.

The whole business of acting has been very good to me and I have thoroughly, thoroughly enjoyed it. Even at this age it's important to keep active, to be a part of something you genuinely relish, whether it's a career or some other interest. As far as I'm concerned, I'm still looking forward to a good deal more of this acting business.

July 27, 1990

Mr. Bellamy passed away on November 29, 1991, at the age of eighty-seven.

Apache, Oklahoma, is her home and her vocation. As chairperson of the Fort Sill Apache Tribe, she remains active in her so-called retirement years. Mildred is tall, erect, and full of energy. But she bemoaned the upcoming chore of getting all her belongings packed up or moved around so the painters could redo her entire house, both interior and exterior. However, she strongly believes in the power of patience, and knew it would all get done. I agreed, but thought it best to beat a retreat to the hotel, where we could tackle the interview in a couple of comfortable lounge chairs. Later, we had supper together — no tape recorder.

In the meantime, planning programs for the tribe and trying to have them approved for government allocations is the main event. Mildred is also well known for her skill and dedication in creating fabric dolls that feature the authentic dress of the numerous Indian tribes. The dolls were all packed away, but I hoped to see them at a festival in the near future.

✳   ✳   ✳

WHEN I was born in the Fort Sill Military Reservation hospital in 1910, I was listed as a prisoner of war. And I remained a prisoner of war until I was four years old. Then, in 1914, we Apaches were set free.

This all had to do with the imprisonment of Geronimo and his followers at Fort Sill, Oklahoma. My father and his parents came from Arizona, and they were held as prisoners, with Geronimo's group, in the year 1894. My mother, who was born in Alabama, was also a prisoner at the same camp. Initially, in various areas, there were about five hundred Apache prisoners, but in the Fort Sill camp the total was a little over two hundred.

When everyone was freed in 1914, our family lived for many years on our allotment in nearby Apache. The allot-

Mildred Cleghorn

ment related to land the Indians purchased with their own money. This money came from their raising and selling cattle while they were prisoners of war. Each adult was given three thousand dollars, and each child two thousand dollars, to buy the land of the deceased Kiowas, Comanches, and Apaches. The money was earned by the Indian prisoners and the land was purchased—it wasn't given to them by the government.

At that time, the prisoners were given a choice of staying in Oklahoma or going to the Mescalero reservation in New Mexico. Two-thirds went to New Mexico and about seventy-two stayed in the area and received their allotments. It was several years before everyone received them. My father purchased eighty acres each for himself and Mother, and fifty acres for me. We farmed crops just like everyone around us, but he never liked farming. Now when I look back, I always think they should have let him raise cattle and horses because he loved and knew how to do that. He also knew how to raise feed, and if they had just left him alone and not tried to teach him how to raise cotton and crops, it would have been much better. Of course, he did know how to raise corn—that was an Indian staple.

Oh yes, I was involved too. When I was going to school, I used to pick cotton, chaff wheat, help plow, milk cows, take care of the chickens, and everything. This went on in high school also. Then my mother got a job as a housemother in a boarding school, the Fort Sill Indian School, and later my father got a job there as janitor and bus driver. Like I said, he really didn't like farming, so they spent their later days in the civil service at the school.

When I was in elementary school, I remember going with my mother to buy a rocking chair; she had always wanted one. In the furniture store there was a Victrola playing music—I had never seen one before. I asked her what instrument the musician was playing, for I was only familiar with the piano which was played at our church. She said it was a violin. Well, that was the first time I had ever been exposed to that kind of music, and right there I said that's what I wanted to play. From then on I was determined to play a violin, even though mother wanted me to play the piano. Maybe she was right, for if I had taken piano lessons first, it would have made the violin lessons much easier. Anyway, when I was about twelve, there was a lady in our town who played the violin, and that's when I started.

You know, in the schools in those days we had contests in everything—arithmetic, geography, music, in glee club, in band and orchestra, in everything. Before I got to high school, I won a gold medal for violin in a competition of the grade schools. Then in high school I won another gold medal for solo performance, and that was in an all-state competition. I also played first violin in our high school orchestra. Later, in the university, I had the opportunity to play with a symphony orchestra, and that was one of my ambitions, to play with a symphony. All in all, I didn't do too badly with the violin.

Another thing I recall about my childhood was that when I went to school the First World War was still on. Both my parents were worried that my father would have to go because they were running out of soldiers. They had already taken married men with no children, so it was possible that those with one child would be next. Every day in school there was something that related to the war. We'd go out with the teacher and go up and down the roadsides looking for peach seeds, tinfoil, and milk glass jars, like the ones that had Pond's cold cream in them. After that we'd go back to class and there, sometimes, a mother would come in with sheets. The teacher would measure three inches off and cut it into strips, which we would then roll into bandages. I'm not sure, but the peach seeds had something to do with gasmasks, and I think they melted the tinfoil.

Each child also got a picture of a big ship, like the *Titanic*. And you know where the portholes were? We were supposed to fill each porthole area with a dime. Oh, we'd just be dying to get a dime and put it there. We'd pin the picture to the wall at home and there were just little dents in the portholes where the family could put the coins in. That was for the war effort also.

The high school I went to was in Apache. No, it wasn't an Indian school, it was a public school. I never went to an Indian school until later. I really didn't know too many Indians because there were only five of us in the whole public school. In fact, when the family went to any places or affairs that involved Indians, I felt left out because I didn't know anyone there. I didn't have any Indian friends, so I begged my mother to let me go the Haskell School after I completed high school. She vowed she'd never have any of her children go to a boarding school, but finally she gave in. Haskell was a two-year school in Lawrence, Kansas, and Indian kids from all over the United States went there. My mother really didn't want me to go and she said, "The minute you get lonesome, let me know and you come right home." Well, I could of died the first two months, but I wouldn't tell her. [*Laughs*] But by the end of October, you couldn't drag me away.

I was going to Haskell, taking a two-year business course, during the depression, and when I graduated in '32, you couldn't find a job or anything. Well, I wanted to work in the Indian service, and finally there was an opening in Nevada. They asked if I'd go there and I said sure, I'd go anywhere—where is it? That was the most godforsaken place, but it was the only place there was a vacancy, I guess, because no one would go there. When I told my mother, she asked, "Where in the world is Nevada?" When I showed her on the map, she just flat out said, "Oh no, that's too far away." But I had to go. Well, I didn't like it in Nevada, I didn't like being cooped up in the four walls, and later I resigned my job and came home. Mother thought I was crazy because I got $1,440 a year and that was pretty good money at that time. But then I went to college at the Oklahoma State University and got my degree in home economics. I got a job in the Indian service at $720 a year, plus my room and board. My mother just absolutely thought I lost my mind. And not only that, I also had to get oriented to the Indian ways.

It was all home extension work, visiting families and relating to home economics and assistance in many areas. I did that for many years until they did away with that kind of work. One thing it did was enable me to work with many different tribes, and that came in handy later when I was making my dolls. Anyway, I then transferred into education and began working in a boarding school in this area, teaching home economics. I got involved in the 4-H clubs, and I want to tell you that we had the largest 4-H club in the whole United States. Every student in that school was a member of the club. It was a well-rounded program in health, home living, livestock, music, speech, and just about everything. You know, the children just loved to compete with each other in everything. They all had gardens and learned to can, and most families fed themselves from their gardens and livestock. I worked with the 4-H club for twenty years, and they gave me a diamond pin for those services.

Yes, the Bureau of Indian Affairs [BIA] had problems, but if it wasn't for them a lot of Indian kids would never have gone to school—exhibit A right here! Because we didn't have money and the BIA gave us an opportunity to get scholarships. Haskell School, for example, was a boarding school and it was free, financed by the BIA for Indian students. That's where I studied business administration. For the Oklahoma State University in 1937, I had to mortgage my farm, myself, and I worked as a secretary in the office of the president. All I had to borrow was fifteen hundred dollars for the three years, because I also had a scholarship.

As far as prejudice goes, heck no, in those early years I don't think I even knew I was an Indian. [*Laughs*] The strange thing is I went to school, college, worked all my life, went everywhere, and there was only one incident. In 1956, when I came back here to find a place to live, there was a house for rent that seemed okay. When my husband and I went to the front door, the woman said, "Oh, you're Indians. I don't rent to Indians," and she slammed the door in our faces. That was the first time that I ever in my whole life was treated that way. It made me so angry I could spit! And it still does.

Oh yes, I've traveled a lot. Once I even went around the world. Let me give you the background on that first. My mother and father were Christian people and they belonged to the Reform Church of America, as I do now. Way back in 1895, a missionary from that church came and saw the conditions of the Fort Sill Apaches, and he wanted to help them in some way. He came back a number of times to Fort Sill, requesting permission to come into camp and talk to the prisoners, but it was not granted. On his last trip, when he got to the gate, it just so happened that this particular guard opened the gate and let him in. After reviewing the conditions there, the missionary returned to New York and reported what he saw and asked the church to sponsor him. And it was the women of the Reform Church who were the ones to sponsor him. See—you don't get anything done unless there's a woman behind it. [*Chuckles*]

So he returned and worked with the Apaches. My mother and father became Christians and I was reared in the church. When the Apaches were given their freedom in 1914, the Presbyterians tried to have us join their group. They were really conservative and they only sang psalms, but without music. Our people were used to having a piano and singing their favorite hymns, like "Amazing Grace," "What a Friend We Had in Jesus," and all those songs. They loved them and because of it they wouldn't attend the Presbyterian church. Finally, the town of Apache and each Indian family contributed twenty-five dollars and we built our own small church. It was very tiny, and they added a

small room for the preacher to stay when he came on weekends. But that was the beginning.

Since then, I've worked for the church and am an elder.
In the late sixties our preacher came to me and said,
"Mildred, you better sit down—I have something to tell
you. How would you like to go on a trip around the world?"
I thought he was kidding, but I said I'd like it very much.
"Well," he continued, "you have a chance to go with our
church group." I guess I near to fainted. This was the time
of that first hunger movement and a group of us—twenty-
seven from various sections of the country—would go on
the trip that would be relating to nutrition, especially in the
Third World countries. The leader of our group said, "You
know, I've sent many nationalities to these various countries, but I've never had the opportunity to send an Indian
to these nutrition seminars. You're a home economist,
would you like to go?" And that's how I came to be going on
a world trip.

We were gone for a few months and visited research cen-
ters, universities, hospitals, and anything that had to do
with food activities or advancement. For example, they
were using sardines as protein and relating it somehow to
soda pop, so that children would be able to increase their
protein intake. Camouflage it—that was the idea. And bul-
gur wheat. At home we would throw it out to the chickens,
we wouldn't eat it, but it proved to be meaningful in a
nutrition program. During that trip, I learned as well as
taught. When we were in Rome, all the televisions were on
and we were able to watch the first American walk on the
moon. It was a wonderful trip in many ways.

I do like to travel. I've been to Alaska, Hawaii, New Zea-
land, Australia, the Fiji Islands, and England, and last year
I spent almost a month in West Berlin. It was right after
they started taking down the Wall and I went out there and
chiseled off a piece of it. I also just came back from Mil-
waukee, all expenses being paid just to play with dolls.
[Laughs] It was the Indian Summer Festival and I displayed

my dolls—sat in my booth while working on them, talking to little kids and big kids, old grandmothers and everybody.

You mentioned that someone said I was a renowned doll maker. Well, I don't know about the renowned, but I do make dolls. It all started way back in the forties when I was working in home extension in Kansas. Since there wasn't any Reform Church there, I went to the Methodist church and joined their women's guild. When they knew about my job, they asked me to give a talk about the Indian lives and customs. I was amazed that they lived all their lives in a town that had a real reservation only about four miles away, yet they didn't know one iota about Indians. They thought I could talk to the Indians there because I was an Indian. I said no, they're Kickapoos and I'm an Apache, but they were still flabergasted that we Indians spoke differently, dressed differently, our legends were different, our creation stories were different, and we were all separate nations.

That's when I decided how to show that we were all not the same, by making dolls that said we were just as different as our clothes are different. I made four dolls in Kansas, representing the four tribes there—then seven more here in Oklahoma for the tribes living here. Now, over the years, I have a collection of forty-one fabric dolls, all different tribes. The trouble is there are thirty-two more to go! Obviously, I'm still working on dolls today. There's a tremendous amount of research involved because all the dress is specific to each tribe and has to be authentic. I do all the beadwork, get real buckskin from Idaho, and pay seventy dollars for a little piece of it. The small, short needles are very difficult to find today, and the quarter-inch wide ribbons of all the various colors and shades have to be accurate, because some tribes don't use certain colors at all. When silver is required, I use real silver, I don't use sequins. The dolls must be as authentic as possible. In the last five or six years I've been to many Indian festivals around the country to display my dolls and answer numerous questions about the tribes. As far as selling dolls—if and when I make some to sell, they are sold for $150 each.

Yes, I did retire in 1970, but not for very long. About three months, I think. They needed a teacher's aide right here in the Apache kindergarten, so I applied for it. They indicated I was a teacher, and I said, "No, no, I don't want to have anything to do with teaching, I just want to play with the kids." So I became an aide and had a barrel of fun, but I also did a lot of office work for the teacher. I loved every minute of it and did that for three years, until I got involved in tribal politics in 1974. Initially, I became secretary of the tribe by nomination and election. Years later, I ran for the position of chairman of the Fort Sill Apache Tribe and was elected. It's a volunteer job, without pay, but I must be nominated and elected from the floor. The elections are held every two years, and although I did have competition, I've been elected these past five times.

As far as government programs, I found that we weren't eligible for any of them because the tribe itself had no land—it wasn't considered land-based. We all had our own land but that was not the criteria. So when a particular law was passed and I found out we could buy land for the tribe, I went after it. We only had a small amount of money in the tribe—something like five thousand dollars. One of our people had eighty acres for sale, but we could only afford to buy two and a half of those acres. But now the tribe was legitimately land-based, and we asked for appropriations to build a house and an office on the land. There was an Indian Action Team, which was an educational program wherein each tribe was given ten thousand dollars. We used those funds to build a building on our tribal acres. My office is there now, and I'm involved in writing proposals for government programs dealing with various tribal activities—education, health, self-government, and so on.

Anyway, those are my so-called retirement activities—travel, an elder in the church, a doll maker, and a chairperson for the Fort Sill Apache Tribe. I think they will keep me busy for a long, long while. But, you know, a lot of it has to do with curiosity. I've been curious about a lot of things all my life. A lot also has to do with the things I would like to do and have, and I'm not talking about material things. Basically, I'm very satisfied with my life.

I also found you have to have a lot of patience. Patience is one thing and money isn't everything. That's the one thing the white man overdoes. Money, money, money—everything has to have a price, and it's got to happen right now. Our Indian people aren't like that, we take it as it comes. We share everything we've got. We share our homes, our lives, everything—we share and we care. We have extended families, I don't care if it's only one drop of blood, you're still my brother, you're still my sister. You can be as white as snow but if you've got that one drop of blood, you're still my brother or sister. And cousins are called sisters and brothers, so you never run out of relatives.

September 11, 1990

JEAN DALRYMPLE

Her background in the theater is one of those all-encompassing ones. Writer, publicist, producer, director, and, in the early years, performer. I visited her in her apartment, across the street from New York's well-known City Center, which Dalrymple helped found in the mid-1940s. During the interview I commented that her life seemed to have a jigsaw-puzzle quality wherein divine providence, or whatever, intervened whenever she had a career change and the appropriate missing piece miraculously made an appearance. Upon reflection on this observation, Jean wholeheartedly agreed.

That and her lack of fear in facing new challenges are among the hallmarks of her dynamic life. Although the books she has written relate to the theater and her career, there was one that surprised me — Jean Dalrymple's Pinafore Farm Cookbook. *When queried about it, her answer was a simple one, "I like to cook." Even that, however, can be traced back to an early challenge.*

* * *

FIRST OF ALL, I must say that my mother died when I was an infant, and I grew up in the home of my grandparents. They were quite elderly, so there was a baby nurse in the household and she was the one who really brought me up. Although Grandmother was fifty when my father was born, she never seemed old to me because she was very spry and taught me games. One game was "Flench," which was sort of a twenty-one game, and we played it for pennies. So she taught me gambling at an early age, and that has stood me in good shape, as my whole life has been one big gamble.

Besides the games, my favorite place in the whole house was the kitchen. Grandmother, however, didn't allow me to enter because she thought the kitchen was no place for a young lady. Mrs. Murphy, who was our cook, was teaching me to cook and I loved it . . . but I had to sneak into the kitchen without Grandma knowing about it. Finally, I asked my father to intercede and he told her, "Let her learn how to cook because when she grows up, she may not have a cook and it's better if she knows how to take care of herself." My grandmother replied, "Oh, that's impossible. She has to make a good marriage, and I'll see to that myself."

"It's a long time between now and when she grows up," my father said. "And the world changes very quickly." He was so right. Anyway, I did get into the kitchen more often. As far as school goes, when I was six years old, my grandmother said that my baby nurse would now be my governess. She was my teacher—no more calling her Nana, and it would be Miss High. She was Scottish Presbyterian and she brought me up in that very strict manner. I owe her a great deal.

Talking about that kind of discipline, there was the time when I was to sleep over at a little friend's house. Our coachman drove the horse-drawn wagon way over to the other side of town in Morristown, New Jersey. When we arrived, it was one of those "dead houses" and it frightened me to look at it. Inside it was also dead to me, and then I went into the bedroom. The room was closed in with very heavy draperies and there was a four-poster bed with a canopy. I told my friend I couldn't stay and if I slept there, I'd have terrible dreams. By this time my driver had left, so her parents had to dig up their buggy and driver to take me home. When I told Miss High about it, she was so angry at my rudeness that she wanted to hit me. But I told her I wasn't rude, it would have killed me to stay there and I couldn't stand it.

In Sunday school, I had produced and directed two plays. One was about Ruth and the other about Joseph—believe it or not, I called that one *Joseph and a Coat of Many Colors.* There was nothing written down, I just taught it to the other kids by rote. This was when I was seven years old. At that time the *Newark Ledger* had a children's competition to write an essay on "Swat the Fly." I decided to enter because this was an important subject—to get rid of the flies. Well, I won the contest and got a check for one dollar, plus some books and other goodies. One of the goodies was tickets to see *Snow White and the Seven Dwarfs* on the stage in Newark. Marguerite Clark was the star, and part of the prize included meeting her backstage. She asked what I was going to do when I grew up, and I said I'm going to know lots of people like you and work with them, if I can. That was really prophetic, in light of what I did later.

A few years before that, my father had remarried and had two children. They lived in New York, but he still ran his lumber and coal business in Morristown. When I was about ten, I went to live with them in New York. The truant officer got after my father to get me into school, and at first they didn't know where to put me because my earlier tutoring had given me a lot of knowledge. They finally put me in eighth grade, and I had a good time because I knew most of what they taught. I didn't know the principles of grammar, but my writing was always correct. Later, although I wanted to go to high school, my father and stepmother didn't, for some reason or other, think it was necessary. Anyway, I was writing and sending stories out but without any great results. Finally, I did send a scenario to William S. Hart, and he sent back a check for fifty dollars. His note said to keep writing for I did have a gift and there was a wonderful scene in the scenario that he was going to use. The enclosed check was to pay for it. I was about fourteen at the time and my stepmother was so impressed, she sent away for a correspondence course in scenario writing. To this day, I know a lot about writing a film.

The First World War was on at that time, and an uncle who hadn't seen me since I was two came to New York. He had been in the Philippines and was now on his way to join the American forces in Europe. He gave me a hundred-dollar bill and told me not to spend it on anyone else in the family. He made me promise to only use it for myself. Well, I couldn't imagine what I could do with it. I had a home, clothes, and my father gave me money to go down to the theater matinees with my girlfriend. Anyway, I carried that bill in my pocketbook for two years, trying to think of something that would hypnotize me into buying it. One day, I was standing on the corner of 181st Street and St. Nicholas Avenue, and I happened to glance up at the building's second floor. There was a sign in the window— *Secretarial Course $99—Employment Guaranteed.*

I knew then that's where my hundred-dollar bill would go. When I went up, the woman behind the desk barked at me, "This course is for high school graduates only." Well, I was really short and wearing a middy blouse and sneakers. I told her I was a graduate, and as I got close to her desk I began pulling the money out of my pocket. She said, "Well, you don't look it." At that point, I laid the hundred-dollar bill on the desk, and she immediately gave me an application.

This was the fall of 1918, and sadly we heard that my uncle had been killed. A friend who was with him at the time gave us the story. He said the war was over and some Germans in a nearby trench sent a farewell salute by throwing a bomb over toward their trench. The Americans were not paying any attention, and it exploded right where they were eating breakfast. My uncle was killed . . . the date was November 11, 1918, Armistice Day. It must have been fate.

Well, getting back to the secretarial course. I had a lot of fun there. In the eighth grade I was always the leader of things, the editor of the paper, the little mother, and so on. The same thing happened here, I was the head of this and the head of that. It all seemed preordained throughout my life, people always turning to me to get things done. Anyway, the course was about six months and at completion they sent me to a job in Wall Street as a stenographer. I advanced very quickly, and after a year or so, I was able to get an apartment of my own just a few blocks from my family. Then an actor fell in love with me.

Because I was sort of a stepchild in the family, there was a lack of affection. My father was much more interested in his new family than he was in me. My stepmother liked me very much and was always very good to me, but she never hugged and kissed me the way she did her own children. And I used to get down on my knees and say, dear God, make somebody love me! So when the actor said he loved me, I gravitated toward him. I really didn't care for him, but fortunately Dan Jarrett was a very nice and good man. I met a number of his friends from the theater, and that was interesting because of my feelings about writing stories. Dan was going on a six-month tour with Tom O'Shea, a well-known actor who had put together a repertoire of the best scenes from a number of plays. A week before the tour, Dan called and said the actress in the troupe had married and left the tour.

That's when Tom O'Shea said, "Gee, I hate to have a stranger traveling with us for six months. Why don't we get Jean to go with us? That would be wonderful." So Dan asked if I would go. He said it would be a lot of fun and there would be a lot of material for my writing—the people we'd meet would be much more interesting than the ones in Wall Street. It was only a small onstage part, as a maid, but there was also offstage dialogue I would have to do. When I asked my boss, he said, "Well, my dear, if I was your age, I'd grab it. But I'll give you just six months' leave; you've got to come back because you're valuable to the company." And that's how I got into show business . . . with a maid's uniform and the one line, "There's Mr. Shea now." There was also an "afterpiece" to the show. That's where some of the cast from the other various acts get together and do a spontaneous bit after the main performances are over. It was a big-time show, with Paul Whiteman and his band, Morton Downey, Sr., as the singer, plus comedies, skits, and our own act. Anyway, a couple of the comics and I did an afterpiece act and I really enjoyed it.

But Dan was right, the show people in the other acts were interesting and there was lots of material to write about. One day I told Dan that I liked show business very much, but I didn't want to work for someone else and why couldn't we have an act of our own. Dan shook his head and said it would cost twenty-five thousand dollars to get an act written. But I said that wasn't necessary, we could write one ourselves. I said I was a writer and he was a very witty, funny, funny man and I already had a good vaudeville skit idea for us. I showed it to him, and much to his astonishment, he said it *was* good. So we wrote it and when we got back to New York, he showed it to his agent, who loved it. Of course, the agent wanted Dan and an experienced actress for the skit—not me.

So they put it together and it opened in Fort Lee, New Jersey. I felt the actress did a good job and got her laughs, but she wasn't right for the part. She was too actressy, not real enough. Anyway, they played a few other places and then suddenly our agent, Max Tischman, got a request for our skit to play the big time—but only if I was in the lead. Max couldn't understand how the Keith-Albee talent scouts could request me. "You've never seen Jean in anything; in fact, she's back working in Wall Street." But they said, "Yes, we have. We saw her in Los Angeles in an afterpiece with the two comedians. You put her into the skit and we'll play it on the regular circuit." That was my first production and it went on the big-time circuit, with Dan and me as the team. By the way, Max told me all this only a short time ago, before he died. He never admitted this to Dan, because he felt Dan was jealous of me, so he simply said the whole thing was his own idea.

In my next production, there was a disagreement with my ideas for casting. This fellow, Archibald Leach, had always wanted to act, but he had never been on the professional stage—only in school plays in England. He had first joined a troupe of acrobats and became a very good acrobat himself. Then he became a very fine stilt-walker. In fact, that's exactly what he was doing in New York, walking on stilts and advertising Luna Park in Coney Island. When he wasn't on the job, he would hit the agencies looking for acting parts, and they finally sent him to me. Well, I wanted him at once, but Dan and Max didn't want him at all. They didn't like his cockney accent. So I said, let's make him English in the skit, what difference does it make as long as he's got the personality we need. "The Woman Pays" was a vaudeville skit about a girl who's engaged to a sort of homey guy, nice and proper for her to marry. Then she meets this handsome, handsome man who is rather worldly, and she falls for him, etc., etc. Well, the agencies kept sending me Rudolph Valentino types, and I said no. I finally used Archibald Leach, and he was a big, big hit in the part. Of course, he was later known as Cary Grant. He was one of my first discoveries, and Jimmy Cagney was another.

I wrote another skit called "In the Park," which was about a sailor on leave who meets another sailor and a girl in the park. They join up and then there's the usual business of who winds up with the girl. I wanted to have some dancing, where all three danced—like a little musical comedy. Dan and I went to see a small musical revue downtown and amongst the male dancers was a wonderful redheaded guy, with a tremendous personality. He really stood out, and I said I'd like to get him for the part. Dan objected, "You need an actor, he's just a hoofer. We have to have actors because we're doing sketches and people expect to see good performers." Again I disagreed and said let's get him because he's got the exact personality we need and he's also a good dancer. We went backstage and I told Jimmy what we were doing and would he leave this show if we put him into a vaudeville skit, with billing. He agreed, and later when the skit went on he was an enormous success. It started his career. Right after that, he went into a big show and he was off and running.

Much later, when Cagney and I talked about it, he said, "I never really knew how to dance. I just did what I was told and made it up as I went along. Even in that big dance sequence in *Yankee Doodle Dandy,* they gave me a choreographer. I had no idea what he was talking about when he would name the various steps I had to do. So I just followed whatever he showed me."

About this time, I began to realize that "talkies" were going to put an end to vaudeville. Not because the public preferred films, but more because the theater owners could get a better return. They could rent a couple of talking pictures for virtually nothing in those early days, rather than having to pay a great deal of money for a bill of vaudeville. Even today, they say people got sick of vaudeville. It's not true; people loved it until the last minute, and they still do.

So I started to think about myself and what I was going to do. I was happy producing our little skits, but I wasn't happy with some of the plays I was able to act in. In those days, the first time you heard the play was at the rehearsals. Many were badly written and I knew they wouldn't succeed, so those were the ones I left after the first full run-through which enabled me to hear the entire play. Since we weren't paid for rehearsals, it meant maybe going without a paycheck for four weeks. And, unlike today, plays didn't have very long runs. If one played more than a year, it was a smash success.

Well, I don't remember how I got it, but I did get a job with Fitzpatrick Pictures—writing, producing, and directing two-reel films. I did a whole series on astrology, amusingly. I had an astrologer as the main character, along with a husband and wife. One of them would be devoted to astrology, and the other would pooh-pooh it. I used all my talented friends who were out of work from vaudeville. I was getting five hundred dollars a week in 1928, which was fabulous money, but it was because this was a new, booming industry. In the meantime, I had written a play with a part in it for myself, and I gave it to Dan to put some amusing situations in it because he was a very funny man. And I went ahead, keeping very busy with the two-reelers, writing and producing them in the studio. One day, Dan walked in and said he had sold the play to John Golden, who was a very, very big-time Broadway producer. But Golden wanted to rewrite it and put his name on it, and apparently he always did that. I agreed to take my name off since I was working and Dan was not, and they both went off to rewrite it.

Many weeks later, Golden sent me the revised script. Well, I was horrified—they had vulgarized it and it was terrible! I sent Golden a note—"I'm very happy my name is not on it." He called and asked, "Now, why would a nice girl like you send a snippy note like that to me?" I told him how awful the script was and we agreed to meet and review it. We looked and I said this page was okay, the next page okay, the next okay, and he interrupted, "See, so it's okay— right?" I said yes, because those pages are the ones *I* wrote. [*Laughs*] Anyway, I showed him all the vulgar and bad parts and he suggested we both rework it until it was producible. I did this for Dan, so that the play would be produced. While reworking it, Golden suggested I shouldn't play the part I had written for myself. When I protested, he said, "Yes, you are good, but you're too good and you don't have the mind of an actress. When you walked out on plays you didn't think would succeed, that's not the way actresses think. I don't want you in the play, because you'll be a hit in it and you'll be an actress the rest of your life." He continued, "You really should come and work for me after you finish with Fitzpatrick. Get into the Broadway theater, which has a little elegance and class to it, and learn my end of the business—that's what you'd really be good at."

And that's what I did! I never acted again, because I realized it actually wasn't my greatest talent. I didn't particularly like doing it, although I enjoyed the laughter and the applause. Putting everything together, writing, and getting it on, that I did like. So, you see, once again there's another piece of my life that fell into place—a very positive career change. I worked with John Golden for many years and did everything, it was marvelous experience. Strangely enough, I knew how to do anything he handed me. Once, when our press agent left, John asked me to do the publicity and I objected because although I could write, I had no idea how to get it into the papers. In fact, I didn't even know what a press release was. John pooh-poohed all that, gave me a list of all the famous newspaper critics, and said, "All you have to do is make friends with these guys. Call them and say you're my new press agent and you'll give them any information they need about what I'm doing. That's all you have to do." That's all indeed! Of course, I would have been thrilled to meet any and all of those famous people. So I worked all night and the next morning, writing an individual note to each of them, basically saying what John had mentioned. A day or so later, their columns were all about *me,* saying Golden had a new press agent and it's our old friend from vaudeville, Jean Dalrymple.

The next day John came in and said, "You were supposed to publicize me and all I see are stories about you!" But I only did what he had told me to do. [*Laughs*] Later, one of the columnists, Ward Morehouse, came to see me, and when we finished talking, he went into Golden's office and said, "Well, I came to see your new press agent and I want to warn you—I'm going to marry her one day." And would you believe it, about a year or so later he did!

There's a story here. When Ward and I were seeing each other, we wrote a play together and he sold it to Warner Brothers. Well, they hired Ward to go out and write the scenario, because he had a well-known name and was a famous newspaperman. After he was out there awhile he called. "I don't know what I'm doing out here. This isn't writing. We have meetings and I don't know what they're talking about—do you?" I said I did, remembering my scenario to Hart and my correspondence course. From the course, I knew all the gobbledygook connected with it and I began to tell him some of it, but he said he couldn't do it and I should come on out. I couldn't because of my work, so Ward flew back to New York and told Golden, "I warned you I was going to marry her one day and I'm going to now—because I can't live without her, and I can't earn my living without her." So we married and went to Hollywood to work on the scenario together. Golden was furious and said, "She threw herself away on a mere newspaperman." But I couldn't have been happier.

After the film, we returned to New York and I started working for Golden again . . . he had gotten over his peeve and wanted me back. Some time later, a friend returned from Europe and mentioned a film he had purchased there, *Maedchen in Uniform,* and he wanted me to publicize it. Golden was unhappy, but I told him I wanted to do it. I handled the film like a play because I didn't know any better. I scheduled two performances a day, and the critics all received opening-night tickets, just like a Broadway show. It had kind of a big-time aura about it, and everybody was impressed. It was a big, big hit! Then others started to ask me to publicize their efforts. Tallulah Bankhead only wanted me for her new show and, before you knew it, I had an office and other personnel. Musicians and performers were next, and I became a manager or publicist for many—José Iturbi, Leopold Stokowski, Joseph Steinberg, Lily Pons, and Grace Moore were a few of the top ones. In fact, I was Iturbi's manager and publicist for fifty years.

For the war effort, the Treasury Department asked if I could do a series of concerts to promote the sale of war stamps. They felt I was the only one who could do it because of my relationships with all the artists. I said okay, and we put on four huge concerts, all with big names, that were very successful. We used the Mecca Temple in New York, which had been closed and used only for the city's civil service exams. At a big celebration party, Mayor La

Guardia and council president Newbold Morris discussed the need for a center where the average New Yorker could go for good entertainment at a reasonable price. They asked my opinion about the temple, and I said it was a beautiful theater, and all it needed was a good coat of paint.

The next thing you know, Newbold and I began raising money to refurbish Mecca Temple. One day he reported there was sixty-five thousand dollars, and could we start with that. I agreed and started to plan some programs, but I then became so busy with my own work and a new Broadway show that I lost track of the activity for the temple. I was lunching with the head of the group of investors, and after filling him in about a new musical starring Mary Martin and some other great talent, he agreed to back it. Then he said, "Okay, I've helped you with your project, now you have to help Newbold Morris and us with the Mecca Temple. I understand you've been too busy to come to meetings, but there's one today and I want you to come with me right now to tell our board what to do. We meet and just sit there." I did go and told the mayor and the board they should get someone to run the operation: "I couldn't do it, but maybe I could help. There's someone in Newark who's doing almost the same thing you want done with the Mecca Temple, and he is looking to move on to something else." The mayor took the phone number and immediately dialed him to make a date for the next morning. He got the job as director.

I quickly publicized him and the project. But instead of making him feel good, he was scared to death—the big city and all that. In the end, I had to tell him many of the things he should do, and some I did myself. I had a wonderful time doing it. I even gave the Mecca Temple a new name— the City Center of Music and Drama. Everything—ballet, drama, musical comedy—they were all there for a top price of two dollars. This fit the original concept that Mayor La Guardia wanted for all New Yorkers—"a place of good entertainment at the lowest possible prices." Over the years we also had a million children attend performances for only twenty-five cents a ticket.

Later, out of the clear blue, a group from the St. Louis Opera Company came to New York and asked me to form an American Opera Company—I could even call it the Jean Dalrymple Company. I said no about my name, but I listened. It seemed all their backers were in the army, and it was suggested that another opera company could more easily be started in New York. They would make all the sets and costumes available. To make a long story short, I suggested it to Mayor La Guardia, and just like the last time, he immediately phoned the director of the opera company in St. Louis. They had a long conversation, and then he turned to us and said, "We have an opera company!" It became the City Center Opera Company.

The mayor had always complained about the high price of opera, and when we got it started at the City Center, opera seats went from 85 cents to $2.25. Top prices for ballet were $2.00, plays $1.50, and concerts $1.00. Although the City Center had a three-thousand-seat auditorium, at those prices every performance wasn't a financial success. Large donations helped, and for the numerous revivals of Broadway plays, entire casts were only paid the Actor's Equity minimum—$57.50 a week. Additionally, many of the leading players donated their services. Leopold Stokowski, who began the New York City Symphony, not only worked without pay, but he often personally contributed large sums toward the concerts.

Everyone wanted the center to be a success, and many of the top people in their fields willingly contributed their talents. After Stokowski, Leonard Bernstein, who was only twenty-six at the time, became the music director and composer of the symphony. George Balanchine and others created a ballet company that was amongst the finest anywhere. And our theater audiences were treated to the great talents of Gertrude Lawrence, Helen Hayes, Orson Welles, José Ferrer, Maurice Evans, Paul Robeson, and numerous other grand stars. The City Center Opera Company had a wonderful first season and over the years it won international acclaim. Yes, there were plenty of ups and downs along the way. Some of the downbeats were painful to all of us, but the successes were extremely gratifying.

Would I consider myself a founder to the City Center? I think so. Especially with Mayor La Guardia and Newbold Morris nudging me along the way in those early days. I publicized it, got the director, named it, got the opera company, had my client the Ballet Russe de Monte Carlo make their headquarters in the City Center, and even set up the Tuesday-through-Sunday performance schedule. Previously, there were no theater performances on Sunday, a leftover from the blue laws. My many European friends had always complained about the no performances on that day, so for the City Center schedule I proposed the Tuesday-to-Sunday programs. I had already done that for my own theatricals, and the weekend activity just made our business. The City Center was a great success, and I remained involved for many, many years. I think my book *From the Last Row* lists something like twenty-five years. You know, with all my activities and directorships I was always a volunteer; I was never a salaried employee.

In the meantime, of course, I pursued my own business of publicist, writer, producer, director, and manager for the next three or four decades. And I also wrote the six books, during the sixties and seventies. I used to dictate from nine to eleven every morning to finish a book. I had a young lady who was very good, and she would go home after the dictation, type it up, and bring it in the next morning. Then I'd edit it and give it back to her, plus another two hours of dictation, and that's the way it went. But in the forties through the seventies, I must have produced about one hundred productions, some of which I also directed. Practically every theatrical star, at one time or another, was involved, and I loved it all.

Once, a long way back, I was in California, working for

José Iturbi. He was in one of those difficult moods, and I walked out on him for a while. While I was out, I thought in a bitchy way that I would like to get somebody he looks up to and work for him—that might give him a jolt. Suddenly the phone rings and it's Stokowski's manager, who says, "Jean, Stokowski's out here doing *Fantasia* and he's like a fish out of water. He needs an old friend like you— would you do a little of your wonderful publicity work for him and make him feel at home?" I said sure, it was exactly what I had been dreaming about.

We met at his place and had a long talk about what he was doing and how I could help. At that point, the Chinese houseman came in with a large plate that looked like a salad, but there were a lot of strange things, in fact one section looked like worms. It turned out to be sprouts, but I had never seen them before. Stokowski noticed and asked, what did I usually have for lunch? When I said I was usually too busy, sometimes a sandwich and glass of milk, he exploded. "Oh God, you're killing yourself, don't you realize that?" And he then gave me a big talk about a salad every day and what I should do to take care of my health, especially since I hadn't been taking care of myself at all. He convinced me and started me on a health kick which I've followed all my life. One thing surprised him—my skin. He didn't know how I could have such beautiful skin when I've never eaten correctly. I told him it was hereditary.

Speaking about skin brings up another story, the time I met George Bernard Shaw. He also complimented me on my skin, but I said that *his* skin, what little one could see of it because of his huge beard, was wonderful, and he was ninety-four years old. Well, he wanted to know how did I and other girls take care of our skin. I mentioned I use a night cream to take off my daily makeup and then a moisturizer on it. In the morning, I do this and do that, and then the other thing. He said, "You're wasting your money and ruining your skin. Do you know that men have better skin than women, and do you know why? The men *wash* it with hot water and towels and things like that. Their skin is nice and clean and it's cleaned every day. Women never wash their faces. They put cream on and then wipe it off with some other gook." He continued, "You should begin tomorrow. Get yourself a nice, mild soap and wash your face. Then rinse it twenty times in cold water. After you dry it, put on a dot of any kind of oil—salad oil, baby oil, any kind of oil. Not because the skin is dry, because it's taut." He told me this in 1948 and I've done it ever since. He also mentioned a prayer—*let me live a long time, but not long enough to be old!* He was ninety-four, but I don't think he liked it. Anyway, those were the two men who worried about my skin.

What I'm doing today started a long time ago. One day in 1940, Rachel Crothers called me and said, "Jean, we're going to get into this war sooner than people think, and I'd like your help in starting a stage relief organization." She had started a Stage Women's War Relief in World War I and wanted to follow through for World War II. She said I knew how to get things started, and would I go ahead now? I agreed and said I'd call certain big stars and then publicize them being with this group and others would soon join. That's what we did, and that's how the famous American Theatre Wing got started. In those days, this organization raised money to take small children out of London during the blitz. We also did a lot of knitting for the soldiers, refugees, and children. It started and ran the well-known Stage Door Canteen, along with many other activities.

Today, I'm still involved with the American Theatre Wing—actually since 1940. Now, of course, we have other functions. There's the Saturday Theatre for Children, an important activity which has its own auditorium where the productions are staged. We sponsor the Tony Awards, which generates a lot of money to be spread around various theater activities. There are the hospital shows, where theatrical scenes are staged with name talent.

Two weeks before the Tony Awards, we have a Tony Award Time Party, and I get some talent together and put on a show every year. I'm still doing that. Then there are the seminars for the Theatre Wing on "Working in the Theatre." I'm a moderator on that. I'm also still a volunteer press agent for the organization. I still do some writing, and if something came along that would excite me, I'd love to produce. Today you have to fall in love with a show to go through what you have to go through to get it on—raising the money, finding a theater, getting the talent, and so on. It used to be a pleasure to be in the theater, but it really isn't anymore.

No, there isn't any particular driving interest that sustains me. It's really just me, and that's a bit complex. As you noted, however, everything just seems to fall into place when I need it or when I'm making a career change, or whatever. I will say that I've always found things easy to do, even when I know nothing about it. Anything that was handed to me, I'd say okay and I'd do it. I just seemed to naturally know how to do things. Sol Horok once called me Lady Hurok, because he said I was a bigger impresario than he was.

I believe that each one of us is sent into life to do something that we do well. If we do it, we're happy doing it. If we don't get into that thing we were sent here to do, we're miserable. And we do other things and don't do them well. Some people have never had the good fortune or whatever it is to find it. I feel I've had it from the very beginning.

October 2, 1990

DOUGLAS FAIRBANKS, JR.

When we met at his New York office, he was hurriedly trying to finish a sandwich and beverage at his desk. I suggested he relax while I look around. His office walls and shelves were crammed with the memorabilia of a highly active and multifaceted life. Theater, films, and television were, perhaps, the major areas of his active professional career. But there were many other Fairbanks activities — writing, lectures, foreign affairs, military service, business, and innumerable public service committees and associations, both here and abroad.

The varied honors and awards attest to this diversity and would fill a few pages. Militarily, there are the Legion of Merit (U.S.A.), the Distinguished Service Cross (U.K.), the Croix De Guerre with Palm (France), and many, many others.

Even now those well-known personal attributes remain — Fairbanks is a handsome, gracious raconteur with a genuine warmth and immaculate attire. The flyleaf of his autobiography proclaims Fairbanks as an American Prince of Wales.

✻   ✻   ✻

I WAS BORN right here in Manhattan—in fact, on Broadway, which is very rare for anyone in the acting profession. Even at that time, Broadway meant the height of theatrical careers. I guess it was that way before I was born; after all, my father was a star on Broadway before he ever went into films, and that was a long time ago.

In those days, plays didn't run for years and years to be a success. In fact, if a play ran from three to six months, it could actually prove profitable. Running a full year and more would be considered a blockbuster, even on a national tour. Obviously, not many of these specifications would fit Broadway today.

Apparently, at that young age I was spoiled by a doting mother and not overwhelmed with attention by a father who was constantly occupied. And I wasn't the healthiest child around. Scarlet fever, pneumonia, pleurisy, whooping cough, measles, and bronchitis, to name a few, were some of the maladies. But I survived.

When I did some research for my autobiography, I found that when I was six months old, the family spent a summer in England, and then we all moved back here to the Algonquin Hotel. Dad acted on Broadway for the next few years and then went on short national tours. When my father was in Chicago in a fairly long-running play, I was taken to a matinee to watch him. Mother and I were in a box, and it was great to look around at everything and everyone. To a three-year-old, the play was definitely not the thing. But somewhere along the line, I did notice my father in a love scene with the leading lady, and I sort of yelled out, "Look what Daddy's doing to that lady." Well, everybody roared, audience and players alike. It stopped the show for a few minutes.

The next year, 1914, we were in London. The best part of that to a four-year-old was watching the changing-of-the-guard ceremony at Buckingham Palace. There were days when I march-trotted alongside them, near the fifes and drums. That was really fun. Later that year World War I started, but I didn't realize or understand what it was all about. In a short time, we went back to New York with my new governess, Dedie Dowd, who would later become practically a member of the family.

After that, my father got signed for his first film, and we were off to meet him in Los Angeles. I expected to see cowboys and Indians in the West, and I was disappointed by it all. Later, however, back at the studios, I did meet some real cowboys and Indians, and we shook hands, posed for pictures, and I even got a cowboy hat. To a young boy it was really something. The studio, when the picture was completed, thought it wasn't very good, and they decided to keep it away from their major outlets. But a new theater was opening in New York, and the owner wanted it because Douglas Fairbanks was a New York star in the theater. I'm sure you guessed the ending—of course, it was a smash hit!

By the way, I was pretty chubby as a kid. They even called me Fatty in the so-called proper school that was picked for me to start my education. That school really bothered me for years—it was the Hollywood School for Girls, and there were only a few other guys besides me. One boy there was Joel McCrea. Later, Jean Harlow and Jane Peters (Carole Lombard) started there.

In the meantime, my father was making one film after another—short and entertaining, but nothing classic. And there were plenty of rumors about his romance with Mary Pickford, "America's Sweetheart." Even my mother wasn't fully aware of its extent. Soon, however, their marriage came to an end, but I was told that my father would see me often. By then, America had entered the war, and we kids were playing soldiers and sailors instead of cowboys and Indians. We also collected tinfoil, rolling it into huge balls, and the girls helped by making bandages.

We had returned to New York, where my parents' divorce was concluded. Later, my mother married her old beau from Pittsburgh. I went to Collegiate School, a semimilitary school founded way back in colonial days. Then Dad, Charlie Chaplin, Mary Pickford, and D. W. Griffith formed a partnership to produce movies—they called the company United Artists. It shook up the entire industry. Soon after that, Mary Pickford got her divorce and she and Dad were married.

So within a few years, I went to school in New York, California, London, Paris, plus some private tutoring. In Paris, I met Gertrude Stein, Ernest Hemingway, Louis Bromfield, and many others. Although I was only thirteen, I was nevertheless impressed. Quite often I played tennis with Maurice Chevalier. My mother said, "The reason we are living in Paris is because it's less expensive than New York or Los

Angeles." A theatrical agent who knew Mother suggested he could get a movie deal for me, so she agreed to let him see what he could come up with.

A contract for one picture was offered, more or less on the basis of the Fairbanks name. There was also some ulterior motive of revenge on the part of that producer—because of losing my father and Mary Pickford when they started their own company. Well, we went to Hollywood, and I completed the film. It wasn't any great shakes, and I was fired. Although I was tall for my age, I was only thirteen. Later, the studio gave me another chance doing small bit parts and walk-ons, and I occasionally served as a second assistant cameraman. In those days, that meant turning a crank on a silent movie camera when shooting long-range action shots. You also had to carry film boxes and camera cases in the location areas—over hills, across deserts, or whatever.

Once I did get a good bit part which also included a scene that I really botched up. It meant jumping from a plane, pulling open a parachute, and landing. I insisted I should do it and they didn't need a double for me. Up we went and I painfully crawled out on the wing, small step by small step, all the while holding each strut tightly. Frankly, by this time I was scared, and when I looked down—I froze at the wing tip. I couldn't jump, couldn't move! Finally, I crawled back. They had to repeat the scene with a double, who jumped and floated down safely. Of course, when my mother heard about them letting a fourteen-year-old kid do that, she flipped. Not long after, my option was dropped and I freelanced at the lesser studios. Unfortunately, they didn't pay well, they finished pictures in two weeks, and they worked long hours. Not too pleasant!

Finally, something better came along. I interviewed and won a part in *Stella Dallas* for Samuel Goldwyn. It starred Ronald Colman, and when it was released, it was a big hit. Even the lesser roles, like my own, got the benefit. Other parts came along, and I also took drama lessons to learn about all the other aspects that would help my acting. John Barrymore was one of my favorites, and I had met him years back at the Algonquin. I'd been on a number of his sets, saw him on the stage, and even tried to look and dress like him. So it was great when I was to do a small bit in a picture with his brother, Lionel Barrymore. As it turned out, the film wasn't any good. But the next one was with Will Rogers, and gradually there were more and more small bit parts in better films. In the meantime, Dad had been making the good ones—*The Mark of Zorro, The Three Musketeers, Robin Hood,* and *The Black Pirate,* which was the first full-length Technicolor feature ever made.

But everything wasn't all roses with me yet. There was a period with no parts in sight, and I got a few side jobs—directing screen tests and writing subtitles. Finally, I talked a friend into having me do a hit play in Los Angeles. We put it on together at the Belasco Theatre. When it was known that my father and his wife, Mary Pickford, and Charlie Chaplin would be there, the place was sold out. Fortunately, the play got the applause that night and the next day the reviews were all good. After everyone had left the performance, however, it was only Chaplin who stayed and gave me both praise and some helpful suggestions.

I also received a congratulatory note from Joan Crawford, and that later developed into an interest between the both of us. After the Los Angeles success, the play went to San Francisco. I worked late there and Crawford worked late in the Hollywood studios. But we kept in touch and managed to see each other occasionally. When the play was finished, I returned to a few not-very-good films. Finally, I got my first lead, in a film called *The Power of the Press,* directed by someone only a few years older than myself. He was Frank Capra, who in later years became one of Hollywood's top directors. Our film was a success! Then MGM cast me in *A Woman of Affairs,* with Greta Garbo and John Gilbert. That was a good supporting role, I even had a death scene to do. I had to admit that things were looking up.

Within the next year or so, the romance between Joan Crawford and me flourished, and we were married. Her career had taken off, and MGM considered her their newest star. There was plenty of publicity about our marriage. Soon after we had become close, Joan had requested that I call her Billie, and I always did. We both kept busy. Billie made a number of films that year, and I completed a series of movies with a new young actress—Loretta Young. She became a longtime friend. In between films, I managed short runs with plays as often as possible.

One of the films with Loretta Young was a football story, and we used actual players from the USC team. Among that group was one player named "Duke" Morrison, and a few years later, I got him a part in a film of mine. After that, he decided to stay in films and use the name of John Wayne. In 1930, things picked up, and I was cast for *Dawn Patrol*, with Richard Barthelmess. It was one very rough, tough picture. Long hours, nights, cold locations, boxed food, and all that goes with that kind of project. In the end it was worth it—the picture was a big hit, both here and abroad.

For the initial period, movies with sound simply meant they had sound effects—like horses running, engines roaring, the slam of doors closing, and full musical scores in the background. Then everybody got into the act and things moved very fast, until in a short while you were able to see all-talking pictures. Of course, that changed everything in the business. Studios now had to have solid walls, equipment had to be quiet or baffled, and for a while cameras had to be put into booths, along with the cameraman! Sound people were something new, and they were still experimenting. Shooting took hours and hours longer. We couldn't make films in three or four weeks anymore; it was a whole new and exciting era. Actors and actresses now had to talk, and theater talent was suddenly in demand. Those of us who had started on the stage were okay, but some of the silent stars had big problems and, perhaps, no careers.

Well, all this activity in Hollywood was going on during

those terrible days of the depression, but there was plenty of work in certain areas. Like they said, "If you had a job, you only read about the depression—if you didn't have a job you really lived it." I took a supporting role in *Little Caesar*, with a fine stage actor named Edward G. Robinson. It was a gangster part, pretty unusual for me, but I wanted to show that I could do it. The film was great, and Robinson became known as a real tough guy. Off the screen, however, he was a very gentle man and hated to play these villains. But it paid well! As for me, well, I signed a new contract—a starring one.

That year, although I did four films, only one was a hit, two others were so-so, and one was a flop. Billie was doing much, much better. Finally, though, Hollywood started to feel the pinch of the depression, and studios cut back on their film output and reduced their personnel. I felt it also. I even made two films in the French language; it was a first for foreign-language films from Hollywood, but they were only fair. Not long after, Billie hinted about a separation.

While she was busy concentrating on her role as Sadie Thompson, in *Rain*, Laurence Olivier, Robert Montgomery, and I started to horse around together. Once I set up a lovely girl to meet Olivier, and they honestly became interested in each other. Well, I got the use of my uncle's apartment and offered it to Olivier. I had another key, so when he and the girl were together there, a huge stuntman I knew was sent in to demand, "What are you doing with my wife?" Laurence Olivier jumped up from the couch, took one look at this giant of a guy, and fainted dead away. When he came to, we all roared, had a drink, and I was forgiven.

My next films were some of the better ones. I costarred with Katharine Hepburn in *Morning Glory,* for which Kate won an Oscar. Then I starred with Loretta Young in a fight film, *The Life of Jimmy Dolan.* Other players in that one included newcomers John Wayne and Mickey Rooney. And in England, I played my first major character part—

the mad czar, Peter III, in *Catherine the Great,* for Alexander
Korda. By that time, Billie had filed for divorce, which
would become final in 1934.

Catherine the Great opened in London and Paris. It got
good reviews, and they acknowledged my character role as
a great change of pace. One of my teenage crushes was on
Gertrude Lawrence, the fabulous international stage star.
We met in London and became very good friends, even
romantic ones. We starred together in two plays, one that
didn't do well and the other which wasn't a big hit, but
seemed to please the audiences. In the meantime, I was also
trying to get my own film company started, and I finally did
get it under way with a film *The Amateur Gentleman.* Elissa
Landi was my costar, and the reviews were favorable. In
one part of that film, there was a scene of a bare-knuckle
fight which I was supposed to win. Well, I had invited
friends, my mother, and her husband to be part of the
shouting extras. At the climax of the fight, one of us was
just a bit off of correct position, and this giant's fist connected with my jaw and it was lights-out for me. I was out
cold! But that's where the joy of movies comes in; we did
another take—and I won!

My company, Criterion, did another film with Valerie
Hobson and myself, which made out fairly well at the box
office. But with all of that, I still had to make a decision to
leave Criterion, which I did. Fortunately, Zanuck asked me
to return to Hollywood and play a supporting role in *The
Prisoner of Zenda,* with Ronald Colman. My dad said, "The
supporting role of Rupert, the villain, is one of the best ever
written. Take it." Zanuck convinced me I was lucky to get
it after a somewhat less than successful few years in London. The rest of the cast was marvelous, and when
released, it was a smashing success and everyone connected with it benefited.

I starred in *Joy of Living* with one of the finest actresses
around—Irene Dunne. It was light entertainment and fun.
Then another light comedy with Danielle Darrieux and

right after that, *Having Wonderful Time,* with a friend, Ginger Rogers. That was Red Skelton's film debut, and Lucille Ball's small part was a success.

Cary Grant invited me to play in *Gunga Din.* They already had Victor McLaglen and Joan Fontaine. When I read the rough script, I could see Victor as the old, tough sergeant, but the other parts were of two young sergeants and I didn't know which one Cary would play. I finally asked him and he said, "Whichever one you don't want, I'll do. I want us together and the three of us will make this a much better picture." I never had anyone make such an unselfish proposal, but Cary was like that. In the end, we tossed a coin for the parts. So we spent many weeks fighting off the thugs in our fort, in the California desert at the base of the Sierra Madre Mountains. The picture and all of us got great reviews when it was released in 1938.

At this time, I became more interested in government and world affairs. After a London trip I returned to the States on the *Queen Mary* and was able to meet Anthony Eden, who was going to America to address the American Manufacturers Association. It was his first trip to our country. After a few get-togethers, someone in the party encouraged me to ask Eden if I could peruse the rough script of his speech, and he agreed. I studied it all day and marked some suggestions and comments that would make his thoughts clearer to an American audience. Later, he noted that half my suggestions would be incorporated, and I was pleased. In California, I had joined some foreign-policy study groups, and I talked and learned from many distinguished people in that field. In the New York and Washington groups, there was Franklin Roosevelt, Jr., Walter Lippman, Cordell Hull, Harry Hopkins, and others. FDR Jr. also had me visit with his father in the White House, strictly a brief social meeting.

In Canada, the Governor General was an old friend who remembered my previous suggestion to have the king visit the United States. It would be the first such visit for any

British monarch. Naturally, there were a lot of political areas to be cleared away for that kind of occasion. Not long after, however, President Roosevelt issued an invitation and the king and queen did come over. They visited the World's Fair in New York, Hyde Park, and Washington. They were a big hit with the American people. I feel I played a small part in that occasion. Of course, some thought I was a pest; others thought I was looking for publicity in the field of foreign affairs. But over the years I had met a lot of influential people, and I kept trying to make others see what was happening in Europe. Our film industry and much of the business world tried to remain neutral about any of the European problems that were developing.

During that same period, I had met Mary Lee Hunt. After her recent divorce, we had become interested in one another, fallen in love, and agreed to marry. Although we set a date, the film director I was working with warned me they might not be able to give me that day off. As the time came closer, he said I might get off before two o'clock—the wedding was set for two-thirty. Boy, was I steaming! Well, that day came and I got to the studio early. I don't think my acting that morning, or the accent I was supposed to use, functioned very well. At ten-thirty, the director came over and said something like, "Okay, Doug, you can go now. That working late idea was all a hoax. We cleared the schedule a long time ago so you could leave early." I didn't laugh too much, but everybody wished me well and gave me a scroll with all their signatures. Anyway, in spite of all that, it was a lovely wedding.

The completed film was fairly good, but the next one was a dud. I wasn't under contract and free-lancing wasn't any fun. By this time, Hitler and Stalin had gotten together, and shortly thereafter they invaded Poland. England then declared it was at war with Germany, and everything came to a standstill that day. After that, however, the war just seemed to plod along, and people started to relax again.

In December, a day after my birthday party, Dad suffered

a heart attack and died a few nights later. He was fifty-six and it was a loss to all of us. Newspapers all over the world had headlines about his death. Paramount rearranged the shooting schedule on *Safari* and gave me several days off.

A few months later, I was working in a new film, *Angels Over Broadway*, with a new starlet, Rita Hayworth. Mary Lee gave birth to a pretty baby girl and we named her Daphne. But then the phony war in Europe became real! Hitler invaded Norway and Denmark, and some of the other small countries. Then he invaded France and it surrendered. Now England was being bombed and their ships sunk.

The United States wanted to help, but not get involved. I became one of the vice presidents of the White Committee to Aid the Allies, and made numerous trips to Washington to meet with President Roosevelt and Cordell Hull. The committee made many proposals, and we tried to counter the isolationists. I made broadcasts to Britain and to our national audiences, and lots of people didn't like my getting involved. Later, the White House approved a South American goodwill tour for me, which would relate to "cultural relations." The real purpose, however, was to sound out these countries for their reactions to our being attacked, or to our involvement in the war. And would we be able to use their ports, if needed, to repair our naval ships. The trip lasted two months, and I understand my reports were well received. Later, I reported directly to Cordell Hull.

Earlier, because of my sailing and boating hobbies, I had applied for a commission in the Naval Reserve, but it was mandatory to have a university degree. However, if I took some exams and completed a correspondence course, it would be possible. When I returned from South America, I reported to the Navy Department and became a Naval Reserve Officer. A few months later, I was called to active duty. Since I had no training, they decided not to have me shuffle papers, but to get out on a ship's deck and learn what it's all about. After some initial training I was assistant gunnery officer on a destroyer in the North Atlantic, to and from Iceland. We did see some combat action there. When the U.S. declared war, I was transferred to the flagship of the Atlantic fleet. Later, there were all kinds of transfers, assignments, and plenty of action with amphibious and other crafts. In fact, I was the only U.S. officer operating with the Royal Marine Commandos in the English Channel.

I think I served on every type of ship the navy had, even their rubber boats. And I've been in the waters of the North Atlantic, the Mediterranean, the Aegean, Northwest African waters, the Arctic Ocean to Murmansk, and so on. Yes, there were awards and medals and that sort of thing, simply because of all the campaigns, combat areas, and battles we were in. All told, I think it was six years. There were narrow escapes—the bombings in London, I saw some of the blitz there. I had almost every adventure there is, short of being killed. Once there was a fellow next to me in Yugoslavia, our shoulders were touching, and during a barrage of shots the top of his head blew off. I didn't have a scratch.

The strange thing is, I've had every finger of both hands broken, I've had legs broken, my ribs broken—everything from the movies, nothing like that from the war. It's amazing. I did a lot of my own stunts in the films, almost all of them. Of course, they weren't done off the top of my head; we rehearsed everything carefully. I had a stunt choreographer who would tell me, "No, Doug, you can't do this because it's beyond your ability," or "You can do this but we have to rebuild the set for it," and so on. Sometimes we worked out things weeks ahead of time. But I generally didn't want to do too many, because my father made it a thing, and I only did about six films out of eighty that had all these stunts. I didn't want to swashbuckle like he did; I wanted to make my own style and didn't want to be an imitation of anything.

After the war, getting back to work in films was something I wanted to do. Fortunately, *Sinbad the Sailor*, with Maureen O'Hara and Anthony Quinn, came along in 1947. The next year it was *That Lady in Ermine*, with Betty Grable and Cesar Romero, and there were a few others in that period. Nothing classical, just light entertainment, I think that's what this period called for. There was a film overseas with Glynis Johns and Jack Hawkins, *State Secret*. And, of course, television was extremely popular. So I had guest spots with Jack Benny, Bing Crosby, Kate Smith, Edward R. Murrow, and many, many others.

In the fifties, oh, for about five years, I hosted and produced a series of 160 one-act plays for TV. It was an anthology series and in the U.S. it played on the networks as "Douglas Fairbanks Presents." Some were also featured on the "Rheingold Theatre" and other programs, both here and abroad. I only acted in about forty of them. The scripts covered all areas, from light farce to psychological studies, and there was an occasional murder yarn. Filming in England gave us all the castles, mansions, villages, and narrow, winding streets we could ever use.

I guess for the next few decades there was something of everything. There were a number of TV specials with so many talented people—Greer Garson, Anne Baxter, Sir Michael Redgrave, Lilli Palmer, and others. I even did a few "Love Boat" episodes, one of them with Sammy Davis and Carol Channing. Of course, there were the talk shows—Carson, Griffin, and the rest, not only in the U.S., but many overseas ones.

One of the areas I liked best was the theater, especially playing the lead in *My Fair Lady*, which was a revival of the original. But over the years, I starred in it for a total of four revivals. In most of the cities we played, it broke records. Another one that had the same number of revivals was *The Pleasure of His Company*. I didn't play in the original cast, although the author told me he wrote it for me, or with me in mind. Those four revivals played in the U.S., London, Ireland, Australia, and Hong Kong. There were a number of others I toured with and thoroughly enjoyed.

It's true that some people get bored and give up on life, but not if you're doing a variety of things. My father had some ideas on that. He had the body of an Olympic athlete at fifty, full of energy and vitality. I remember him saying by the time he reached fifty, he ought to die—there wasn't much point in going on because you begin to decline. He used to have a facetious remark for people with a career of any kind—"They ought to be shot at the height of their career." He told John Barrymore he should have been shot after his Hamlet. Of course, knowing my father, all this might have just been the kind of remark he used to amuse people.

My interests, fortunately, have been wide, and my activities reflect it. In addition to films, theater, and TV, there's been radio, narrations, singing—I surprised you there—public speaking, and travel, as well as government and foreign affairs. Not politics. I don't relate to partisan politics at all, you know, Republican and Democrat. Funny thing, when I'm abroad people will say, "Now tell us the difference. Here we have conservative, liberal, socialist, and so on. They're easily defined by the name of the party. But Republican and Democrat, what does that mean? What is the difference?" And I'd say damned if I know—I don't think they know the difference themselves. Sometimes it's really interchangeable. There are years when the Republicans are liberal, some years they're strongly conservative—and vice versa with the Democrats. I'm much more interested in international affairs, because I've been mixed up in it on a high level from the president and secretary of state. It began under Roosevelt, then Truman, and some of the others, though I didn't know Nixon very well. And I've had missions assigned at various times, as well as made addresses to various government departments both here and abroad.

My activities today take up a lot of time. There are business involvements, directorships, article writing, and lectures to various colleges and associations. Additionally, I'm trying desperately to complete the second book of my autobiography. The first one, *Salad Days,* concluded in 1941, so there's lots to write about yet. I've got to confess, I haven't touched it in weeks—too busy!

Well, I've always been interested in things, maybe too many things. I'm interested in a vast variety, some having no connection with one another. And sometimes, for no purpose at all, just for the fun of knowing about it. I don't do it deliberately. I do it (a) some of it because I have to, and (b) because I'm interested. Maybe it's a sign of empty-headedness. It's like an animal who constantly sniffs around at this and at that. Kind of childlike as well, sort of an immaturity. Hm-m. I think that last one sounds better than all the rest.

September 26, 1990

JOE FLIEGER

*To this day Joe retains the "cowboy look" and the soft, roll-
ing gait that goes with it. We agreed to meet in the town of
Oracle, Arizona, and he would guide me home from there.
It wasn't a ranch anymore, just a large, open, comfortable
place he built after his ranching days were over. At the
house there were great photos of Joe on bucking horses, in
rodeos and Wild West shows, and at his ranch house built
into a cave. There were numerous silver award buckles and
many other well-worn mementos of forty-two years of
ranching.*

*He talked about those days slowly and deliberately, but
with never a memory hesitation. I enjoyed every bit of it
and wanted to hear a lot more about that lifestyle. But Joe
said he was writing a book about it and if I really wanted to
know more I'd have to wait and buy a copy. The manuscript has since been completed, with publication scheduled
for the near future.*

*   *   *

NEW BRUNSWICK, Canada, was my original stamping
ground. Dad drove a dray which he used for deliveries and
to clear snow off the roads. I helped whenever he needed
me. When I was sixteen and a half, I left home to go west
and become a cowboy in British Columbia. That was in
1918, and that first year I worked harvesting the fields
because all the able-bodied men were in the army. So we
kids, the teenagers, put up all the grain that year.

I stayed in British Columbia for ten years, working on
ranches, breaking horses, and performing in cowboy
shows. In 1928, I went to New York with California Frank's
Wild West Show, and we played mostly in eastern Canada
and the eastern United States. Also worked on the 101 Wild
West Show in Oklahoma, where I played a sheriff, rode two
bucking broncos every day, and also did an act as the

"drunken cowboy." Part of that act had a little trick riding
to it. I would put my feet up by the front of the saddle and
stand up while racing along. Then I'd drink a bottle of beer
and throw it away; pull off the bridle and throw it away;
pull out my six-shooters and bang away; then almost fall
here, almost fall there—and the crowds in the South
thought it was really funny.

In 1929, I went to Phoenix to ride in the winter rodeos
there and in Tucson. When I saw people running around
in their shirtsleeves in February, well, that got me. The last
winter I spent in Canada, the weather was sixty-five degrees
below zero. It usually ran forty-five to sixty-five degrees
below for six weeks with never a break in it. I was hauling
logs then and one of the other guys—who was hiding out
there—told me all about this climate and how the cattle
and horses were out running around during the winter.
You didn't even have to put out any hay for them all winter,
and by God, that's the kind of place I was looking for. You
know, in cold country, you have to put up the hay all summer and then you put it out all winter.

So I came to Arizona in '29 and I stayed. When I hit Phoenix it wasn't a very big town, and Tucson, well, there were
only 34,000 people then. Today, Tucson is more like
634,000. In 1930 I rode in every rodeo around Arizona and
even in Nogales, across the border.

Of course, that was the depression and it was hard times
all around. I got by now and then because I was able to
break horses and that got me jobs that other cowboys
couldn't get. It was rough, though. In '32, I'd put my stuff
on a packhorse and visit ranches all over. They'd all say,
"Yes, we'd like to put you on but there's no money."
Nobody had any money! They had horses to be broken, but
no money to pay for it. One ranch after another, it was all
the same story. Although it all started in '29, it was much
worse a few years later. I remember it in '29. We were playing the Coliseum up in the Bronx, in New York, and when
it hit, people were jumping out windows, committing sui-

cide—bejesus, the whole country was going haywire right then.

Well, anyway, I finally got a job on the Three V's Ranch in Seligman. I rode from Winkleman to way up there, about 360 miles. I camped out nights, and when we got there I had $1.35 in my jeans, my horses were hungry, and I was too. This ranch had a reputation for having some of the rankest horses in the cowland. "We don't want no cowboys," they said, "heck, we got cowboys coming out of our ears. If you can ride the 'rough string,' you got a job."

The "rough string" was made up of horses that were already broken, but they were mean, high-spirited, and spoiled. "Well, I'm gonna tell you something," said the foreman. "If you can't ride, you better not go up there. Those guys are big and mean!" I looked him right in the eye and said, "If you got a horse out there that I can't ride, I'll just eat the S.O.B., hide, hooves, tail, and all—and then I'll walk back to Winkleman!"

You know, I was desperate. I had to have a job then and I'd been riding for years—in the Wild West shows I rode two bucking horses a day, so I was in good shape. I had lots of confidence in myself, and hell, I'd rode buckers in Prescott, Phoenix, and everywhere else; I didn't think a ranch horse was gonna buck me off. So I said let's go, and I sat there while they brought the horses in off the Colorado River.

I could see the cloud of dust coming down the valley, and this big guy coming down with them reminded me of the pirates I used to read about as a kid. A big black hat, red whiskers down to here, and wild wet hair down his back; boy, he sure looked like a pirate. And those 150 horses! Well, he walked over, looked me up and down, and said, "Who're you?" I told him what I was there for, got my saddle, and he pointed to an old gray horse. The other cowhands started giving me the works. "Bet you five he throws him." "Bet you ten he can't stay on." "You know, that's old Fiddler, he killed the last three men that tried to ride him."

I was saddling, you know, getting ready. Hell, I wanted to ride him. I needed that job and those damn guys don't know me and I don't know them, and if this thing bucks me off I oughta walk back to Winkleman. So I eased up onto Fiddler, hit him with the quirt, and away he went. Never even offered a buck! I just ran him way up there and ran him back and said to the boss, how's that? "Oh, hell," he said disgustedly, "just turn him loose." Well, I gotta tell you, that horse bucked every day after that! I think I must have caught him by surprise that first time.

So anyway, I went to work there. And every day that boss tried to get me bucked off. He was determined to get me down. Finally, he told me, "Joe, you're the first man that ever worked here that I didn't get on the ground." I worked there five months and saved my money. Got sixty dollars a month and my board—regular cowboys only got fifty a month. Well, then, I sold my two horses, went back to Winkleman, got ten head of cows and a bull for twenty-five dollars each. There was a cement tank off the road back aways, so I found out who owned it and bought it for $150 so there would be a watering place for the cows. You didn't buy acreage then, everything was in public domain, you just had to have a place to turn your cattle loose—but there must be water available for them.

I rode around awhile and finally found a little cave back there. I ran the wild hogs off out of the cave and threw my bedding down and that was home sweet home. That was 1932, and twenty years later I had five hundred cows. If you count the bulls, heifers, and the calves, it was closer to nine hundred head. Some years after I started that spread I got married. We had to move to a bigger cave then—that was the fourth cave since I started. I finished the walls in there, chopped a bathtub out of solid rock, and built sort of a regular house. Part of it was inside the cave and the whole front of the building was set on the outside.

I remember that little cave where I run the hogs out of— I had a cot for a bed. One time I got up, swung my feet around, and just where I would put them down was a six-foot diamond rattler, all coiled up. Well, I jumped back, hit my head on the cave wall, and knocked myself out. When I came to I got a shovel and did away with that snake. Boy, if I hadda stepped on him, I wouldn't be here now. It's lucky the cave was cool because that snake had hardly got to moving around yet.

It's a funny thing, but all the times I was in the rodeos, Wild West shows, and breaking horses, I never got really hurt. I got bunged up, knocked up, and stomped on, but didn't get really hurt. On my own ranches (for forty-two years), though, when I got banged up with horses, I shouldn't even be sitting here. Altogether, I should have been dead about fifteen times—there was six times with horses, six times with men, and three times with snakes that could have done me in. Once I roped this steer and the big stallion I was on was yanked down on top of me. I was in the hospital bed for twenty-seven days and couldn't move.

Or there was the time in '35 when I was racing down the hill and the outlaws were shooting with those 30-30 slugs whizzing by me. I didn't have any gun so I just kept going! And then when my neighbor was murdered in '36, they said I did it and I'd get the chair. Everything pointed right to me as the killer.

When they wheeled this neighbor to the hospital and they said he was dying, he said, "Joe shot me." His wife came into the court, pregnant, laden with kid and crying, pointed a finger at me, and shouted, "That's the S.O.B. that shot my husband." And then the guy who actually shot him, he came in and said he talked to me that day and that I came back later and said I took a shot at the dead guy. Boy, that noose got a little tighter then!

Sure he was lying, and only I knew it. What really happened that day was this guy came walking by my place when I was chopping wood, and he said, "Well, I got him. I blew his guts all over—you oughta heard him holler."

Well, that took the air out of me, I tell ya. It's true the guy who got killed and I didn't get along too well, and that certainly wasn't a point in my favor. You know, once I got my ranch working good, all the others wanted it. But I wouldn't sell out to any of them. So now with this problem they all thought they had me. And that real killer, he didn't say boo!

Anyway, they arrested me that night, took me over to Florence, accused me in court the next day, and then threw me into a cell with a couple of murderers. The plumbing was all broke to pieces, the steel door just had a little crack in it, and that's where I stood all night, trying to get some fresh air. I was going a little haywire trying to figure out what I was doing there. The next day they took me to court and set my bail at twenty-five thousand dollars. Well, my wife and friends put up forty thousand dollars, but they wouldn't turn me loose. That day the two deputies took me back to the prison, walked me up the thirteen steps, and showed me the electric chair. One of them said, "That's where you're going to wind up."

After a while in jail, I was worried about my dog, but my lawyer said I better worry about myself, because that was the worst case of circumstantial evidence he ever saw. That night I thought about it and asked my lawyer to try and get me into the same cell as the real killer—they were holding him as a material witness. That was a toughie, but somehow he did get me into that cell, and I asked this guy why he was doing this—what did he have against me? "Nothing," he says. "But the sheriff lied to me. He said you—Joe Flieger—told him that I had killed this guy. So I got damned mad and said no, he's a liar, Joe did it." He continued, "Well, then they patted me on the back and said son, stay with that and you'll be all right."

So he got to talking and tore the whole thing apart. They couldn't get me out of there fast enough. That sheriff, he wanted to shake hands with me, but I wouldn't do it. You know, they found cigarettes where the killer was waiting—

hell, I don't even smoke! There were tracks to my place in the canyon, a size nine boot—and I wear a six! Yet that damn sheriff was saying it was me. But he got his come-uppance later.

You see, way back in '28, when I was with California Frank's Wild West Show, there was this gypsy fortune-teller. Even though I didn't believe in that stuff, she insisted, said it wouldn't cost me anything, that I was a good guy and all that. Well, she took my palm and told me every-thing that was going to happen to me from that day on. Everything came out like she said—where I was going to go; what I was going to do; how I was going to make a living; who I was going to marry; and all the trouble I was going to get into. She said it was all going to turn out all right in the end, and that I was going to live to be ninety-three and enjoy every minute of it.

And I gotta tell you that when those outlaws were shoot-ing at me, and when the sheriff was after me, that gypsy was on my mind and I was thinking, hell, I hope she knew what she was talking about. Another thing at that time was the gypsy curse! She said, "You will make enemies along the way, but if you cross my palm with a silver dollar, I will put a curse on them." So that's what happened to the sher-iff and all those other guys—it was pretty spooky—the curse worked and bad things did happen to them.

Years later, there was this farm—ranch on Aravaipa way that was owned by a man from Chicago. He bought it, built a big, fancy eight-room house and a large swimming pool. I had always wanted to buy up there but didn't have the money. Well, after he died, I did buy it. I sold my farm and desert ranch and moved up there. It was about fourteen miles from the highway and about as high up as you could get before the rocks stopped you from going up any further. We ranched up there for quite a while, but when the mine opened, it was hard to get cowboys to work for us. They were able to get bigger money there, so there weren't very many who were available to help us out. But we were there for some twenty or so years, and then I sold it and left in 1973.

You know, I got a down payment for that ranch and then it took years of litigation before a final settlement was negotiated. The people we sold it to then sold it to a doctor from California for about six times our price. The doctor then went bankrupt and the bank took over, but then it was sold again. In the meantime I still had the deed, and I must have gone to court about a hundred times to try and finalize the whole thing. Altogether it took nine and a half years of litigation before it was done.

During that time, we moved to Catalina, where I was gonna raise racehorses to race there. But the track went haywire and then I lost my wife. I moved back to Oracle and had this present house built by a contractor in 1980. In fact, while here I was still going back and forth to the court about that ranch sale. After one of those heated days in the court, I was sitting at home that night and I noticed a car stopping out there at the gate. Well, I got up and walked to the screen door and BANG! a bullet just parted the hair on the top of my head. The car zoomed off and even though I was sure that shot had to do with the court case, there was no way to prove it, so I couldn't do anything. But I felt pretty good about not getting killed—it was damned close—and again I remembered what the gypsy had said . . . gosh, I hope she keeps being okay!

I've been retired for quite a while now. I've got a big-screen TV and cable, so I get to watch the wrestling and boxing shows, the horse racing, and all the rodeos. I belong to a senior citizens' group and have been a member of the Mountain Oyster Club in Tucson for thirty years. When my birthday comes along, we go down there and have a big party and dance.

A while back, I met this lady at the senior club. Lillian lived in a big house alone for a number of years and I had been doing the same. Well, we got together. It's made a big difference since we met. We just hit it off, just like that. We were married on New Year's Eve, just three years ago.

In '87, we drove up to Canada for the Calgary Stampede, where they were having a reunion of all the rodeo contestants who had competed in the twenties and thirties . . . I had been there in 1924. This time I was the oldest one there and all those who had competed in my day were all gone. Anyway, we had a great time, saw a lot of my buddies' relatives, and did a lot of eating and some good dancing.

I can't tell you any more of all the things I went through because I'm working on a book of my life, with a young writer who comes over every Thursday. Lots more than I told you . . . heck, we're over three hundred pages now. It should be published next year sometime. I gave it a pretty good title—*Dreams Come True for Cowboys Too.* Yeah, there were plenty of other stories. I didn't tell you about the time this guy had his gun right in the middle of my belly and he was sweatin' and shaking something terrible. I had my gun out too, but boy, his shaking really scared me—any jarring would set that gun off! Uh-uh, you'll have to read the book to find out what happened.

Anyway, Lillian (she's gonna be eighty next year) and I have a great time together and we're enjoying every minute of it. We keep busy. We go to all the horse shows and rodeos, and we love to dance. You know, you get a good western band playing, you eat and drink, and you just whoop-er-up!

September 28, 1989, and
July 18, 1990

LILLIE HARRINGTON

At the Cochise Hotel in Cochise, Arizona, she is the manager and does all the cooking, cleaning, laundering, and whatever else is needed in this antique-filled, from-another-era, former rooming house. Lillie has been running the Cochise for over twenty years. Her well-known brusque manner — she herself calls it "crotchety" — has been highlighted in many feature stories about this 106-year-old hotel.

Our interview took place in the hotel's dining room and then in the kitchen while Lillie was baking huge, delicious corn muffins. It didn't take me long to realize that the sometimes irascible, defiant, impatient tone in her voice really reflected the rugged personality of a hardworking, content-with-herself, pioneering woman. I drove down to Cochise twice because I enjoyed the ride and I liked Lillie.

* * *

I WAS BORN in Arkansas. Don't remember too much about those days because we left there when I was eleven. My father was a farmer, and all us kids had to work in the fields from the time we were six years old. He raised cotton, corn, peas, and lots of other stuff, and we all had to help. There were eight of us children and one other, but that one brother, he died as a baby.

There were farms spread out all around us, and we lived a few miles from a small town. But us kids had to work from daylight to dark, so there was no time to play much. We always had plenty to eat because my father had orchards, grapevines, a huge garden, and cows to give us the milk we needed. So we never went without. As far as school goes, well, at that time there was only three months a year, and I didn't even get to go to school until I was eight years old. When I was eleven years old, in 1918, we moved to Phoenix, where my father got a farm there. We all worked on that farm too.

My mother, my poor old mother, felt she had gone to the hot place, sure enough. She would have went back to Arkansas anytime if she could have gotten there. She lived to be ninety-three and a half. That farm was about a half mile from Sixteenth Street. If you know Phoenix today—it's a city of over a million people—maybe our farmland wouldn't be too far from the middle of that city now. North Central Avenue at that time was only paved wide enough for two vehicles, and I think today it's six or eight lanes wide.

Even though I was eleven years old when we moved to Phoenix, I had to go into the first grade in their school, because I had gotten such a late start in Arkansas. I caught up, though, because I graduated from the eighth grade when I was seventeen. Then, right after that graduation, I got married. It was after the end of the school year, July 24, I think. I married a cowboy. His father owned a homestead this side of the Rincon Mountains and there was a 160-acre homestead available near him—so we took that up for ourselves.

Then I helped my husband drive a herd of thirty-eight wild horses from the Rincon Mountains all the way up to Young, Arizona, over 150 miles. We swapped eight head of horses for a homestead in Young, but we only lived there around eleven months. We had to give it up because the house didn't have a roof. So we went back to Phoenix and worked on the Porter farm for a while. We couldn't stay away from our Rincon homestead too long because you had to be on it and make a certain amount of improvements. Well, then, when my first son was born in 1926, we decided to move there permanently in 1928, and we all lived there for over twenty years after that. Not much in conveniences, of course—there were kerosene lamps, outdoor toilets, and that kind of thing. I had three children—two boys and a girl. Lost the girl in 1980. Now, there were seven grandchildren, and I still have six. There are fifteen great-grandchildren, unless there's a new one that may have just come along. One of the grandsons married a Mormon, and, believe me, they're producing children.

It was rough on the homestead because we were five miles from the nearest neighbor. The school was also five miles away, and we couldn't afford to run back and forth with the kids. My oldest boy was eight before he went to school. That's when the school board bought a bus, and they hired my husband to drive it all around this area. He would pick up the kids all around and then stay at the school until it was time to bring them back. After they graduated eighth grade, they had to go to Benson for the high school. My oldest boy, who was barely sixteen, had to drive twenty-five miles to get there.

So, anyway, after twenty-three years, my husband and I split up. I was really upset. I had never really worked outside the house. After all, I was raised on a farm and we were poor people—the very thought of trying to get a job—what kind of a job could it be? I certainly didn't want to do housework [*chuckle*] . . . I still don't like housework.

Well, some time ago, I had gotten acquainted with a woman who worked at a hotel restaurant in Tucson. She told me one of the girls was getting married and was leaving, why didn't I apply? I met the owner and told him I had never been in front of a counter more than twice in my life and I certainly never had worked behind one. He said, "Well, you can walk, can't you?" I said I certainly can, and that's how I started. It was one of those places where the boss cooked the burgers and other stuff . . . he was at one end and in the back, and I was at the other end so you had to yell in the orders. Well, for a few days he kept saying to yell louder 'cause he couldn't hear what I was saying.

It didn't take too long before I got wise to the whole job, and then I never looked back. I figured from now on I could take care of myself. If I couldn't work behind a counter, well then, I'll do something else. I never even thought of sitting down and letting my kids support me. They haven't had to support me one dime! I've been working steady since 1949, and there was only one month when I was out of a job.

Anyway, that waitress job was my first job, and the kids and I moved into Tucson. I had sold the milk cows but the other few cattle needed to have their water, at least once a week. So I had to run out to the homestead on a Saturday night to make sure the pump would supply the water and then hustle back for work on Sunday. My husband had taken his share of the cattle, and it was up to me now to take care of the rest. I worked at the waitress job for a number of years until the hotel was sold and we all had to leave.

Across the street from the hotel was the Porter Company; they sold saddles and other western gear. So I got a job there in their shipping department—I wrapped all the packages and carried them off to the post office. Stayed there for three years until they hired a manager from outside the family and he brought his own people in. Then there was a short time in a drugstore and a not-too-long time at a truck stop. At the truck stop, the cook got mad at me and that was that. In those places, the cook bosses the outfit. So, anyway, that was the one month I didn't work. Well, I worked like heck, but not at anything that would bring the money in.

I had gotten married again, but that didn't last too long. He was starting to tell me that I couldn't do some of the things that were helpful to my kids. He wanted what money I made so he could go fishing, or to the mountains, or something. He didn't have guts enough to quit picking on me about what I was doing with the kids. Well, I just told him I had them first—before him—so I finally just moved out. After that, I bought a small lot in Tucson, and friends and neighbors helped me to build a little house there. I put all the siding on the house, put in the wire for the plaster, and they did the plastering because I had never done that. About that time, the month I didn't have a job, I saw an ad for someone to run the PX at the Marana Air Base. I got out there quick and got the job.

By that time, I decided the running back and forth to the homestead to take care of the cattle was getting to be too much. So some of the neighbors out there helped me to round them up and get them into the truck. When I was moving them up the chute to go into the truck, one of those old cows ran by me and kicked me, dislocating my right knee. Well, that was a Sunday and I had to get to work on Monday. So I drove all the way to Tucson with my left foot ... braking, clutching, and giving it the gas. Luckily, the doctor was in his office. He saw me drive up and yelled for me to get out and come in. I said I can't, I can't walk! Well, he came out, threw me over his shoulder in a firearm's carry, hauled me into the office, and plunked me down. He yanked that knee back in and said go to bed for a day or so. I said nothing doing 'cause I got to work in the morning. If I didn't go in, I wouldn't have that job.

While working at the air base, I met the groundskeeper there, and we got to talking and visiting. After a while, I thought that it might work out. So we got married. But it didn't work at all. He was too critical—by gosh—of everything. So it lasted about eight months.

The owner of this hotel, my boss, is Elizabeth Husband. Well, her father, William Fulton, established the Amerind Foundation [American Indian] in Dragoon, Arizona. It's a museum, library, and a research center about the archaeology of the Southwest. After the air base job, I worked as the family cook in the Fultons' home at Amerind for ten years. My first husband's older brother, who had come in from California, was also working there as the yardskeeper. Well, that's who I got married to ... number four! It's only after the wedding bells that you get the problems. He didn't like his job and he wanted me to quit and let's— you know—just go and wander around. Gosh almighty, I did all that with my first husband, and I was not inclined to do any of that again. Gee, I had a good job, a good place to stay, and he wanted me to just take off. So he took off! That marriage only lasted six months. After that, I said to heck with it. I'm not tying myself to anyone anymore! I'll just run my own business.

Like I said, that was a good job. When I first went to work for the Fultons, they would spend eight months back east and then four months in Arizona. Soon they turned that around and only spent three months back there. When they were east for those three months, we got paid half salary and didn't do anything. I stayed there for ten years until the Fultons passed away. After that, I went to work for their daughter, Elizabeth, to manage the Cochise Hotel . . . that was in 1969.

She bought the hotel in 1959. It had originally been built as a rooming house for the railroad workers way back in 1882. Well, she had to do a lot of fixing up, and she also added bathrooms to each room. There are three rooms with double beds and two suites (two connecting bedrooms). The most people that can stay over is twelve, and that rarely would happen. Elizabeth didn't take any guests until 1962. By that time all the fixing up was done and a lot of the antiques were put in. There's even a gift shop with old-time things, toys, cards, lace knickknacks, and some books. She says she hired me because I could do plumbing, electrical, and carpentry work, as well as cook. Well, I did do everything, even helped Henry put in that sewer pipe this morning. Course now, if we get more than four or five people, I have a lady who comes in to help me.

We don't get too many people overnight, but they do come from all over the country . . . maybe a dozen or so a month. If you do want to come, you have to make a reservation and tell me what you want to eat at the same time. Otherwise, no food. I only cook chicken or steak, and no matter if it's lunch or dinner. For breakfast, it's bacon, eggs, and biscuits. Lunch is at twelve or one and dinner is at six—period! No changes. Breakfast is at seven-thirty, unless I gotta go to town, then it's at seven. Everyone sits at the same table—family-style—and except for the steaks, you pass the platters around. We do get people in for meals only, some parties and get-togethers too. Breakfast is $3.00, chicken is $6.50, and steak is $9.00. This whole thing is no money-making operation, but it's been kinda fun all these years.

We're not fancy, not by a long shot. There's no air-conditioning, no swamp coolers, no fans, no phones in the rooms, no TVs or radios, and the Southern Pacific railroad is right in front of the hotel. But those who have come have enjoyed it. Must be the good food, I guess.

Elizabeth goes back east for the three summer months to Connecticut. I closed the hotel and went back with her to keep house for six summers, but no more, the house is too big and I'm getting too old. I'd rather stay here and keep the hotel open all year. Fortunately, I've had good health, and in spite of riding bucking horses and running under trees and getting knocked off, I've never had a broken bone. I've been really lucky, healthwise, so far. My gosh, you see so many people, half my age, and there's something wrong with them—that makes it terrible.

Some say I'm crotchety, and I say sure! I don't let anybody get by with anything. The reason John said I was crotchety that time was when I had twelve people at the table and I was by myself. He was eating with the rest, but he got up walking and started following me around, asking questions. I finally told him to "go sit down and eat!" I sometimes have to say that because there's always one or two that may want to sit somewhere else and I'm running back and forth, so I yell, "Sit down! I don't care where you sit, just do it!" You know, Elizabeth says I may occasionally offend guests "because people are used to staying at places like the Hilton and they're not used to country-type people. But after a while, they adjust. Lillie's just Lillie, and everybody loves her." Aaaah, my bark's worse than my bite, that's what it is.

You know, I only serve chicken or steak. So for those who

want chicken we put their plates on the table because that will be served from a platter. But for the steak eaters, the steak is put on their plate in the kitchen, right off the grill. Well, sometimes the person who wants the steak has a plate in front of him and there's confusion. So I say, "For heck's sake, move the damn plate!" And then there's the problem of how people want their steaks cooked. Every once in a while I have to think they don't know what they like. The last time we had twenty-four people from the Sun Sites community for dinner, one of the men ordered his steak rare. When Mary brought it to his place, his wife said, "You don't like rare steak." He turned to her and said, "Yes, I do, that's just what I ordered." It's remarkable when a wife doesn't know how her husband likes his steak—isn't it?

But, really and truly, I've had very few people come in these twenty years that I felt like they really shouldn't have come because they were unhappy with it. Most all of them were pleased to stay here, and most of the time, when I do pick on one and say "Sit down," the others will think it's funny and we'll all have a good laugh. After all, when you have to pass the potatoes, the peas, the bread and butter, it's the quickest way to get to know one another. Every once in a while someone will ask why can't I sit down with them . . . I just say, "The work sits right there in the kitchen and waits."

One magazine article mentioned that I don't encourage the guest to stay more than one or two nights. I guess that's so . . . but, you know, there's nothing much to do around here. I've had people who reserved for three or four nights and by the second night they're ready to go. So that's why I tell people they can't stay more than two nights. After all, Cochise is a tiny community, and there's nothing you could do around here that would keep you occupied for any long time.

I see you noticed those bottles hanging out back there. Well, you can bring your own wine or whiskey here, and when people left the bottles, I started to string them up. I think there's about 163 strings, with something like ten bottles to a string—all kinds. Don't like the stuff myself, so I didn't contribute any bottles.

These two books in the kitchen, by Dick Francis, they were given to me by a friend. I've read all his books; he's really a good writer. You know something, I've been reading books since I was fourteen years old. In the past twenty years it's the mysteries that have been my favorites—good murder mysteries and detective stories.

Some of the writers, though, have so many darned nasty words in them and such silly psychological junk—it gives me a pain. Others go round and round in circles; they describe the whole countryside instead of doing anything about their characters. I like mysteries, but they have to *be* mysteries. That's why I also stick with some of the old writers; with them a murder mystery is exactly that. The clues and characters aren't easy or crazy, and reading them is entertaining. Agatha Christie and her detective fellow, you know, Poirot—they're darned good.

I was trying to read another writer who was hipped on women's lib, and I couldn't stand it. Well, I think that's all right. If a woman is turned down on a job that she can do as good or better than the other applicants, then she *should* have the job. But some of this other ranting around is just ridiculous. Now, spy stories, I got tired of them in nothing flat. Their characters were out of this world. They could *do* anything, *be* anything—just a bunch of unbelievable superpeople. I don't think very many real spies were able to get out of the spots these writers dream up. But, let's face it, it's everybody to their own notion. That's just how I feel.

You know, I've got no real complaints. I certainly don't feel downtrodden or anything like that. There have been some rough times, but everybody has those one time or another. That homestead in the Rincon Mountains gave us some of that. When my father-in-law passed away, he had joined his place with ours, but even the total of eight hundred acres wasn't enough to run any decent herd of grazing cattle. So, after twenty-eight years, back then, I had that land all cut up, surveyed, mapped, and put the parcels in the children's names and let them take care of it. They still own some pieces, but they've sold off a lot to people who now live there in house trailers and so on.

Here at the Cochise, Elizabeth and I get along real good. She doesn't know too much about running this, but once in a while she comes up with a suggestion. If it isn't good, I just ignore it and she never says anything anymore about it. I know she's been wanting to make the dining room a no-smoking area, but I'm not giving up my cigarillos just yet. I only smoke a pack in four or five days, and I've been doing that since some time in the fifties. Still feel okay, as far as I can tell. I'm still in good health, and that's important. Staying active—*that's* important!

I think the young people of today are . . . well, most of them . . . it's not their fault they didn't have anything to do when they were growing up. But so many of them have got the wrong attitude, as far as I'm concerned. By gosh, if you didn't inherit money, then you've got to work! So many of them seem to think that money ought to grow on trees. Well, this business of hanging about and depending on somebody else, I don't believe in.

July 27, 1989, and
June 25, 1990

Like many other blacks in the South, Hardy Howard finally went north, where "separate facilities" for everything didn't exist. Not physically, perhaps, but there were barriers. During our meeting, his bright smile, cheery manner, and honest forthrightness were a strong reflection of his feelings about the past and the present. I enjoyed the hours we spent together.

Hardy retired last year from his many, many years as a truck driver. His retirement came at an age when the majority of retirees had already finished working one or two decades earlier. Time for fishing and gardening was welcome, but standing still held no appeal. Even now, there's a face without wrinkles and a body that is trim and plenty energetic. Hardy looks as if there's a lot more to come.

*   *   *

MY MOTHER married a man in a little place called Talbotton, Georgia. He was a farmer, and when she became pregnant she went back home to her mother in Tallahassee, Florida. That's where I was born in 1904. It was a midwife who recorded my birth in the Bible, and that was the only record of this event.

We went back to Talbotton, where I went to school until the eighth grade. The school was way out in the boondocks, and I had to walk five miles to the Methodist church, which had this one-room schoolhouse. There were only eight children in the class, and the preacher taught us our ABC's and all that. The white folks' school was right across the street from where we lived, but I had to walk that five miles to the colored school. I'll never forget the time when I was a little older and had some button-up shoes. I didn't want to get them muddy walking to the school, so I tied a string around them and put the string around my neck with the shoes on each side of my chest. Then I walked. Living con-

HARDY HOWARD, SR.

ditions for blacks were horrible down there. At that time I didn't know when all this prejudice started, but you had a fountain where you could drink out of and it was marked WHITE. Across the street was the one marked COLORED. And it was the same thing with the toilets. *Everything* was like that.

We also had to work on the farm. If my dad had planting to do, Mother and I had to help plant, and we had to help the same way when it was time to gather in the crops. You had no altervatives; it was forced on you—we all worked on the farm because we were sharecroppers. You slept on the floor. Even if you did have a mattress, it was something filled with straw. You took pieces of cloth, patches, and made quilts 'cause you didn't know what a blanket was— you never had the money to buy one. Flour used to come in cloth bags, and you'd take the flour sack and make a lining for the quilt, then you'd stuff hay or chicken feathers in it. We cooked in the fireplace because there was no stove. There were the frying pans, with legs, and we cooked grits, fish, and everything else in them.

When I was thirteen or fourteen I went to public school, but I also worked in a hotel. With my bicyle I'd leave school at eleven-thirty, get to the hotel to serve the meal and wash the dishes, then go back to the school. If it wasn't cold in the morning, I went to school. If it was cold, I had to get to the hotel first and start the fire in each room that was rented. There were twenty-four rooms in all; sometimes ten or twelve or more were rented. There was no central furnace in those days; each room had to have a separate fire. This work included all seven days a week, and I was paid three dollars a week.

At fifteen or sixteen I went to live with my aunt in Atlanta, Georgia, and went to school there. It was a colored school—I never went to any school in the South that wasn't colored. And even in Atlanta, things were pretty much the same. If you went up to Mitchell Street to buy a hat or some shoes, once you put any of them on—it was yours! For a hat, the black man would have to put a string around his head to get an idea of size. Your shoes and feet were the same way. They measured your feet crossways with a string and then longways with the string. Then the shoes were measured and if you put your feet in them, they were yours. That's just the way they did it. I remember it just like the date today.

I also went to Clafton State College in South Carolina and took some agriculture courses at night. I learned how to plant grass on cement and to keep it winter-grown. [*Laughs*] I went to the college for about a year and half and learned a lot about agriculture.

This fellow I was driving for paid me six dollars a week and fifty cents a day for a place to sleep. He was a salesman for an overall company and didn't know how to drive. In Cleveland, Tennessee, I dropped him off at a hotel and walked around looking for someplace I could stay for fifty cents the night. This white fellow walks up to me and says, "You got more nerve than most blacks I see around here. The last black I saw—you see that dam over there with water running over the top—well, he was swimming, trying to get over it." So I said, you don't like black folk here? He glared at me and said, "That's right!" Well, I went back to the hotel and told the salesman that we had better get out 'cause there was no place for me here. He checked out and we left for Knoxville, where I might find a deacon's or preacher's house that would let me stay the night. Those were the kinds of people we blacks depended on for lodging. There were no motels then and only a few hotels—which they wouldn't let us in anyway.

Later I left South Carolina and went to Detroit, but I didn't like Detroit and went to Cleveland instead. That was in 1929, and within three days I got a job driving a truck for a food wholesaler. But even in Cleveland, a black couldn't go downtown to a good restaurant and eat. However, things were cheap then, and I could buy a weekly meal ticket from one of those small Greek restaurants for three dollars. That gave me three meals a day, seven days a week. Ham and eggs, beef stew, liver and onions—anything they could cook cheap. I bought those tickets for the first three years I was in Cleveland. That was also the time of the Wall Street crash and the bank failures. In the Carter and Homestead hotels downtown, eight, ten, or fifteen people jumped out the windows and committed suicide because they lost all their money. The banks were closed, nobody could get their money.

When the banks opened again, some of the people only got nine or ten cents on a dollar, others got nothing. The Union Trust was the highest payer in Cleveland—they paid sixty-six cents on the dollar. You know if all that money they absconded with . . . it would almost be the same thing now, people losing their money with the savings and loan banks, if the government hadn't guaranteed their accounts. But even now, it looks like the people will still be the losers 'cause they are the ones who are gonna pay for the S&L bailouts.

Anyway, in the thirties, you really got the depression. Unlike what Hoover said, there wasn't gonna be any two chickens in every pot, or two cars in every garage. But I had a job, and I worked at it diligently. I was driving a 1918 chain-driven Mack truck with solid rubber tires. You had to get out and crank it up to start it, and at night I had to take a candle to light the kerosene headlamps. It also had isinglass shades to roll down and cover the side windows. If it rained, you had to move the windshield wipers by hand to clean the water off. The truck couldn't go over twenty-five miles an hour. The only way you could get it up to thirty miles an hour was if you were going downhill. I used to have to drive to Akron, Canton, and Youngstown, and it would take me something like five or six hours to get it over there. And those solid tires—wow—all the roads in Cleveland were made out of red brick, and you went bumpty-bumpty-bump all the time.

But I liked the job, and little by little the bosses would

teach me to do different things. Saturday, the warehouse was closed and I'd go to their homes and cut the grass, trim the trees and shrubs, paint, wash the walls, and anything else. I learned a lot and got paid for that work, so I added to my income. At that time, they didn't have two-wheel hand trucks and you had to lug everything. The truck would hold up to four hundred cases of foodstuffs, which had to be loaded and unloaded by hand. These were wholesale groceries being delivered to all the grocery stores, and you had to load and unload and carry every case. I learned how to handle them. I'd take two cases on my shoulder and one case under my other arm, and walk as far as necessary. All the streets were narrow and sometimes the truck would be too wide to get between the streetcar tracks and the sidewalk. That meant going around the corner, unloading the cases, and carrying them around the block to the store.

A funny thing happened in 1935. I caught the clearing house numbers that day and won twelve hundred dollars. Well, I wanted to take the other five drivers down to the union hall and pay for all of us to join. It only cost $7.50 each to join, and $1.50 a month dues. They said, "No, we have too many men out of work." But I said we've *got* jobs. They still said no. The next year, the union called a statewide strike and requested a seventy-five-cents-an-hour pay, plus time and a half for overtime after forty hours. It didn't bother me 'cause I was working and not in the union. One day, with a big truck and two helpers, I went downtown on a delivery. And like I said before, you had to lug everything on your back—100-pound bags of sugar, 108 pounds of poppy seeds, 134 pounds of salt, 100 pounds of flour, and so on. They all had to be walked into the stores.

The union goons came in a big Packard car, and they were gonna beat me in the head for working while the strike was on. A big policeman who knew me told the goons they weren't going to bother me, or else. Well, they complained they wanted all drivers and helpers in the union. I said, "Hey, guys, we tried to join last year, but they wouldn't take us in because there were too many people out of work." Then they told me, "We'll let you in the union for nothing—can you get the rest of the drivers in your shop to join?" I said I could, but only after I finished working. And I did, I took them down to the union hall and we all signed up. The boss wasn't too happy about that because we were only making thirty-five cents an hour before joining the union. Signing a contract meant a higher wage and overtime after forty hours.

Well, after that, things changed. Before the contract we often worked ten or twelve hours a day. You got there at six in the morning and went from warehouse to warehouse picking up various merchandise. You brought the three hundred or four hundred cases to the main area, unloading and stacking it away and then picking out your orders that were to go on your truck. You loaded them and by that time it was nine or ten o'clock at night. You were paid for every hour you worked. But now they stopped you from working longer than forty hours in the week, so they wouldn't have to pay the overtime rate.

After a while, though, they didn't worry about my overtime after forty hours. I handled all the C.O.D. deliveries because they knew all the money would be there. They got rid of the drivers who would deliberately scratch merchandise on the truck and then sell it, or the ones who would try to pad their hours. In the long run, honesty pays better dividends than anything else. I had the keys to the warehouse and the codes to the alarms, and I was back to working whatever hours were needed. Later, two other wholesale companies were going out of business, and we took over their people and accounts.

The war was starting to involve us, and people were being drafted. I was told, "You better get a job that's essential to the war effort or you'll be classified 1A and go into the army." Well, I went to work for Thompson Aircraft and got a job as a polisher of valves. Then they made me a pivot man to teach the new guys, because I knew how to do it before I went there. In the B-17, B-29, and others, they had sodium-filled valves and you had to polish those interiors so the sodium could go up and down smoothly. Otherwise, the valve would get hot and split off. I worked there from 1942 to 1947, working eleven at night to seven in the morning. At eight, I would go to the wholesale grocery company and work until about five or six in the evening. But I had three kids, and in order to support them you had to work. There wasn't any big money in those days. I made eighty-five cents an hour at the plant, but you could also get a bonus if you had good production. At the grocery company, they paid me $1.65 an hour driving a truck—a much better truck than the old Mack one.

I also became the warehouse boss for a number of years. I knew every product, every customer, and the bosses felt I was absolutely honest. We didn't have any stealing of merchandise off the trucks, especially in the thirties, even though the people were hungry in those depression days. After the war, though, you had to be on the watch for that kind of thievery. In fact, many years later they put locks and gates on the trucks, and you had to lock up while you were delivering. There was only one time I had anything like that. It was when I was delivering five cases of peaches to a school. I parked a way back and carried three cases to the kitchen, leaving the other two cases on the tailgate. When I got back to the truck, the cases were gone. Then I heard a tap-tap, and it was the lady across the street, tapping on her window. She pointed to a basement staircase near the school. I hustled down the steps, and there were two boys sitting on the cases of peaches. I told them they should be ashamed because the peaches were for the school.

But that was the only time something like that happened. Now you look around and what do you see? Would you believe that in the last twelve days here in Cleveland there's been twelve bank robberies? You know, the banks tell their employees, "Don't run the risk of getting hurt or killed. So if someone comes in and wants to rob the bank—give them the money!" I guess that's progress.

In the late fifties, three or four of the wholesale grocery companies decided to get together and form a new, big company called Seaway. Well, I've been the warehouse boss at my company for many years, but I went to my people and said, "I think I ought to quit the warehouse and drive a truck instead." They couldn't understand why and tried to talk me out of it. I explained that the bosses from the other companies would start bringing in their own people, their sons, their relatives, and they're not going to take orders from a black man. I didn't want to be fired or pushed out by that kind of thing, so it would be best if I went back to the truck—the truck would never learn to drive itself. It's where I started and it's where I'd like to finish. My bosses couldn't see it, but they finally agreed and okayed it.

Well, I have to tell you it worked out just like I said. They brought in their relatives and good friends, and I don't think I would have lasted six weeks. I did go in and ask for a two-wheel handtruck because my back was starting to feel some of this, and they said sure, why didn't I get one before. They did have handtrucks in the forties, but they were the big, iron-wheeled ones, with iron ribs and solid wood—must have weighed almost a hundred pounds themselves. So this time I went out and bought an aluminum one for my truck. I enjoyed the driving and knew all the shortcuts to the nearby communities. And in all my years of driving, there hasn't been any real accidents. One time in Canton, a lady tried to pass me on a bridge, even though there was a solid line and a no-passing sign. She hooked her bumper into my rear bumper, and we blocked off the bridge. The police gave her a ticket because it was her fault. You always have to be careful, whether you're driving a truck or an automobile—you have to drive for the other person too. I don't care how right you might be in an accident, you can be just as dead. That's something the average person doesn't really think about. Give the other guy some leeway so you can stop if it's suddenly necessary, and that's been my attitude all the time.

I like to help others, and I have a good story for you on that. I was on my way back from upstate New York, and there was a car on the side of the road with a white hand- kerchief on the antenna. It was snowing lightly, and I braked to see if I could help. There were three nuns in the car, and one of them said, "Yes, we need help. We have a flat tire on the car and a flat tire in the trunk." So I asked them for six dollars and I would take both tires and get them fixed. It was only a few miles to the next town, and the mechanic fixed both tires in twenty-five minutes. I drove back, put one tire in the trunk and one on the wheel. At their request, I gave them my name and address. A few weeks later, I received a card of congratulations and one hundred dollars. One of those new bosses mumbled some- thing about it being on their time and maybe even hinted something about the money. I said, heck, I did my twelve stops, didn't take a lunch or coffee break, and didn't waste any time—did you really want me to pass up those three nuns?

It's the original owners and their sons, who are in the business now, that I relate to. Their families have always accepted me as I am. If one of them gets sick, I'll go visit in the hospital. If one dies, I'll go sit shiva with them. If they have a wedding or any kind of an affair, I'll get an invita- tion. I always take a lady with me, so I have someone to con- verse with. Let's face it, some of their friends may not care for us to be there, but *they* care! I can sit at their table and eat with them and when I get through drinking, they're not going to break the glass. This is the way it's done and I appreciate it, because it's nice to be treated good after being treated bad so long. One time I was invited to a wedding of one of the sons at this very good hotel in Cleveland. When the doorman saw me and my wife come up, he pointed to the rear and said the help went in that way. We were turn- ing around to leave, when the groom's brother came up and said, uh-uh, these are *guests*.

I've worked for these families all the way back to the first time I came to Cleveland, through all the mergers and their growth. I retired last year, at eighty-five, after sixty years with them. And one of the biggest merchants in Cleveland, who has four stores, wanted me to come work for him now. He offered $525 a week, forty hours. It isn't because he actually likes me, but because he knows that I know everything about groceries and that I'm honest. That job meant getting there in the wee hours of the morning, seeing that the stores get their deliveries and that all merchandise is checked in right. But I didn't want any more of punching a clock.

Quite often, since retirement, I get up in the morning at five and drive up to Muskogee Lake to go fishing for four or five hours. I've got a dog, named Hannibal, and he weighs 162 pounds. He has to be walked twice a day, and if I don't get up, he'll come in and get me going. I have three, four, five lady friends, but I don't want to get married again. I've been living alone since my wife died in 1981. My garden is a very big one, there's sixty pounds of green beans in the freezer, and I'm giving away tomatoes like it's going out of style. Maybe that agriculture course was pretty good, after all. But there's work also. Like I said, punching a clock is out and I like to work—just like to do it whenever I feel like. So now I have three or four select accounts that I do landscaping for. Cut their grass, trim the shrubs, fertilize, and all that. I just load up my mower and edger into the station wagon and take off for their places, but it's the kind of work I like and I do it on my own time schedule.

I feel good to be as old as I am, and when I think back, I never had any problem walking or going up stairs, no false teeth or hearing aids, no nothing like that. Maybe it was all that lifting on the job—even today my lawn mower weighs about a hundred pounds and my edger about eighty, and I lift them into the wagon all the time.

Yes, I do some volunteering work at the Metropolitan Hospital, twice a month, with people who are paralytic. I help exercise and pattern them. I've always believed in helping wherever I can. You know, what you get out of life is what you put in. Measure unto others as I would have them measure unto me. Anybody I can help, I don't care if they're white, black, green, or gray—anything you want, if I can do you a favor, I'll do it. And this has been my logic since I was a little boy and I haven't changed from it, even today.

September 19, 1990

When I called his office as a follow-up to my letter, G. A. Larriva was very crisp in his response. "No interviews in my office," he said. "I'm much too busy and have only one secretary. You will have to call me at home after six, or on weekends." Fortunately, we did get together at his home, where he was a most pleasant and cooperative host. In addition to our interview, we perused many photos of his family: his wife, his children, and his grandchildren. Family is very important to him, and this feeling was nurtured in early childhood with his numerous brothers and sisters.

Although law is his present profession, a greater portion of his working life was devoted to sales and entrepreneurship. And he notes, "There's a relationship between the art of salesmanship and law, especially when addressing a judge or jury." Like many older professionals, he has strong negative feelings about the present trend of advertising by lawyers, doctors, and others in the professions.

G. A. prefers to be called by his initials, simply because there have been so many unrelated variations of his given names—Genaro Amado.

*   *   *

MY PARENTS and their family lived in a small mining town at the bottom of what is often called the Mexican Grand Canyon—Batopilas, Chihuahua, Mexico. That canyon is so deep that at the top it's cold, and on the bottom, where our town was located, tropical fruits such as mangoes and papayas would grow. The steepness of the canyon walls protected us from the strong winds and the cold air. There is a river that still runs through the town, and this also helped with the vegetation and humidity.

There were rich mineral deposits in the area, and my father, Don Leonilo, and his partner, my uncle Don Victoriano Martinez, owned and operated a few small mines.

G. A. LARRIVA

In addition, my father used to say there were two other mines they owned—the *only* two general stores in town. After the ore was mined, the gold and silver were extracted and put into small bars. In those days there were no banks in the town and there was no railroad at the bottom of the canyon. Until the time the bullion bars could be hauled to the railroad terminal at the top of the canyon, my father would bury the bars in the ground in many different places—not all in one hold. One very good reason was that Pancho Villa and his bandits would come through the town at various intervals and clean out whatever they could lay their hands on—stores, bullion, and whatever they considered useful to them. They would also torture people to make them divulge where bullion or valuables were buried.

When it was time for a shipment of the bullion bars to the terminal, a posse of armed miners would be rounded up to make the trip to the top of the canyon. The canyon walls were so steep that the only practical means of travel were mules and walking. It would take a number of days to make the trip, and the Tarahumara Indians (indigent to the location) were needed to guide, set up the camps, prepare the food, and take care of the mules. They were used because they could outrun and outwalk both the men and the mules. There were no roads, just trails, and when existing trails were overgrown or washed out by the rains, the Tarahumaras would work to reestablish them. Those footpaths would wind around the mountains, climbing more and more steeply at every turn.

I was only a toddler at the time, so all this is what my father and the family told me. You know, it's pretty much a fact that we were forced out of Mexico by Pancho Villa and his bandits. My father and my uncle were conservatives, as was anyone with means, and the periodic raids of the bandits kept stripping them of their belongings. My father and his partner were at one time or another the top "politicos" of the town, and that in itself placed them as prime targets for Pancho Villa and his revolutionaries, and this endangered their lives as well as their belongings. During one of these raids my father was put into the jail by Villa, who was torturing people to find out where the gold and silver might be buried. My father told him where a few bars were, and then where a few others were, but he wouldn't tell him where the main cache was hidden. "If I do, then you'll kill me," he said. No matter what they did, he wouldn't tell them. Finally, one of the jailers was a man who had worked in my father's mines, and he had always been pleasant to him. My father said, "You know I'm Don Leonilo, and my word is good." When the guard nodded, he continued, "I'll tell you where it is if you let me go and give me a horse, and let me take one bar that I can carry in my hand." The guard agreed, and that's how my father got out and took us to Arizona.

Our family at the time consisted of eight children, four boys and four girls—two other boys were later born in Arizona. The girls had been sent ahead earlier, and we all joined them. This was in 1911, I believe, *before* Arizona became a state. Incidentally, the little bar my father carried was worth twenty-two hundred dollars and he deposited it in the Consolidated National Bank (the forerunner of the present Valley National Bank). In Mexico, my father was a wealthy man, considered a millionaire. So now he would have to start over again with just that one bar of bullion. As to what happened to that guard in Mexico, we never did find out. Since Pancho Villa got all the rest of the cache, he may not have punished the guard—but we don't know.

We immigrated through Nogales and came to Tucson, where I spent my early childhood. Frankly, I don't recall too much about it, and some five years later we went to live in Nogales, Arizona, where I attended both grammar and high school. Our family believed in education, but the thought of ten children going to college was overwhelming. By that time, my uncle had died, and my parents took his children, three boys and a girl, and brought them up as their own. My older sister did go to college in California, but my older brother and other sisters had to work with Father to help support the brood. I was fortunate to win a scholarship as a result of a competitive test given in each county of Arizona. The prize was one thousand dollars, which was big money in those days. It was payable in installments of $29.90 for each month that I attended college. If you didn't attend all four years, then you would not be entitled to all of it. That scholarship enabled my father and older brother and sisters to pay for my brother to go to college at the same time, and the two of us enrolled together at the University of Arizona in Tucson. My scholarship money really paid for food, because the commons charged thirty dollars a month for three meals a day and you could eat all you want. The dormitories, if I remember, were very reasonable. There was no tuition for residents and resident Mexican aliens, but we had to buy our books and other necessities.

I had been working since I was thirteen—first in a hardware store in Nogales, where I was an export manifest clerk and typist; then in a branch of an electrical appliance and contracting concern, where I worked throughout my high school years—after school, on Saturdays, and during vacation times. I kept books, answered the phone, sold small appliances, and when the boss was out of town, I even handled the routing of electricians to jobs. So at sixteen, when I started college, I was already experienced with three years of work behind me. Fortunately, when I graduated high school, that appliance store in Nogales was closed and my boss became head of the Tucson main store, and I was able to get a part-time job there for fifty cents an hour to start. I did some bookkeeping, collected bills from door to door, and did a lot of typing. Believe it or not, that did help with my college expenses. There was some help from home, but I think the total help I received from my father and older siblings was about $975 for *four* years of college—which I repaid as soon as I could after graduation.

I graduated in 1929 with high distinction and elected to Phi Kappa Phi, with a bachelor of science business administration degree and a major in accounting. I was able to accumulate 145 units of credit (125 were required for graduation) while working twenty to thirty hours weekly during school term and full-time during vacation. In those days, the enrollment at the university was about sixteen hundred students—today it's something like thirty-four thousand. There's an interesting earlier aspect to that accounting major. During what they called University Week, the state of Arizona conducted competitions in the county high schools in various subjects. I became state champion in bookkeeping at the age of thirteen, and then at fourteen I became the advanced bookkeeping champion of Arizona. For a little town of five thousand people, we in Nogales got four out of five awards in bookkeeping—and that included the whole state. My brother was one of the four Nogales winners.

You asked about my father and what happened with him after we left Mexico—how was he able to take care of the family? After being a wealthy man in Mexico, with servants and everything else, his chief endeavor was to *feed the family*—ten children and four cousins, Father and Mother, and two old retainers brought from Mexico, whom we considered family. The first thing Dad bought was a one-horse wagon. Then he went to the neighborhood farms to buy corn, beans, and other produce which he later sold to the grocery stores. After a while he opened his own grocery store. In a few years he sold the store and went to Nogales, where he started to trade in hides. This was the early World War I period in Europe, and that was good business. Then he opened a money-exchange and currency-exchange business. In the meantime, he had built a home for the family, and we all moved to Nogales, Arizona, in 1916. Each state in Mexico had its own currency and there was also the Mexican national currency, so he bought and sold dollars for people coming to Arizona or going to Mexico.

Today's peso, for example, isn't worth much. Before we came to Arizona, however, the peso was worth $1.26 because of the bullion in them. Well, my father got into banking by trading coins and bills according to the market price for the day. The markups might be infinitesimal, but if you do enough of them, you can make money. He would have a telegram on his desk every morning from the Chase National Bank in New York, with the latest quotations.

At one time, and I know this for a fact because I was working for him, he began to separate the old, heavy Mexican pesos (the "dobies"), which were worth more for their silver content than as a coin. He bought them at various prices: two for a dollar, forty-six cents, and then for a long time forty cents each. There was also some devaluation along the way, but in time he collected about a hundred thousand coins. During the war they went up as high as a dollar and twenty cents each because of their silver content. He sold all his coins at a dollar and fourteen, which meant he received $114,000 for his coins. His collection probably cost him between forty and sixty thousand dollars, so he did get some big money and was able to get back on his feet. He purchased real estate and built up a reasonable estate, until he became very ill and spent a lot of money trying to get well. I always said he died of old age at sixty, the poor man—he worked himself to death taking care of his large family and his partner's as well.

After college I went to work as the office manager of that same appliance store where I had worked part-time during college. Although this was 1929 and the country had just gone through the crash on Wall Street, Tucson didn't feel this for a few years due to the growth taking place. Times were basically good then, though we would feel the depression some years later. My salary now was $200 a month, but I was given an additional $40 a month if I had the statements on the boss's desk by the tenth of the month. By this time, refrigerators, radios, and other applicances became available, and sales were good. Additionally, commercial refrigeration was developed, and the people who were making big money were the salespeople. They worked on a commission basis, and sales were no problem since it was a new and growing market. I was cutting their checks for $800 a month, up to $1,500 a month. So I went to the boss and said, "I want to sell!" "Well," he replied, "you know how we start rookie salesman, we give them $15 a week drawing account against commissions earned—and that's it, until they sell."

In a few months I was making $600 a month. I went up from there and later became sales manager. This gave me my own commissions, plus an override on all the sales by the other salesmen. I was married in 1930, and later changed jobs, but I kept working in appliance sales and sales management for the next five years. Then my old boss called and needed help. His repossessions were coming back almost as fast as his sales, and he was going broke. So I joined him for a few years, increased his sales by 250 percent, and stopped those repossessions by suing some of the purchasers to make them pay—and the word got around.

Now it was 1939 and time to start my own business. I had already trained [two of] my brothers to be first-class appliance repairmen, and I took one of them with me to start a retail appliance store. I had saved $5,192, and my dear wife was very supportive. She went back to teaching to help out. After one year I had done fairly well, and I think my net worth went up to $7,800. At that time pressure was put on my suppliers to discontinue selling me major appliances, especially refrigerators, which were one of our main lines. Well, like any good salesman I looked for something exclusive to sell, and since I couldn't buy from the present distributors, I decided to try to buy direct from the factory. There was the Stewart-Warner line, the only refrigerator with a separate freezer for frozen foods, and since it was being sold by a discount house in Phoenix, nobody really wanted the line. I put in a request for a distributor's franchise for southern Arizona, and when I met with their representative, he said, "Mr. Larriva, you need a net worth of at least $50,000 to be a distributor." Well, I really had to use all my sales technique in this situation. "That's simple," I said. "We now have a net of $7,800. My experience in the field is worth $25,000, plus what I have taught my brother and junior partner is worth another $25,000. Altogether, that's a total of $57,800, so you see, we meet your requirements and have $7,800 left over!"

The rep looked back at me. "You have a lot of guts. Okay, you guys got it if you give me the first check!" So we immediately got refrigerators that we could buy at more than 50 percent discount. I traveled to the other nearby towns and set up some dealers, but in Tucson we sold both retail and wholesale. Over the next number of years there was rationing, World War II, and then the postwar demand for appliances. We had earlier stocked up refrigerators in a warehouse, borrowed money to pay for them, and as the rationing eased, we sold them fairly quickly, and at a good price.

That was also a period when the GIs were returning and looking for jobs. I decided to teach some of them how to sell, using the display area in my warehouse. They offered to pay but I said no—I'm going to teach you and then get you a job. I trained them to sell refrigerators, freezers, and radios, and my competitors laughed because all these items were rationed. But, sooner or later, rationing would end and there would be ample merchandise available, and if they knew how to sell, then the dealers could give them jobs. If they worked for my dealers, it would be *my merchandise* that was sold. And, of course, it would also make sense to keep the best students for our own wholesale business.

The students had to learn some of the basics—they weren't selling a refrigerator, they were selling a service. They had to be on the buyer's side, and they should interpret the product in terms of the buyer's needs. Sell what will do most for that buyer—does she entertain, is the family large, does she buy in quantity, and does she buy the weekly specials? Then show the customer that she could *not* afford not to buy the refrigerator, because she saved more each week than her installments. Another technique is to keep the prospect saying yes. Will this one look better in your kitchen? Do you need the larger freezer? Do you prefer the deluxe model? Are weekly installments better for you?— just keep asking other relevant questions that relate to the "yes" principle. Then ask for the order at least six times. There will usually be some objections when you ask—just *answer* them! If you don't know, find out—but don't lie! There's a lot more, but I just wanted to give you some idea of what I was trying to teach them.

Whenever I sold an appliance, I always asked the buyer for another recommendation. If it worked out, I would give them a modest gift for the referral. I used to give a bouquet of flowers, but being a young man that could possibly cause problems, so I stopped that. Anyway, one woman pointed down the block. "She's one who might need a refrigerator, I can't remember her name, but that's the house." Well, I followed up the lead and told her that a friend said she was in the market for a refrigertor. She said, "No, I'm not—I can't afford one." She had a big family and needed a large refrigerator, but there was no room in the kitchen. I pointed out the electricity would cost less than the every-other-day ice, she would save by shopping in quantity, and her spoilage would be less costly. All the savings could go for a less expensive model, and we found a place for it in the living room, around the corner from the kitchen door. Yes, I did sell her. Later, when I brought the gift to the lady who referred me and told her all about it, she said, "Mr. Larriva, that wasn't the one I told you about. It was the one *next* door." It was my error, but don't laugh too quick. I went back a day or two later and sold that one also. This illustrates one thing—mind over matter—if you *believe* in what you are doing, you can be considerably more convincing.

When Stewart-Warner sold out to Admiral, I decided to go to Crosley because they had radios and the exclusive Crosley "Shelvador," a refrigerator with shelves on the door. The Crosley franchise was held by a wealthy distributor. But we had a very good service department—one that could best carry out the obligations of their factory warranty. After they checked our excellent Dun and Bradstreet ratings of the past five years I told them, "Your present distributor is worth millions and I'm only worth $44,000—but we *both* pay our bills well. So what is it you want: to frame a letter of credit on the wall, or to *sell* merchandise? We pay our bills just as well as if we had millions—but we can turn your merchandise over and over and will make the sales!" They decided to give us a chance. "But look," they warned, "business is pretty bad, we can see what's going on over here." Nevertheless, I went ahead. I built a larger warehouse than I needed, in Phoenix, and rented half of it to the RCA distributor, so he paid for all of it. I left one brother in Phoenix and I stayed in Tucson. Within a short time our sales of Crosley appliances exceeded those of the former distributor—and from approximately $25,000 in radio sales a year they had, we increased sales to $1,000,000 as the Crosley lines widened. Years later, however, they sold out to Philco, who had to guarantee there would be spare parts available for the Crosley appliances. That's when we sold our spare parts back to the factory for $120,000. Then, after a short while, when Philco tried to tell me how to run my business, I decided to retire.

While I was in business, I never had any money. I was running all the time to be able to finance my dealers and keep up with the expanding lines. Now it was different. We sold the spare parts back to the factory, liquidated the local business, and sold the Phoenix warehouse for a good price. So for the first time I had money, and here I was, retired at fifty-four. But a man as active as I was really cannot retire. When you've been a statewide distributor, met lots of people, attended conventions, won trips and cars, and that sort of activity, it's a big difference from just working on a job. It's the big leagues, by comparison. Anyway, who's going to hire a has-been that's fifty-four years old—although I couldn't go to work for someone else either. So I bought real estate with the money from the business, and I figured I'd stay retired. By the time I was fifty-six, I was going crazy.

My wife said, "You always wanted to be a lawyer, why don't you go back to school?" But I told her I was too old. To make a long story short, she and my daughters talked me into it, and I graduated from the University of Arizona in the regulation three years with a juris doctor's degree. That was in 1967, and I've been a lawyer ever since. After I graduated, to get experience as a trial lawyer, I had to take assignments from the court at $250 a case. Practically all those cases the judge assigned were criminal cases, the kind of law I was really not interested in, but had to handle to acquire experience. Usually these defendants were not charged until the police and the county attorney had assured themselves they were guilty. Nevertheless, they had to be furnished counsel. So here I was handling burglaries, assaults, and all varieties of that type case. And although many of them were not cooperative in giving you truthful details, you have to defend them to the best of your ability. That brings up a case that I must say I was not proud of at all. It was a capital offense case—forcible rape. I tried to get out of it, but couldn't. That defendant absolutely stonewalled me, wouldn't easily give me any information. I had to dig it out, piece by piece, recording it in jail on a tape recorder—and made him sign an affidavit that I was to defend him on that basis.

Anyway, he was acquitted. It has a lot to do with my picking the right form of jury, because they are the ones who have to determine whether he is guilty or not. But there were other aspects, even though they had photographs showing scratched knees, torn clothes, and some blood. The victim had previously had relations with the defendant, she was pregnant—by a married man—and in the final analysis *she* was being tried, not he. It's a system that many people bitterly complain about, and there's a lot of validity to their concern. As I said earlier, this was one case where I didn't feel very proud of myself. In fact, I quit right then and absolutely refused to do any more criminal work—and I haven't since! The defendant said, "Thanks." And I told him, "Thank the jury." Later, when we were alone, I said, "Take my advice, do me a favor and get out of Arizona. Stay away from here, I never want to see you around here again." I do not doubt he was guilty, but I never knew. If you're going to defend someone, you don't ask—you just explain the things you're going to do to the best of your ability. All told, I guess I spent about $2,000 in time and work, for a retainer of $250. But I got experience that I really didn't want.

In contrast to that case, there was another that I was proud of. Someone started a school to teach GIs how to fly. He opened shop in Texas, then New Mexico, Arizona, and other places. He'd go broke in one state, change the name, and start up somewhere else. A couple of GIs wanted to get their money back, and I got interested because I thought someone should. It was a civil case. Both he and his lawyer kept stalling as long and as hard as they could. In fact, his lawyer was being partially paid by free flying lessons. Well, it took five years, but I finally got him. He even said on one occasion, "You know something, you know more about my business than I do." He may have been right, because if I wanted to win, I had to know everything. To collect a judgment of $5,000 for my clients, however, was murder. I had to apply for supplementary proceedings to do so, and when I threatened to take some of his personal valuables, he finally agreed, just to get me off his neck. I think I spent at least $5,000 and only got $500 for my efforts. But it was worth it!

At the present time, my field is general law, no specific specialty. You see, I've owned a lot of real estate and still do, so I'm quite familiar with that aspect, as well as leases and contracts. Then, since I have an accounting background, and like to protect myself from Uncle Sam, I'm pretty informed about tax laws, estate planning, and trusts (both revocable and irrevocable). At present, I also represent two of the largest credit unions in Tucson—accounts which I've related to for the past fifteen and twenty years. I don't claim to be an expert in everything, but I do have expertise in many areas. I don't advertise; people just come in to me from referrals and I have all the business I need. I even get referrals from other lawyers. As far as the advertising goes, I'm against it. It makes our profession a business, and I don't think it really enlightens the consumer. Referrals are a better indication of whom you will be dealing with.

One of the biggest accomplishments that gives me great satisfaction is that my dear wife and I have believed strongly in education. I have always stated, "Money you can lose. Education you cannot—and if you do, then you are 'nuts' and won't know the difference."

No one could have done what I have without the constant loyalty, love, and encouragement of my dear wife. Together we have paid for over sixty years of college—for ourselves, our immediate family, our relatives, and help for others. There are now three successive generations of Larriva Phi Kappa Phi's from three universities: Arizona, Texas, and Arizona State. I am most proud of our having established a Larriva-Francies scholarship, funded at the University of Arizona, so that the product of the fund will give scholarships for others.

As far as my own life goes, I definitely do believe activity has a lot to do with longevity. I feel if I hadn't gone back to school to become a lawyer, I would have died. You know, I actually felt sick when I was retired (working only a few hours a week, collecting rents), and I used to get stomach pains frequently. The doctor couldn't find anything wrong. "I think you're a workhorse," he said. "Maybe you should go back to work." And that's when I went to the university for my law degree. I actually felt better.

I still work eight hours a day and sometimes, when necessary, on Saturdays also. In addition to my own family and relatives, I've always enjoyed and been interested in people. Some people, I don't charge anything, and some people I don't want. I also enjoy my work. Another fact that keeps things interesting is that I don't specialize in just one aspect of law, it's the diversity that keeps you on your toes.

January 19, 1991

BARBARA BARONDESS MACLEAN

BARBARA BARONDESS
MacLEAN [83]

*Her eyes brighten, her smile widens, and her voice quickens
as she describes all the projects still to be done. The immediate one is the upcoming annual "Torch of Hope" awards
ceremony for her nonprofit organization. Various tables are
strewn with stuffed envelopes, still to be addressed, containing the invitations and an appeal to join the foundation.*

*In the near future are her plans for a second book—
almost completed—and later books on interior design and
cooking. Although bothered by a back problem, she nevertheless continually pops up from her chair to show me photos, bits and pieces relating to her forthcoming activities,
and other meaningful mementos. The stimulation is there,
the energy is aroused, and the enjoyment is constantly
reflected in the radiance of her features as she talks about
them. It's infectious! And when I asked her to pose for a
photo, she slipped into her favorite outfit—that was a fun
surprise.*

* * *

THE BEST THING about my birth is the fact that I was born on
the fourth of July, the greatest day in the history of the
United States. It has made me uniquely proud and grateful
for my heritage. I realize, because I've lived so long, that
none of us has any choice on where we're born, who we are
born to, what our religion is, the color of our skin, or the
shape of our body.

As a young child I always felt somewhat like an outcast,
because my parents took me on a trip, when I was six
months old, to visit my grandparents in the Ukraine, in
Russia. They expected to stay a few months and we were
talked into staying five years, because my grandfather
claimed that if we left sooner, I would never remember
them. So my parents agreed to stay the five years, and my

109

grandfather was lavish with all the luxuries he gave to Mother—beautiful clothes, fur coat, and servants. He even built a house with American conveniences for us, and Mother enjoyed all the things she would never have had in Brooklyn. The only comfort we didn't have were bathrooms with running water. We had a number of outhouses, well hidden in a part of the garden, and in the winter there were the chamber pots.

But Father stilled dreamed of America. After I was five, however, my mother was pregnant, my grandmother was sick, and the First World War broke out. This put a definite, temporary halt to our return to America. Unfortunately, that "temporary" halt lasted many more years. In the meantime, America had entered the war and I grew up as the little American curiosity, with no one to teach me English. With my private tutoring I was learning French and German, and Russian, of course, was our everyday language. In the summers we would all go to Grandfather's country house, set in the woods near a river. The countryside was beautiful. We swam in the river and picked berries and flowers in the fields.

At that time, the early years of the war had no effect on us. Later, we saw lines of ragged German prisoners, and then, within a few years after that, the Russians were fighting each other in a civil war. Things changed rapidly, for the worse. We didn't go out at night anymore, and, finally, I didn't even go to school. Father gave me lessons at home. There were guerrilla gangs looting everywhere, and we had to go into hiding in the cellar of one of our workers. Weeks later, when the food ran out, Father decided to go and search for more. I followed behind, being careful that he didn't see me.

His luck ran out when two bandits stopped him, and when he said he had nothing to give them, one whipped out a gun and fired a shot at him. Without thinking, I jumped out and threw myself at my father, putting my arms around him. They were so startled, they fired another shot and ran off. The second shot hit me in the shoulder. Blood was everywhere and my father was unconscious. I ran to a house and when someone answered, I pointed back to Father lying on the ground, and then I fainted. A few days later, I was in bed, bandaged and with my arm in a cast, and Father was in the hospital with a bullet wound through his vocal cords. Although he might lose his voice, the czar's doctors decided to put a silver tube in to help him breathe—perhaps it was the world's first tracheotomy. It was many weeks before he came home, and then he couldn't talk at all. A pencil and paper became his only means of communication until about six months later, when he could whisper in a voice that was raspy and hard to hear, or understand.

Those bandits who shot us were part of Petrula's gang, who raped and killed all over our region. He was one of the world's first terrorists, and a few years after that, when he was in Paris, a young boy named Schwartz tracked him there and killed him. Schwartz was never tried because no one wanted any part of Petrula, and the boy was exonerated.

In the meantime, World War I ended, but the Russian Civil War continued. Mother had been pregnant and she delivered another baby sister for me—now there was Rosalie, who was six, and Ann, who was nicknamed Nucy. But it was time to do something, and Father decided we'd go to America very soon. We all knew it wouldn't be easy, but at the same time we were all excited and ready to go. To sneak out of Russia meant taking nothing with us. My father signed all his property and possessions to his sisters and brothers—that is, whatever was left that the Bolsheviks hadn't taken. Rubles didn't mean anything; gold and jewelry were what we kept, and the jewels were sewed into our panties, to be used very sparingly along the way.

On the Russian New Year, we got into a hay wagon and traveled that night—it was cold and the snow was all over. It took two weeks of travel to get to the border, and each night we slept in a different barn and traveled in a different wagon the next day. At the Polish border, Father decided it would be two wagons, he and I in one and Mother with the children in the other. Well, they caught our wagon, put us in prison, and the sentries went out to get the other wagon. Mother kept telling them I was an American, and somehow they let us go. But in the next town, Father was thrown in prison until we could prove our rights. He was there for months, wasting away, and during that time Mother contacted the American ambassador in Warsaw, to get my birth certificate from New York. In those days there were no electronic overseas communications, so it took over a year and a half before the papers came and they issued my passport.

In the meantime, my parents received Polish passports because they convinced the authorities that the Ukraine area of their birth had belonged to Poland at that time. The American Red Cross gave us clothing—ours were in tatters by that time—and we went off to England to set sail for America. In Liverpool, as we were boarding the boat, a very unfortunate incident occurred. Father was ahead of us, moving up the gangplank, when my sister Nucy suddenly broke away and Mother took after her. Father had the passports, and when he couldn't answer clearly about his name, the officer had him and the rest of the family step aside. Although Mother tried to convince them he wasn't sick, the boat sailed without us!

Then we went to London and my mother talked to and begged those at the American Embassy, [telling them] that Father was not sick, that he had his intelligence and could support his family. He couldn't talk clearly, but he could hear, read, write back, and understand. Finally, the English government and our embassy approved our voyage. The next boat out had no space other than steerage accommodations, and that's why we had to go through quarantine and ended up in Ellis Island. At that time, Ellis Island was like a dungeon on the inside, and they called out, "Men to the left—women to the right." Here again, Mother became frightened because she knew they wouldn't understand Father's inability to speak and they might send us back.

I had my passport and they couldn't deport me, but I was underage and required a guardian. They acted just like my mother thought they would—they thought Father was an invalid and that meant holding him. They wanted me to leave with my New York relatives acting as my guardians, but I refused and said I was staying with my family until they let us all out. It was a mess, and we stayed for *two weeks* in Ellis Island while they tried to figure the whole thing out. My relatives finally got in touch with Judge [Louis] Brandeis—another version of our Barondess name—and the justice asked President Harding to intervene. A few days later, a telegram from the president arranged for our release. As far as I know, I believe I was the only American ever detained at Ellis Island.

Brooklyn was a complete disappointment with the shabby buildings and tenements. Nothing like the open fields, rivers, and the luxuries of Russia. Somehow I forgot all about the horrors of why we fled. Here, I didn't understand the language, couldn't read any of the signs or books, and didn't even know what all my families were talking about when they spoke in English. And then in school, they put me in *kindergarten!* Everybody thought I was a dunce or something, but they said I would learn faster and could move up into the other classes as soon as I knew some of the language. And they were right, for I was only in kindergarten for two days. My knowledge of French and German were a big help in learning the alphabet. I graduated from eighth grade within seven months after I had started, but I was far from fluent in English.

In the meantime, my father had bought a small candy store with money that came from selling whatever jewels we had left from our escape. He was a very smart and sensitive man and knew how disappointed I was with our area of New York. So, not long after we were there, he took me on a trip through Central Park, Fifth Avenue, and the places where the wealthier people lived. It was different and beautiful. He taught me many things, and in his own way, he was a philosopher. Father was considered a half-Jew and Mother was Jewish. When he had an argument with her about my religion, he told me, "Everybody in the world is climbing the same mountain to one God, and whether you are crossing yourself, praying on your knees, or putting the mezuzah on the door, you have no choice on how you're born. But when you're eighteen or nineteen and old enough to choose which rituals you like and believe, then you can decide what church you want to go to."

About education, I also remember him saying, "It's stupidity to waste your life. If you learn you earn respect and you'll make a living. You are what you learn and you make your living by what you earn." I went through high school in two years, but didn't take the exams to graduate because I never did learn how to spell properly. You know, the things foreigners have trouble with—when is it *i* or *e*, *oo* or *u*, and so on. The simple words gave me the most trouble; the difficult words like *psychology* I learned by photographing them in my mind. But I went out and got my first job in a bank as a Burroughs machine operator, and I didn't have to speak very much English. And then I won the beauty contest . . . let me tell you about becoming a beauty queen in the Modern Venus contest.

I was swimming in a pool with a friend, and suddenly someone started to yell at me. I swam over and asked if he was yelling because I didn't have a cap on. He shouted back, "No, but how can a girl be so stupid and get herself so wet when she's supposed to be in the beauty contest for Miss Greater New York?" I protested that I wasn't in any beauty contest, my parents wouldn't like it. "Oh my God," he said. "I saw the other seventy-five girls in the contest, and you could easily walk off with it." My girlfriend whispered that maybe I should do it, but I said I couldn't, I'm all wet and I don't even have the right bathing suit. The man groaned. "There isn't enough time to change—the contest starts in four minutes. Never mind that the stripes of the suit go the wrong way, it's your face and figure they'll be looking at!" Again, I protested that my parents wouldn't approve, they wouldn't like it at all.

"Your parents wouldn't know if you lose, unless you told them about it. If you win, they'll forgive you. And besides, there's a thousand bucks in it for the winners." With that, he and my girlfriend pushed me towards the hall, and he slapped a #4 on my arm. My birthdate was the fourth and this was August 4, one month after my nineteenth birthday. Well, the judges started chopping off the numbers, and finally, there were only three of us left. I said to myself, gosh, I'm going to get the third prize. But they mentioned third place, then second place, then *my number* for the first prize. I was speechless! I became a celebrity overnight. Thirteen papers had me on the front page, and Fox Movietone News had it in the theaters. It was unbelievable. [*Laughs*]

The Schuberts put me into my first play on Broadway, and all their publicity people featured my winning the beauty contest. The play was a success and I was in it for six months; all the while I kept studying English and visiting other producers looking for parts. Well, I was in five plays in five years, with the last one running for two years. I played the ingenue lead, opposite Frank Morgan, in *Topaz*. Then Irving Thalberg ordered a screen test for MGM. He wanted a second test, but I said only if we could do it in Hollywood with the best professionals. I was willing to pay my own living expenses while I was out there. We did the test, and I got a part in *Rasputin and the Emperor*, with all the Barrymores in it—Lionel, Ethel, and John.

When I was playing in *Topaz*, I was offered a job on the *Morning Telegraph* newspaper to write a column, which I called "Little Bo Peep on Broadway." I wrote it for two years, and Walter Winchell thought it was very funny. Once he was trying to get an interview with Greta Garbo, but he had no luck. So he wrote that she had big feet. And I wrote in my column that it was pretty hard to tell a woman's foot size, and as small as I was I'd bet I had bigger feet than Garbo's. Well, Winchell said, "You're such a smartass. Now that you're writing a column, you're impossible! I'll make you a bet," he continued. "I'll give five hundred dollars to your five, that you'll never get near her yourself." I said, "You never can tell, Walter—I'll take that bet."

Three or four years later, I'm on the MGM lot and I had just finished a picture starring Clark Gable and Jean Harlow. MGM offered me a small part in *Christina*, with Greta Garbo, but I kind of objected to playing another small part. I called my agent and reminded him about my Winchell bet. If I could get that interview with Garbo, then he would have to announce it nationally that I had won the bet. Well, my agent surprisingly negotiated a six-week deal for that part, at fifteen hundred dollars a week. I worked with Garbo, got the interview, and Winchell did announce it all over the air. I also sold the story to a movie magazine, and they headlined it BARBARA BARONDESS, I ACT WITH GARBO. Wasn't that worth it, for a girl who only made five pictures and whose name wasn't really on the screen yet? Well, it created a furor. At first they all resented me, but I got the money and I got the fame. Even the *Hollywood Reporter* headlined BARBARA BARONDESS WITH GARBO. How could they miss me?

Five years and many films later, I said I've had it. I didn't want to be remembered for some of the sluts I played. And at the same time, Douglas MacLean asked me to marry him. He was a big producer, and I didn't want to be in the same business, competing. I wanted to find a way to develop whatever talents God gave me. I already drew and painted, and I got excited about interior design because my husband had such fantastic taste. A short while later, he offered me the lead in a film he was producing, but I said no. "Everyone will think I got that part because I'm your wife. I sell the talent that's in my head and not in my body, and since I'm sleeping with you, I don't want you to give me the lead." He told me I was crazy. In the meantime, I went back to college, UCLA, and studied interior design. Eight months later, someone called me for a little job, and I did it. Edgar Bergen saw the results and gave me my first big decorating job. From then on, you couldn't stop me! I did two million dollars' worth of business in my third year. Some of those clients included David Selznick, Jennifer Jones, Louis B. Mayer, amongst many others. Mayer asked, "How come I didn't meet you when you were at the studio?" I said, "Mr. Mayer, I was afraid that if you liked me, I was a dead duck, and if you didn't like me, I'd be a dead duck. So I thought it was better not to meet you. I'm not afraid anymore, because *I* choose my jobs now."

During World War II, I taught first aid for three years. In a sense, that was my guilt paying off because I was in a country where the war did not physically affect me. And all along, I kept up my design work—not only in interiors, but also in other fields. I designed fabrics, clothes, and even manufactured my own line of clothes. I've also been copied for years without any credit. In fact, I'm donating clothes I designed between '46 and '52 to the Brooklyn Museum— about eight-five garments. With my own designs, they were labeled Barbara Barondess MacLean. That addition of MacLean went back to the beginning of my decorating business, when I asked my husband his opinion—Barbara Barondess or Barbara MacLean. He said, "Barbara Barondess is a very fine actress, and they'll be confused. Barbara MacLean could be anybody. Barbara Barondess MacLean—if they see it written, they'll never forget it." When I asked how he could be so sure, he responded, "Because you have incredible taste. You've learned more about design and antiques in two years than I've learned in a lifetime. And you're obsessed with working. Your father was right, you live like a condemned woman who has only six months to live."

Not too long ago a young man came to see me and said, "I understand that you designed the first knickers, the first short-short, the first off-the-shoulder dress, and the first bubble dress—all those clothes and you don't get credit, even though you changed the American silhouette?" I said yes, and that young man just shook his head. But I did show him some of the old ads which featured those changes, and I'd like to show them to you. Here they are . . . Macy's, the first fabrics I ever designed, for Schumacher and Company; and here are ads for Saks Fifth Avenue and others— Barbara Barondess MacLean, clothes of distinction; Barbara Barondess MacLean, the clothes of tomorrow; BBM, the clothes of today; and so on. And here are my clothes in various movies—worn by Loretta Young, Gloria Swanson, Mary Pickford, and Marilyn Monroe.

Talking about movies, here's an interesting story. There was a young girl, about seventeen, who used to sneak into the theater in Cleveland, Ohio, to see me play various leads. She wanted to be me and she talked her parents into coming to New York, where she lied to agents about having played my parts in Cleveland. She was caught by an agent who said, "You're a liar! You didn't play any of those parts." She started to cry and asked how he knew. "I know," he replied, "because I was the one who sent Barbara Barondess to Cleveland to play them. With your imagination, you should write." Later, this young girl wrote the story for the film *All About Eve,* and I was invited to the preview screening.

All of my designing and decorating continued for a period of about forty-three years. My clothes were worn by Elizabeth Taylor, Norma Shearer, Jennifer Jones, Jeanette MacDonald, Gertrude Lawrence, Teresa Wright, and many others I don't even know who purchased them in stores like Saks Fifth Avenue, Bergdorf Goodman, Neiman-Marcus, I.

Magnin, and the like. In addition to the ones I previously mentioned, my interior designs included commissions for Jane Wyman and Ronald Reagan, Errol Flynn, Gary Cooper, Robert Taylor, Norma Shearer, Ann Miller, the Beverly Hills Hotel, Romanoff's Restaurant, Schenley Industries, and numerous others over the years.

Since I mentioned Gary Cooper, let me tell you about him. When I first arrived in Hollywood, the one actor I had a crush on was Cooper, my favorite. One day a group of us went into the commissary, and when I turned around in my seat, I found myself staring into the fabulous blue eyes of Gary Cooper. No one said a word or introduced me, and I turned absolutely crimson with excitement. A producer, Jack Cummings, who was seated at the table said, "Look at Barbara, she's blushing." I was so embarrassed that in an effort to be sophisticated I blurted out, "Well, one Cooper in the hand is worth two Cummings in the bush." They all went hysterical! I realized when they were laughing so hard that I had said something which could be misconstrued as suggestive. I wanted to cry with embarrassment, and I ran to the ladies' room to pull myself together. When I returned, Cooper was gone.

A few weeks later, I was making a test at Paramount. I was wearing a nun's uniform with all the rosary beads and crucifix, walking along and mentally rehearsing my lines. Suddenly, someone pinched me on my bottom. I was so enraged, especially in a nun's uniform, that I whirled around and shouted. It was Gary Cooper. He laughed and said, "I couldn't resist it. Come on and let's have a cup of coffee." I told him it was a terrible thing to do, it was sacrilegious and I wasn't going anywhere with him. But he charmed me and I relented.

Three or four years later, I was sitting in Romanoff's with a client. I had just picked up a new chinchilla jacket from the furrier and had put it down on the seat next to me in the banquette. My client and I were talking when I sensed someone about to sit down next to me. Suddenly, there was a scream and I turned—it was Gary Cooper. He had sat on my jacket, and the furrier had inadvertently left a large pin in it. Cooper looked at me, all the while rubbing his bottom. "You finally got even, didn't you?" [*Laughs*]

As you've noticed, there are a lot of mementos around the rooms. The one you're looking at now is an antique, it's a cover over the john—a "Marilyn Monroe sat here" memento. It was in my house in Beverly Hills, and it became famous because Marilyn Monroe and Joe DiMaggio lived there for many years. The bed they slept in was also an antique, it was over a hundred years old when I bought it. It was built originally for Nathaniel Hawthorne. Six months ago I sold it to the Japanese, and they bought it because DiMaggio and Monroe slept in it and are two of their favorite celebrities. It's going into a museum in Tokyo, and they paid me $60,300. After deducting the expenses of the press agent and the people who arranged the sale, the remainder goes to my nonprofit foundation. I'll tell you about that in a moment.

You know, I did retire once, when I was sixty-five, I guess. I went to Palm Beach and bought a beautiful house, with palm trees, oranges, grapefruits, the works. After three or four years of that life, I was bored and decided to return to New York, where I continued some of my designer work. At a certain point, however, I wanted to return to the theater and do something for it. After all, athletes can run around in the park to keep in shape; a singer or dancer can practice in a basement; but an actor can't do a damn thing without a playwright, a character to develop, a director, a theater, and an *audience*. And that's why I started a nonprofit foundation in 1981—the Barbara Barondess Theater Lab. For professional actors, especially for the ones who don't forget their origins, they stick to it, they're dedicated, and they spend their lives creating illusions for people that need it. Everybody has to get away from their troubles for a few hours in the theater or in a movie, where they may make you laugh or cry, or teach you something.

In one way, the foundation is to say bravo to my father and mother for bringing me up the way they did, and to keep the Barondess name alive. Its main purpose, however, is for the professional arts in the performing and visual aspects. This includes directors, playwrights, actors, actresses, and, some time later, designers. The foundation also teaches communications and projection. The speaking theater is slowly dying. All that we bring to Broadway today are the five- and ten-million-dollar musicals, many of which have been tried and proven in London. We build theaters for them that can never be used for the speaking theater, they're too big. That's why the lab gives lectures and staged readings, with some of our best actors and actresses. We do produce a play when we can afford it, but costs today, even for a two-character play with a minimum equity contract, can easily reach seventy-five thousand dollars. And that's when the top actors and actresses work for peanuts—a few hundred a week—just to practice their craft.

So every year, the foundation has a "Torch of Hope" awards ceremony. The award is a statuette of glass, along with a check for five hundred dollars. There are five categories, and this November 1990 will be the first time the ceremony will be on TV. Preceding the awards will be a fashion show of my original designs of the forties, all the spectacular ones and all handmade. They are the group of designs going to the Brooklyn Museum and hopefully, the Metropolitan. The individual award categories are for a playwright, a director, an actor, an actress, and one person who is a philanthropist or runs a nonprofit theater. In the past, the winners have included Morgan Freeman, Estelle Parsons, Geraldine Fitzgerald, Geraldine Page, Jean Dalrymple, Milo O'Shea, and many others in the nonprofit theater areas. This year's ceremony will be a benefit, and we hope to raise some funds to start workshops for our members. I'm an unpaid, full-time director, and the members of my board are all wonderful volunteers. I want to leave the foundation as wealthy as I can. I take nothing for myself because I don't need a sable coat, or jewelry, or any of the things I needed when I was young and active in those professions. You see, I've learned something very valuable, and you can quote me, "A shroud has no pockets."

Yes, the directorship is practically a full-time job and it takes a lot of energy and I love it. I'm also writing—the first book of my autobiography was *One Life Is Not Enough*, and the proceeds go to my foundation. Hopefully, the second volume will be out soon. Then there's another I'm writing. Gable . . . Harlow . . . Monroe played *A Game Called Fame*. After that, maybe a cookbook, because I like to cook, and a book on interior design. If I'm ever on record as a writer, that will be my greatest achievement. I want to leave something behind that gives people inspiration so they live by the golden rule.

Today, too many expect the world to give them everything, and they're not willing to work for it. I want to leave the inspiration to keep working and to keep learning. I was born in the first decade of my century, and I'm still here doing all this and knocking my brains out. It's my century and I hope I can live out this decade to the next century— the year 2000. If I do, I'll feel I did my job.

September 24, 1990

MARY PEYTON MEYER [84]

She suggested we meet at the McDonald's in Vandalia, Illinois — it would save me going to her home in St. Peter. Mary cleared it with the manager and wrote that we could talk there. But when I arrived, that outlet was a beehive of activity, and we eagerly beat a retreat to a community room in one of the local banks.

Tiny, pert, gray-haired, and the epitome of a grandmother — that's how I spotted her in McDonald's. Energy, fast talk, and a great down-country sense of humor are what I discovered at the bank. A knee operation still bothered her, and she limped a bit. But that didn't stop her from substitute teaching the day before our meeting. She is known by many people in the surrounding communities because of her gossip column in the Vandalia Union-Leader *newspaper. This year, however, the tables were turned and she has been featured and interviewed in the national media. But all that hasn't changed her one bit; she's still the same no-nonsense person she always was, and that's refreshing.*

* * *

FAYETTE COUNTY in Illinois has always been my home, and I guess I've lived in this vicinity all my life, within, oh, about eight miles from where I was born. I went to the Frogtown school as a child, and I also taught there later. Frogtown's a little place and you don't dare bat your eyes or you're gonna miss it. It used to have almost three hundred people, a tavern, a few churches, and the schoolhouse. Now there's nothing there but a few houses and the old schoolhouse, which is about ready to fall down but it's still there—made of bricks, you see.

I went to high school here in Vandalia. You probably didn't go by it, but it's over there, and they made it into a place for old people to go. I visited there once and it's really

MARY PEYTON MEYER

nice—a rooming house for old people. When I graduated from that high school, I wrote for a teacher's certificate and I passed. I was tickled to death and I went out and got me a school that next day for the fall session. Before that they put me over here in the Washington School to substitute for a little and I thought I was really doing something. I got five dollars that first week to substitute. You know, in those days you didn't have to go to college to be a teacher. Later, I had to go to school taking night courses and some correspondence courses. I also went to Charleston College to keep my certificate up.

Well, in the country I taught for nineteen years in the one-room schoolhouses. I had grades one, two, three, four, six, and eight. The next year it would alternate a little to grades one, two, three, four, five, and seven. And if I told the kids to sit down, they'd sit down! Nothing like today. The kids came from all the neighboring communities; sometimes I'd have as much as forty of them—that was when there was an oil boom around here. Yes, we had a potbellied stove, and there was gobs of woods in the back where we could get fresh kindling, although I also brought corncobs from home to get the fire started. The coal shack was right out the back door and we'd get the buckets filled up and the kids would help carry them in. We had big wide floors, and there were four brooms which the kids would use to sweep up. They'd help wherever they could, and that meant a lot to me.

I had a Ford roadster with a rumble seat and the kids would pile in, as many as could fit. I'd take them home because it was on my way, and they sure loved riding in that rumble seat. When the roads got icy or muddy, I couldn't drive the car, so I went around on horseback. But I could only carry one little girl that way and she always rode with me; the rest just had to hike. I've stayed all night with many of them. I'd be riding horseback and they'd come out and say, "Mary, it's just too bad to go home tonight, so you'll have to stay overnight here." Then we'd play cards all night until midnight and get up the next morning to get that fire going.

The school was in a German community and it was hard for me at first, because I had the lower grades while the in-between ones would go to the parochial school at St. Paul. So I depended on the kids that got confirmed, the older ones, because they'd help me with the little ones who couldn't speak English. But they were all good kids. Of all the kids' parents from our school, there's only one mother left, and she celebrated her one hundredth birthday the other day. That's really good—really good.

That Frogtown name comes from the pond that was about a quarter mile from that town's school. No, you couldn't hear the frogs croaking in the day, but you could hear them at night and that's when we weren't in school, thank goodness. When I taught there, I would take those kids, as soon as we could finish our lunch, up to the pond and go ice-skating. And the minute I blew that whistle to pack up, they'd follow me back to school. We'd all get a drink, go to the outdoor parlor, and come back in to work. I would never do that with kids today, not the way they are now.

As I said before, they were all good kids. There were plenty of things that happened during those years, but it's hard to remember them. In the second grade we used to tell stories before the regular class got started. Would you like to hear a few? I had one little boy who was always ahead of everybody else and he told this one—which was true. He came up one day and said, "Did you know Lassie had only one pup last night?" I said, one pup only, why that's not much of a dog to only have one, they usually have several. He said, "I'll have you know Lassie didn't cooperate with Rover very long."

Another little boy came up one day and one of his stories was, "Do you know how to catch a bear? Well, you might get where there's ice sometime and you better know." He was very serious about it. "You go out to the pond and cut a hole about this big. Then you take some Del Monte sweet peas and sprinkle them all around the hole. Put some detergent on 'cause the bear'll smell you and if he does, he won't come out. Then you hide. It may take quite a little while, but you just hide and be real quiet. When that bear comes out to take a pea—you kick him in the icehole." [*Laughs*] Oh, those kids, they really could tell you some stories. When I asked who told him that, he said, "Well, Mom told it." It really isn't anything bad, if you just laugh at it.

During the depression, things went pretty bad. I was teaching one of those years for forty-seven and a half dollars a month and glad to get it. We were farmers and weren't able to raise much. I took what money I could get and bought molasses and poured it over straw for our cattle to eat. My husband was sawing wood for other people and he had an accident—cut the top of his knee off. The doctor came every day, and at that time you didn't have any kind of insurance. You just couldn't afford that kind of thing. The knee got worse and he went into the hospital. I went there every night. Like I said, there was no insurance—we couldn't pay the doctor or the hospital, couldn't hardly keep up. Just then, the school board came to me and said they were going to raise my wages to sixty-seven and a half a month, and I thought I had the world by the tail. In those days, you could buy something for that.

It was hard though. We tried to milk the cows and ship cream, but we couldn't get much out of that. That year we didn't have many crops either. When he was hurt, of course, he couldn't farm, so we hired a boy to help and I got out and helped too. When we were done and I thought I could manage myself, I paid him. All except ten dollars, which I promised as soon as I could. That same day, they came and put a lease for oil on our ground and paid us ten cents an acre for ninety-seven acres. They paid a full ten dollars and boy, that money really looked good. I handed it over to the boy who worked for us and said, "Okay, we're all paid off now, and thank you."

Now I still have about three hundred acres of that land. A lot of it is kind of hilly and has to be pastured. I've got a good tenant farmer and he has two grown boys. Before he came, I had some other people there and they were just taking me. They were there for twenty-five years and got two-thirds to my one-third. I was going broke slowly. Now our agreement with this tenant is I get two-fifths to their three-fifths. We do have to buy a lot of fertilizer, lime, and whatever to keep it going, but that's the way the world goes. We've just had a lot of bulldozing done, with the backhoe in there for a week, and that cost a leg and an arm. But it had to be done.

As far as the gossip column goes, I write for the *Vandalia Union-Leader,* right down the street. It's published twice a week. I've been a columnist since 1921, my first year in high school—that's sixty-nine years ago! At that time the *Leader* was one paper and the *Union* was another. Well, back then some people told me they'd take the *Union* if I'd be in both papers, so I had to make a copy for each one until they merged. They didn't pay anything for a long while when I started, I just did it for the fun of it. Then they started paying, I don't know the exact rate, although one article said I was paid twenty-five cents a column inch. I have gotten as much as seventy dollars a month, but not too many times—more like fifty or so a month. It's not just a column, it can run two or three columns, from the top to the bottom of the page and sometimes over onto the next page. It just depends on how much news there is around.

I get the bulletins from the various churches about weddings, births, anniversaries, rummage sales, and whatever. I then find out what it's all about and I write it up in my own words. There's lots of things going on in the various communities—people recovering in the hospitals, out-of-state visitors, anything that's positive and interesting. I never do divorces, family arguments, or police business. If I thought it would hurt someone I wouldn't put it in. One time a reporter from Decatur came down here, and we went over to the Frogtown school. Well, the guy who owned that lease drove up and told us to get off that school ground. I knew him and said they'd take his picture and so on. But he wanted no part of it. Well, that reporter tried to get me to write up what that owner had said and how he treated us— but no-o-o, I don't do that. At one time, my reporting area included about five communities and all around. Now it's a little less, but if you told me some news, your name would be in the paper next week, whether it's here, there, or yonder.

As far as stories go, well, it was this year—1990—that I became some kind of story myself. A reporter from the *Chicago Tribune* called and wanted to come down one day. I didn't know him from Adam and I told him there was nothing to see, but he insisted on seeing Frogtown and the like. I just had knee surgery and couldn't walk too much. When he got here, he said he didn't have gas enough in his car—didn't know it was so far out here. So I said for heaven's sake just drive my car, we'll just go! I took him down to Frogtown, St. Paul, Square Town, and St. Peter. He just had a ball—he's from the city. He took that picture, went home, and put all that in the *Chicago Tribune*. Then it was like putting gas on a fire, it just blazed! Sandy Gillis, Johnny Carson's coordinator, called me and I turned her down four times, because with that bum knee I just couldn't walk much. She said she gets ten or fifteen papers every day, wades through them looking for people, and she found me in that article in the *Chicago Tribune*.

Sandy said I should come out with someone and they'd pay the expenses. Finally, Bob, my adopted son, took me. Bob came to us when he was eight years old. His dad was going into the service and he got drunk that night and left him out on the street. The state attorney's secretary said, "Oh, I'll bet Mary will take him in." So we took him in. Oh, he was a problem when we got him. They had put him in a home with some older people and they couldn't do anything with him—he wouldn't come home from school and so on. It was because he'd just been let go and wasn't taken care of. We wanted to adopt him right away, but that couldn't be done until they put a notice in the paper that if anybody wanted him, they would have to appear in so many weeks. Somehow, that wasn't done. In the meantime, we bought him clothes, sent him to school in the country, and things worked out okay. When he was grown, Bob went into the navy and then came home. My husband died and while we were settling the estate, the lawyer said, "I don't see why in the world you don't adopt that boy." And I said, well not at this age! But the lawyer said I could adopt him anytime because his mother and father had died a long time ago. Bob agreed and I adopted him when I was in my fifties or sixties. I don't have any blood relations, but even if I had a dozen of them, I wouldn't think any more of them than I do Bob.

When I had finally decided to go on the Carson program, I called Bob and he said he just couldn't go because he had taken so much time off when I had the knee surgery. I said okay, I'll find someone else. Well, at three-thirty in the morning he called and said, "Mom, I haven't slept a wink—I'm going." And when he went to his boss and asked him about it, the boss said, "That's where you belong."

We flew out to Los Angeles first-class. I'd never flown that way before. They met us with a limousine and they had a sign on the car—MARY PEYTON MEYER. Oh, we were treated like royalty. I told Bob, live it up, we'll never be treated like this again. At the studio they had a special room for me, with my name on the door. Then Sandy took me up to a man who put me in something like a barber chair and put a thing around me. He had a bucket of paint and he smeared it on me. Then I went to the beauty shop and that lady worked my hair all over. I did it before I flew there, but she really fixed it—fixed it really good. Sandy had me get up and walk a little so my knee wouldn't stiffen up. Johnny Carson knew about the knee, and when I got there, he reached down and got a hold of me to get me up there. I never saw him before I got out there, and I never saw him afterwards. I was told to just talk as hard as I could and not to let Johnny get ahead of me. Some kids in the audience, behind Bob, kept yelling out, "Just give it to him, Mary, we're in back of you." I talked about him coming to Frogtown, and when he asked how many people were there, I told him eleven—and if you come out there'll be twelve. He said he couldn't go now but he would take a rain check. That's why everybody at home teases me as if I've got Johnny locked up somewhere. It was fun, I'll tell you that! When I got off the stage, a big guy grabbed me and just whirled me around, and I wondered what's he gonna do with me. He just said, "We're getting you back."

The limousine met us to take us out to eat and I had a paper that was made out so it wouldn't cost us anything at the restaurant. Bob wondered if we should be doing this, but Sandy reached into her pocket and pulled out a roll of money and said, "This is on Johnny." The whole thing was from Wednesday to Saturday, and we had a very good time. They paid for everything—I mean everything, even the calls home. They treated us like a king and queen. Took us to Universal Studios and even wanted to pay an extra day for me to visit relatives in Escondido—but I said no-o-o, and I wanted Bob to get home.

Look here—here's a copy of my check for appearing on the Carson show. I brought the check to the bank and said if there was any trouble cashing it to let me know. They didn't think so. When I went to dinner that night with our local undertaker, he said he wished he had a copy of the check, he could laminate it for me. Well, the bank made a few copies and he did fix one up real pretty. He also asked why I cashed it and I told him, "Well, Johnny's got so much trouble with his women, I'm scared to death he won't have any money anymore." [*Laughs*]

When I was on the show, they asked me how old Bob was and I made it wrong that night, I couldn't think for a moment. I said he was thirty-nine, but he was thirty-eight the other day. I told Bob that's what he gets for calling me Grandma. That's what he does every once in a while, calls me Grandma—so I made him a year older. Also, when we were there, Sandy asked me about my camera and I said we each had one. Well, she got both cameras and took pictures of everything—where they put that paint on, fixing my hair, onstage, everything, and now we have a whole album on it. Oh, we had a good time—a really good time. I enjoyed it because I like to talk and meet people. *You* know I like to talk.

Then when I came home Saturday night, we went out to dinner and to a little string musical show. Sunday, Bob went home and I went to church and took my neighbors out to dinner. They had stayed at my house all that time because they didn't want that house to be left there alone. The next three days I was called to substitute at school. No, the trip to Burbank wasn't my first plane ride. I've been on many others—to Europe three times, to Hawaii, Canada, and South America. My husband and I planned to go traveling when he retired, but he died from cancer before he was old enough to retire. He smoked . . . I hope you don't smoke. No, well good for you! He quit, but he quit too late. He's been gone twenty-one years now. I first met him at that pond in Frogtown—ice-skating. We used to go on several Sunday nights, and they'd build a big bonfire to keep warm. One night we were skating with another couple and the ice broke and we went in up to our waists. Lucky it wasn't deeper, but we still had to break that ice and struggle to get out of there. That taught us a lesson.

Oh, you want to take a picture of me? Well, I hope it isn't like those two newspapers—they each took about sixty or seventy shots, it seemed. Then one even came back to take some more! After school, this photographer took me all over, and when my farmer said we had a new lamb in the barn, this camera guy wanted me to hold the lamb and take a picture that way. There weren't that many animals around anymore; we had to sell most of them four or five years ago. We couldn't get hay then because of the drought and even if you paid for it, there wasn't any hay available. Now we have too much hay! I have a sixty-by-sixty barn and it's piled full of those great big round bales. Can't get rid of it, nobody wants it. Then it's also stored out in the fields and all around. But if you can't get rid of it, that won't help either.

As far as teaching goes, well, you know, I was subbing yesterday and wasn't sure I could meet you today. I go wherever I'm called, the low grades or the high grades. I've taught here at the Lincoln School in Vandalia—kindergarten—some twenty kids in the morning and twenty in the afternoon. I've got to say they were okay. And then there's the kids they bring in from all over the county. They're brought in the morning and returned in the afternoon— they are the slow learners, from about three to five years old. It's a little pathetic, but they're all good kids. In the upper grades, I'd say the junior high is worse than the high school. They've learned a little something by the time they get to high school. I don't go to the high school very much.

You know, the kids today are as big a difference as night and day from those kids of yesterday. When I first started teaching, if I told them to do something, they'd do it. Today they try to do as they please. Now, I don't mean all of them—just some of them. The parents are a part of it, they both work and they're out at night and gone, and the kids are let go from here to there. Again, I don't mean all of them, but there's enough to make a problem.

Now, I have a lifetime teaching certificate and if I pay four dollars a year, I can keep that till the day I die—which I'm gonna do if I get the four dollars. Oh, I'll get it. [*Laughs*] They don't pay too much, we get fifty dollars a substitute day. I sub here in Vandalia and also at the parochial school in St. Peter, where I live. In fact, they called me the other day and wanted to know if I would consider subbing this year. I said I would if I can. Previously, we were allowed to sub seventy-five days a year, and many a time I got those days in before the year was up. For the past two years, we were able to sub one hundred days a year—but I didn't make my full quota last year.

This year it will depend on how quickly this knee gets better. Heck, about twenty-five years ago when we were unloading hay, I fell off a bale and broke my right leg. But that didn't stop me from going to work. I had to go teach school with crutches for about two months. I just kept going, and when someone asked how did I manage to drive—well, I just used my left foot. Oh yes, I'm still driving today. If everyone gets out of my way, I can still drive. *You* better not get in my way. [*Laughs*]

Oh, I'll still be teaching and writing my gossip column, and I'm still doing volunteer work. I've belonged to the Mental Health for years and years. I help out with Fayco Enterprises, where the retarded children are, and I'm secretary to that organization. I belong to the Retired Teachers, and I wouldn't miss their meetings for nothing. Yes, I like to help wherever I can. If it's for a good cause, I'm ready to help anytime, you bet.

My philosophy is never give up, just hang in there and just keep going. It's not all gold that glitters, but just hang in there. There are people worse off than I am and I feel like that every day. At my age I can't complain. Our body is like a piece of machinery, it breaks or tears sooner or later. You know, I was born December 31, 1905, so I don't have much longer to say I'm eighty-four. It's going to be eighty-five soon. Guess I'll just have to hang in there.

September 14, 1990

MITCH MILLER

He has musically touched a majority of people through one or more of his numerous careers. Miller has been a classical oboist, a record company executive, a network music personality, and a symphony conductor with major orchestras throughout this country and abroad. We met in the office area of his New York apartment. The familiar beard had whitened, but the vitality still existed. I was impressed with his easy, energetic handling of both the incoming phone calls and our interview session.

Although widely known for his sing-along format, Miller has received numerous accolades for his oboe and English horn recordings with major classical orchestras. Then, as a conductor, his concerts were a sellout in all our major cities, plus Canada and Mexico. In the last few years, he's enjoyed including the London Symphony Orchestra in his schedule. His love of music precludes any thought of a near retirement.

* * *

ROCHESTER, in upstate New York, was my hometown. Even at that time it was a pretty large town, something like two hundred thousand people. It was a big manufacturing region . . . Kodak, Bausch & Lomb, and a number of others.

As far as schooling goes, Rochester had one of the best public educational systems in the country, including music. I think it had the first music school system in any of the public schools. When other schools went on to include music departments in their curriculum, they plucked teachers from Rochester, who then went to different cities to set up these programs. In our schools they gave you the instruments to use—George Eastman bought them—and you got instructions and class lessons. We also had orchestras and Saturday morning lessons at the East High School

135

Mitch Miller

conservatory. Rochester, sad to say, doesn't have all this today, and yet they were the pioneer.

Although my father was a metalworker and my mother a seamstress, there always was music in our home. We had a windup Victrola, and there were plenty of records, including Leopold Stokowski, young Jascha Heifetz, and many others. In the house, we also had a big, square Chickering piano that my father had bought for fifteen dollars. That was the first musical instrument I played. Later, in junior high school—guess I was eleven then—when I wanted to practice and study on one of the free instruments available, only the oboe was left. I guess the other students thought it might be too difficult. So it was by pure accident that the oboe became the instrument of my career in symphonic music.

I have to tell you that schooling in our family was a very important thing in our lives. My parents, having fled the czarist pogroms in Russia in 1904, were like many of the immigrants of that day—the main thing they wanted was for their kids to have an education. It's no different with the Asians today. My parents worked very hard, and although we didn't have any extra money, we never went hungry either. In fact, we ate very well, because we canned all our fruits and vegetables just like thousands of others in those days. However, the main thing was for the kids to get an education. "In case you had to flee again," my father often said, "what you had in your head nobody could take away from you." That was the philosophy all the time.

So we'd go off to school with the dictum that you study or be a bum. And we all studied! I had two sisters and two brothers. One sister became a legendary public school teacher in Rochester, another sister was a paralegal, and my two younger brothers both have doctorates. And the main point was that if you did anything, do it well—you never messed around. So when I got the oboe instrument, the point was to practice. And I did! When I was fifteen, I was playing first oboe with the Syracuse Symphony

Orchestra, and I had to drive eighty miles each way in an old Model T. I remember there was a hill, called Camillus Hill, and you had to get that old Ford revved up to a running start just to get over it.

Incidentally, Rochester used to be a tryout city for musicals and plays. I was in the orchestra when they tried out *Hit the Deck,* a Vincent Youmans musical with Queenie Smith, and we had this dress rehearsal that ran until about three in the morning. Well, on our break, Youmans comes in with a case of champagne *and* glasses, and everybody joined in. That was my first taste of champagne, at fifteen. Somehow he had managed to find it even though this was during prohibition. I found out later that he did have a drinking problem, but he was a great writer.

A year later I won a full-time scholarship to the Eastman School of Music, and later I began playing second oboe, professionally, with the Rochester Philharmonic Orchestra. With both the Syracuse and Rochester orchestras, I had the wonderful opportunity of playing under the most renowned guest conductors of that period—Fritz Reiner, Sir Thomas Beecham, Albert Coates, and many others. It truly was a golden opportunity. You know, by the time I was sixteen, I was making something of a living with the oboe.

When I left Rochester, at age twenty-two, I was making about $125 a week, which was very good money in those days. Heck, a Ford runabout cost $600, a good hot dog in New York was a nickel, and so was the subway fare and the telephone. I came to New York because I knew there was no future in Rochester and it was the bottom of the depression. I took every job I could get and worked pretty hard. But it was good for me financially and culturally. Fortunately, the depression didn't hurt me in this sense. When the WPA (Works Progress Administration) started these orchestras, the oboe was a rare instrument and they needed oboe players to complete the orchestras. So even though I didn't qualify for relief, I was able to get into one of these orchestras for $23.50 a week. It was a big drop from the regular work, but, believe me, we were able to live on it pretty well.

After that I began to audition around. You know, with music you come in and they don't have to know who you are—you play your instrument, sing, or whatever and you're either good or bad. So then I began to get jobs. In 1934 I went on tour with a symphony orchestra that George Gershwin put together. We traveled the country playing all his major works, including "Rhapsody in Blue," and Gershwin was the piano soloist. At the time, his doctors hadn't yet diagnosed his brain tumor, and they thought the tour would be a good way [for him] to get over his depression. I doubt very much that he could have made any money from that tour; after all, he was just about carrying a full symphony orchestra with him.

Although we were still in the years of the depression, on that tour we got $110 a week and lived on a train. We had our own two cars, just like a circus, and they put us on a siding in the city we were visiting. But we had to pay for our own food and a hotel, when and if we slept in a hotel—it was only a few times, if I remember. And that brings to mind the Lowry, which was a new hotel just opening in Minneapolis. A room was two dollars, and one of us would register. Then, afterwards, we'd take the mattresses off the twin beds and one would sleep on the mattress and another would be on the box spring. So you'd have four people sleeping there. And, funny enough, last year they just tore the Lowry Hotel down. When we were touring the southeast part of the country, it was on the Chesapeake and Southern Railroad; they had a dining car in which you could order seconds at no charge—sort of an all-you-can-eat menu. For a buck and a quarter, you got a dinner with shrimp cocktail, filet mignon, and I'll never forget their baked apples with heavy cream. But we'd always order a second filet mignon and stuff it in our pants to take home and eat it in a sandwich later. [*Laughs*]

One time we went to Sioux Falls, South Dakota. I don't know how they happened to book us there—it was the middle of the week and probably we had an open date. Gershwin, you see, was doing this tour because he wanted to popularize his music. You have to know that in those days the critics never did like his music, and so he wanted to spread it out to the American public. Anyway, when we got the hotel keys, I looked at my key and then I looked at Fred's key and they both looked alike. Then we checked later, the keys could open every door—they were all alike. The next morning we asked the room clerk what there was to do in this town. "Well," he said, "you can always visit the state penitentiary. They have tours there." We laughed at that, but it was true so we went there. As we walked around, there were inmates at the rock piles hitting and breaking them into smaller pieces, and the guard would say, "This guy was an accountant, the other one was a banker," and so on. Boy, [laughs] I wish they would do that with the S&L guys today—they deserve it!

Anyway, in the next year I played with the original *Porgy and Bess,* which ran for eight weeks on Broadway. Here again, Gershwin only got lukewarm reviews. Yet we in the orchestra pit knew we were playing some of the greatest stuff we had ever heard. Today, of course, he's considered one of the tops—I wish we had a few like him right now. So I kept right on free-lancing with other major musicians around New York, and by this time I was known in the musical circle. It still was a case of long hours and not always the best of conditions. Finally, after a few years of that I landed a full-time job with the CBS Symphony Orchestra. That paid better than the major symphony orchestras and, at the same time, gave me the opportunity to play both symphonies and the compositions from films and musicals. I also played extra bits on the side with conductors like Andre Kostelanetz and Percy Faith, both of whom I admired. All this sometimes went into twelve- and fifteen-hour days, but that was okay, it was something I loved.

Interestingly, I played the original broadcast of Orson Welles's Martian scare. Although we were surprised by the public's reaction, you have to consider what was going on at the time. There already was tension in the air, what with Hitler gobbling up those small countries in 1938. Of course, no one stopped to figure out if the Martians really did land in New Jersey—how did a reporter get there so fast? Frankly, we who were there in the studio thought the show was duller than hell, it was only something for Halloween. But Orson was so good, and, then again, when you listen on radio, you have to understand that your imagination takes over—which is one of the great things about radio.

After playing quite a while and earning very good money as an oboist, I sort of wanted to get into something different. Well, luck and a friend were with me, and I got the opportunity to produce some records for a small label—Mercury Records. It went extremely well; I don't know, maybe it was in me all the time, just waiting to get out. But we produced lots of hits and came up with lots of new talent. I even "invented" a children's line of records called Little Golden Records.

A former classmate of mine at the Eastman School was in charge of Columbia Records, and he offered a job where I would be the head of popular records and he told me to go find new talent. Once again it took off. In two years Columbia went from number four in the business to number one. I found lots of new talent, both for Mercury and Columbia—Vic Damone, Patti Page, Tony Bennett, Rosemary Clooney, Frankie Laine, Johnny Mathis, Jerry Vale, Ray Conniff, The Four Lads, and oh, I guess I left some out. They were brought to me as unknown talents and I discovered them; I signed them for the company and guided their careers. And to this day, forty or forty-five years later, those who are still working are at the top of their craft. Rosie Clooney, Vic Damone, Patti Page, Frankie Laine when he wants to work, Johnny Mathis, and Tony Bennett. All of them are considered top artists, and they fill the joint wherever they go.

You know, when I went into producing records I was a classically trained musician, and pop people were not used to that at all. I could look at a page of music and hear it! Also, I introduced new sounds into the pop recordings, from instruments that the pop musicians were not ordinarily using—the French horn, the harpsichord, the exotic drums, and so on. That period of time was really the "Singers' Decade." It was also the era of the Top Forty idea, which governed radio stations' music selection completely because it was a listing of all the best-sellers. Unfortunately, it kind of ruled the airways, and I spoke out and said radio shouldn't be programmed by lists, it should program music for "all the people." Well, I made both friends and enemies with that statement.

In the meantime, I didn't give up the oboe. In fact, I always kept one somewhere in the vicinity of my desk. And I did and have played with all the great conductors of those eras. One Monday, a voice called me on the phone at seven in the morning. The man's voice said, "Michelle Mi-ll-er, this is Leopold Stokowski." Well, I thought it was one of the boys, because I had never met the man, so I made some scatological remark, but without missing a beat he just went on. I finally realized it was him, and he said, "On Wednesday, we are going to record and I heard you on the air with CBS and I want you to play the English horn." So I showed up, and there was one of the greatest orchestras in the world—the best of all the New York Philharmonic, the NBC orchestra, and the best free-lancers. It was called Stokowski and His Orchestra, and we played the Sibelius tone poem for English horn and orchestra. He's a fantastic conductor. You couldn't realize how good he was until you played under him. The English horn, by the way, is related to the oboe, as the viola is related to the violin.

While I was still at Columbia, I came up with the idea of

recording some "sing-along" albums of standard and nostalgic songs. You know, singing together is an American custom, and all the ethnic groups do it also. The Germans had their songs, the Italians sing at every party, and so on. All you did was go to the five-and-dime, buy a piece of music for a quarter, the pianist played it for you, and everybody joined in. This was before radio and television. People always sang. So I had the idea to make it informal—to sound informal is very hard, while at the same time you're trying to get a specific format. So, anyway, in '58 I made it, and I thought it was a damn good record, but you never know how successful something will be. Well, they made three thousand copies and overnight it became a tremendous seller, and this was in the midst of rock and roll. It was simply called *Sing Along With Mitch*, and it shows that there's room for all kinds of music, and a lot of people still don't understand that.

Eventually, there were more albums, and altogether the series sold twenty-four million copies. So, of course, television was interested, and I tried to sell it to CBS as a show. Although they saw that the records were selling millions, they didn't take it. So I sold it to NBC as a one-time shot, but all hell broke loose and it swept the country. "Sing-Along" became a household word, and my Vandyke beard was cartooned everywhere. The program was in color—in very good color—and here I was on NBC and still running Columbia Records. Anyway, we were on NBC for three and a half years with the program called "Sing Along With Mitch," and when it went off the air in 1967, they got twenty thousand letters of protest. But, if you know anything about marketing, they wanted the youth market and that meant our program had to go. It didn't make any difference that we were tops in the ratings. I figured there was no sense in arguing, so I took the whole group and went on a series of very successful tours across the country and as far away as Japan. The TV shows are owned by me, and the tapes are right there above the file cabinets.

No, no, there's no bouncing ball, there never was—the bouncing ball idea was in the theaters to teach you to sing *new* songs. The whole point of the sing-along was to have the lyrics there so you sang them with confidence; there was nothing that pointed out the words. You didn't need that because they were songs you already knew. That would have been too much of a gimmick, and besides, it never occurred to me to do it that way on TV. If you ask any person and they say bouncing ball/Mitch Miller—bet them a hundred bucks and you'll win! [*Laughs*]

After all that, I went back to my old haunts and started to conduct symphony orchestras, and I was very successful with it. I conducted both classical concerts and ones that were a combination of symphonic works and a second half of Broadway and Hollywood classics. Once, by the way, when one of my engagements included the San Francisco Symphony Orchestra during their summer season, it turned out to be somewhat unusual. They said they had a prizewinning pianist from the conservatory and could he be my soloist. Well, I figured a prizewinner, why not? When I got there, I never ran into a more undisciplined musician in my life. It turned out he was half-Polish and half-Japanese. Well, I had to have the soloist, so I spent about four hours with him trying to organize him, because a soloist has to know everything that's going on with the orchestra. He has to be aware of every note that's being played in the orchestra, you just don't chase after it. So I thought we had it pretty well down, and when we got to the concert we barely, barely got through it.

But he had put on a good show banging away at it, and I'm sorry to say that many in the audience, instead of listening to music—they look at it. They see instead of hear. If somebody makes tortured faces, they say ooh, he's creating the music, and it's all baloney—musicians laugh at it. Anyway, the soloist came out to take his bow, not realizing there were about two busloads of friends and relatives from his nearby hometown. Well, they immediately stood up and began to cheer and scream. So, without even taking a bow, he sat down and started playing an encore—which was twenty minutes long! The point was he did this with all the musicians on the stage—they were supposed to go out for intermission. The result was that the concert went twenty minutes longer, the musicians had to be paid over-time, and the so-called good deed became a very costly one. No, I don't recall his name, and I've never heard of him since.

I'm not a disciplinarian. No one has more fun at rehears-als. I make jokes and so on. But it's not a matter of just play-ing the notes. With professional musicians, a gorilla could conduct and they would play beautifully. They'd be together—loud, soft, or whatever—but there wouldn't be any definitive interpretation. So you try to do that with minimal rehearsal, and with most orchestras it will work because they understand. My philosophy is that if you're with a symphony orchestra, no matter what you're playing or who you're playing with—every time you play in public, you are the such and such symphony. You should never let your standards down.

Orchestra musicians in America, most of them have a long season, and most pop conductors are mostly journey-men who happen to have arrangements and don't demand the musical standards that I do. There are musicians who say, "Well, it's only a pops concert, why should we have to work that hard?" It's not the whole orchestra, but if you have five or eight players who have that attitude, that already sets it off. And you have very little rehearsal anyway.

So I run into those conditions once in a while. On the other hand, when you meet musicians singly, they're all very nice. Sometimes, collectively, they can be a horror!

I don't approach life as if there's some good in everybody. If I don't *see* the good, I'm not going to look for it. I've been burned too many times. So now, for a while anyway, I would just withhold my opinion. It's like I told my daughters on dates. I said, "Don't feel sorry for anybody, at first. Let them earn your sensitivity and understanding, and then in the end they will be getting much more than they would have gotten in the first place."

As far as what kind of music do I like, I have to say all kinds. It's like books. You have mystery novels, biographies, big epics, and so on. The question is, are they well written? And the same goes for music—you have to ask, is it well performed? I also feel that concerts should be less formal and ticket prices lower. Music should be available for everyone, and the government could increase its subsidies for the arts, which includes music. I try to do everything I can for symphony orchestras and other musical causes, including fund-raising, appearing on telethons, even donating some of my rare tapes and records for auctions. I must say that music is just as important as health or education . . . in actual fact it benefits both.

I don't have anything against what's going on in music today, except that young people are missing a broad spectrum that's available to them. I have to compare what's available now to a giant smorgasbord—there's so many things in varied music that they can taste and try, but they don't. And that's just like eating hamburgers and fries for every meal. Basically, I don't even mind any of that, all the repetition and caterwauling, it's just that I don't want the kids to think that's all the music there is. It's fine to start with that and then graduate to somewhere else.

In my career, I've met and known all the great pop composers, and the amazing thing is that all of them were in only *one* generation. When you think of it, that's fantastic! Irving Berlin, Richard Rodgers, Rodgers and Hart, George and Ira Gershwin, Rodgers with Hammerstein, Harold Arlen, Jerome Kern, Cole Porter. I'm sure I left some out. When you stop to think about it, they're all dead and still their songs remain at the top—people keep doing them. And yet the only one around today who's in their class is Steve Sondheim. You could take Andrew Lloyd Webber and pluck tunes from classical music that he studied while he was at the conservatory and you'll find his roots for every one of the songs he ever wrote.

I'm fortunate to have always enjoyed whatever I was doing. All my careers were great . . . an oboist, a record company executive, a TV personality, a symphony conductor. And if we come up to date, well, I've been conducting symphonies all over the world for the last twenty-five years. As far as right now is concerned, I'm still very active and busy. So today I'm doing mostly conducting, and I do about eighty-five concerts a year, but not in eighty-five cities. Some cities I may do multiples and so on. Just a few years ago I conducted the London Symphony Orchestra in an all-Gershwin concert, and the compact disc recording was selected as one of the ten best of the year. And the next year the London Symphony and I were at it again with a classical concert. You know, when it comes to symphony or pop concerts, I treat them all the same and enjoy them both thoroughly.

As Ed Murrow's mother used to say, "It's better to wear out than to rust out." It's pretty hard to rust out if you keep on the go all the time. And that's what I do, I keep moving. Especially with the music concerts—I try to reach as many people as possible. My reward is to see their faces come alive. As for me, I don't consider conducting as some sort of work . . . music is my totality and I'm still having a ball.

September 26, 1990

DR. RAPHAEL PATAI

He is a noted anthropologist and biblical scholar, author of many books. His tall, erect frame gives no indication of his having arrived at the octogenarian status. Neither does his intense, enthusiastic approach to the constant research required in his chosen fields.

Dr. Patai's home in Forest Hills, New York, affords easy access to the unlimited resources of information that can be found in the nation's largest city. But parking in New York, even in its outer boroughs, is always a problem. Fortunately, he came out to rescue me—showed me where, and how, to park in what appeared to be a no-parking area. With that trepidation out of the way, the interview was both relaxing and extremely interesting.

Dr. Patai's early years overseas have afforded him many insights into the diversities of the Middle East and the problems that abound. Optimism for eventual solutions, however, has been tempered by the sad fact that over many years, nothing much has changed the basic problems and animosities.

✢ ✢ ✢

PERHAPS you would permit me to start with an anecdote that relates to an experience which, for the fist time, made me aware of the approaches that various cultures have to aging. At the same time, it does have something to do directly with your book. It did occur in the early years of my life, but it is interesting.

This was in 1933, a few months after I arrived in Jerusalem. I had several Arab friends there, and one of them took me to a little library in the Old City of Jerusalem. The director of that library was an elderly Arab sheik, a beautiful man with olive skin, a square white beard, and a white turban. He was very friendly and started to show me the treasures of his library. The room had a very high ceiling,

149

and the shelves of books lined every wall to the very top. Well, he climbed way up the tall ladder and brought down some big, very heavy manuscript volumes for me to look at. I was very impressed, and I said to him, "Sheik Amin, I see that you have such wonderful strength. How old are you?" He replied, "I am eighty, and Allah will hopefully give me many more years."

After we left the library, I said to my friend, "Wasn't it wonderful for a man of eighty to have such strength?" He said laughingly, "Don't you believe him. He's only sixty-five." So what did I learn from this? Simply that it was in sharp contrast to our culture, where people always want to be young, always want to appear younger. We are constantly making great efforts to keep our youth and hold back the years. In *that* culture, old age is considered a value and an asset, so that a man who is sixty-five will actually pretend to be eighty and therefore have more honor, wisdom, and respect. This was the first time I learned that different cultures have different approaches to the phenomenon of aging and to old age itself.

Now to go back to the beginning. I was born in Budapest, Hungary, and lived there for the first twenty-two years of my life. Our high school was a very serious school, and it was there I first learned to appreciate culture. In those days, high school went up to the age of eighteen. Elementary school was four years, from age six to ten; and high school, from age ten to eighteen. After that, one could enter the university. In my high school, which was one of the best in Budapest, we learned no less than *five* languages: Hungarian, Hebrew—because it was a Jewish school—German, English—starting with the age of fifteen—and one hour a day of Latin for eight years. By the time I was through with the Latin of eight years, I knew the language. Even to this day, I can read it without any difficulty. At that time, however, I was unhappy about it, and during one period I screwed up enough courage to ask my teacher about it. You know, in those days we had a terrible respect for, in fact fear of, our teachers—we didn't dare open our mouths. Still, I asked him, very respectfully, why do we spend so much time learning Latin syntax? We will never use it. He replied, "It develops your thinking capacity," and he tapped his forehead.

I couldn't understand his answer at the time, but today, looking back at those years, I really think there was quite some truth to what he said. By the way, in each of those five languages we had to memorize poetry. And to this day I entertain my wife by declaiming to her poetry in Hungarian, German, Hebrew, Latin, and English. [*Laughs heartily*]

The universities in Hungary had a quota system relating to Jewish students. Since 5 percent of the population was Jewish, only 5 percent of university admissions would be available to those students. Most of the Jews lived in the big cities, and being professionals, they wanted their children to attend the university. Most of the Hungarians lived in the villages, were farmers and peasants, and not many were concerned with university education. Nevertheless, although the law was unfair, it was the law. My father was the editor of the Hungarian-Jewish literary magazine, a poet in his own right and a man who was loved and respected by Jews and gentiles alike. As a result, he was quite influential and had many friends among the authorities. With their help I was enrolled in the university, but only after the academic year had already been started.

I entered the engineering department of the university. I recall, some time later, one day I was working alone in a remote room of the main buildings. When I went to leave, I found the main entrance locked. I walked around and finally found a side door that was open. When I checked the main entrance from the outside, there was a notice which proclaimed that the university was closed until further notice—because of disturbances. The next day I read in the paper that during the afternoon when I had been sitting peacefully at the drafting table, several Jewish students had been beaten up, thrown down the stairs, and hurt quite badly. This type of incident didn't endear the university to me, and I decided to change my field of study. For hundreds of years, my family had produced famous rabbis and scholars, and I decided to follow in their footsteps. I enrolled at the Rabbinical Seminary of Budapest, and at the Faculty of Philosophy of the university, and took Oriental studies. I spent my sophomore year in Germany, and at the age of twenty-two I passed my doctoral examination.

My father was not only a poet, writer, editor, and Jewish intellectual leader, he was also the moving spirit of the Zionist movement in Hungary. He had given me a Zionist education, so that from childhood on my great desire was to go to Palestine, or Eretz Israel, as we called the country. Within three days after completing my doctorate, I took a ship from Trieste to Haifa. You know, it is fascinating what little details memory retains. I remember—this was fifty-seven years ago!—that on the day of my arrival in Haifa, I walked out of my hotel room on Mount Carmel, went down to the garden to lie on the grass, something I always enjoyed doing in Budapest. The stalks of grass and the surrounding vegetation was strange, not the familiar flora I knew in Hungary. This, perhaps more than anything, made me aware that I was in a completely different world. Of course, the main difference was in the people. In Hungary I was used to a homogeneous population. Everybody was Hungarian. In those days a foreigner was a rarity in Hungary. Everybody dressed alike—at least in Budapest—they behaved alike, spoke the same language, and [each] was a Hungarian patriot. True, there was a Jewish minority, but the Hungarian Jews felt as Hungarian as the Christians, and prided themselves on being not more different from the other Hungarians as were the Catholic from the Protestant Hungarians.

When I walked out into the streets of Jerusalem on that first day, I saw a veritable mosaic of people, the like of which I had never seen before. First of all, there were the

Arabs, all kinds of them. There were city Arabs with the men wearing the red fez and the women wrapped completely in black garments, their faces covered with black veils. There were the fellahin, the villagers, with their colorful clothes; the bedouin with their rough brown goathair cloaks. Among them were some blacks, the result of past interbreeding between Arab men and their Negro slave concubines. The Arabs were one of the major slave traders almost up to the twentieth century, and whenever they took slaves they converted them to Islam. They treated them well—there never was the harsh treatment that many industrial and agricultural slaves suffered in America. In the Arab lands, they were mostly household slaves and became incorporated into the family and society. Negro slave girls were often the concubines of the men, and if they had children, they were considered the legitimate children and heirs of the fathers.

As for the Jews, who were the majority in Jerusalem, the streets of the city presented an even greater variety. Some were from Oriental countries, whom I had never seen before. They spoke Arabic better than Hebrew. They hailed, as I soon found out, from Yemen and Aden, from Iraq and Syria, from Egypt, Libya, Algeria, Tunisia, and Morocco. There were also Jews from other Muslim countries whose mother tongue was not Arabic. And there were other smaller groups of foreigners. For instance, there was a small Abyssinian colony living on the roof of the Church of the Holy Sepulcher in the Old City of Jerusalem, in little white washed huts. And, of course, there were the British, since Palestine was a British mandate. In 1933 the country was still underpopulated—approximately 500,000 Arabs and about 120,000 Jews. It was a fascinating time to get acquainted with life in that country and to find my place in it. Fortunately, I spoke Hebrew quite fluently, so I had no difficulty attending classes at the Hebrew University. I also knew English. The university was only eight years old in

1933, and I was admitted as a graduate student. In three years I earned my second doctorate, which happened to be the first ever awarded by that institution.

When I arrived in Jerusalem, I knew some Arabic, having studied it at the universities of Budapest and Breslau. After settling in Jerusalem I made many Arab friends. With one of them, Sheik Ahmed Alkinani by name, I met every week for many years either in his house or in mine. He taught me Arabic and I taught him Hebrew in exchange, and thus we learned each other's language quite well. He also introduced me into Arabic society, and through him I became acquainted with many other Arabs, including high officials.

In those days disagreements between Arabs and Jews as to the future of Palestine lay beneath the surface. The Jews planned and hoped that Palestine would one day become a Jewish state. The Arabs planned and hoped to be able to establish Palestine as an independent Arab state. Still, compared to the bloody period that started in 1936, the years from 1933 to 1936 were tranquil, even peaceful. The British mandatory government kept a balance between these two sectors of the population, with the result that both of them were dissatisfied. The situation came to be considered a fact of life in the country. A story circulated in those days was that the British officials were instructed to make sure that both sides kept complaining. They would be told, "Your trouble will begin when one side is satisfied with you. As long as both sides are dissatisfied, everything is fine." From 1936 on the Arab riots brought hostilities out into the open. But by that time the Jews had gained a lot of self-confidence, as shown by an anecdote I remember from those days.

The story goes that the Arabs came to the High Commissioner of Palestine and asked, "Your Excellency, please give us three days of free hand and everything will be solved in those three days." The High Commissioner replied, "Well, I wouldn't object to giving you three days, but just an hour ago I had a Jewish delegation here and they only asked for *one* day for the same purpose."

But, anecdotes aside, those were very tense years, beginning with 1936 and ending in 1939 with the outbreak of the war. The Arabs carried out many terrorist attacks against the Jews and the British. The Jews, at first, followed a policy of self-restraint, of no retaliation in kind. Only when they saw this policy didn't work did the Jews too begin to attack the Arabs. So every day you heard on the radio or read in the paper about Jews and Arabs being killed. The British, who were caught in the middle, also suffered fatalities.

However, this did not interfere in the personal relationships between me and my Arab friends. As a matter of fact, my friend Ahmed and I made a private pact. We solemnly vowed that should conditions become so bad that either of us felt his life was in danger in the place where he lived, the other would take him in and protect him. I lived in a Jewish quarter and he in an Arab one. Fortunately, it never came to that, but I believe to this day that if I had been in danger, he would have taken me in and protected me. What did we feel about the political differences? We both felt that the Jews and the Arabs were two brother nations and they must find a way of living in peace with each other. Well, it simply hasn't worked out that way. It is truly unfortunate that individuals in this conflict can respect and get along with one another, but communities or nations cannot.

In 1939, when the war broke out, the British clamped down very energetically on the Arab terrorist bands. They attacked and killed many of them, and the leaders had to flee from Palestine. Thus it came about that while the world bled, order was restored inside Palestine and there was peace and relative security. We suffered little actually, more psychologically. There were several bombing attacks by Italian planes on Tel Aviv and Haifa, but not Jerusalem. There was austerity. There was also a time when Rommel was advancing in North Africa. He crossed the Egyptian border. If the Allies were unable to stop him, how would the Jews fare in the Nazi-occupied Palestine? Those were difficult times, and plans had even been made for the Jews to retreat and gather on Mount Carmel for a last stand. Fortunately, it never came to that. Rommel was defeated and pushed back.

I lived in Jerusalem for about fifteen years. While completing my doctorate, I taught Hebrew and Arabic at a local high school. After the doctorate, I was awarded a fellowship at the Hebrew University, and that enabled me to continue scholarly research and complete a book on ancient Jewish seafaring. Before the outbreak of World War II many students were coming to Jerusalem from Europe and the Middle East, and most had no knowledge of Hebrew. For them the university set up a program for Hebrew language classes, and I became one of the instructors. I taught there for four years, but throughout that period my main preoccupation was research—studies in the areas of historical and contemporary culture, folklore, customs, and anthropology of the Jews and non-Jews in Palestine and the Middle East. By the time I left Jerusalem, I had six Hebrew books to my credit. Also my first English book, *Man and Temple,* was published in Edinburgh, in 1947.

I had never formally studied anthropology in any university. I learned on my own, from reading, work, practice, and research in the Arab and Jewish communities. In 1945 I founded the Palestine Institute for Folklore and Ethnology, in Jerusalem. I became its director of research, and started publishing its journal and series of books. This work made me known in anthropological circles abroad. In 1947, I was awarded a fellowship by the Viking Fund in New York, with a stipend of twenty-five hundred dollars, a fantastic sum for me at the time. I felt like a millionaire. The fellowship called for a year of study and research in America. In October I said good-bye to my wife and two little daughters, and sailed for New York.

It was on the ship that I had my first encounter with Americanese. I shared a cabin with an elderly Jewish gentleman from Brooklyn. He was on his way home after visiting relatives in Tel Aviv. The first morning when I woke up, I saw that Mr. Gray was already up and about. I said, "Mr. Gray, why are you getting up so early?" So he said to me, "Don't ya no, da oily boid getz da woim?" I said, "What . . . what?" And he repeated, "Da oily boid getz da woim." I was too embarrassed to tell him I didn't understand. Months later, when I finally became acquainted with Brooklynese, I understood what he said—"the early bird gets the worm." It was a great anthropological discovery, Brooklynese English. [*Laughs*] But, seriously speaking, what I learned from my attempts to converse with Mr. Gray was that being able to read, and even to write, a language is one thing, to understand it as spoken—quite another. I was the proud author of a book and several articles in English, but I couldn't understand Mr. Gray. The problem persisted for a few months. I would go into a drugstore and ask for a sandwich and the counterman would ask, "Why aw righ?" It took a number of these encounters until I understood that he meant "White or rye?"

Upon arriving in New York I experienced a goodly portion of what later anthropologists called "culture shock." It started before I even went ashore. The ship arrived in Lower Bay after midnight, to wait for morning before moving into its berth. Mr. Gray and I were among the many passengers who stood on deck and watched the shoreline. "Dat's Brooklyn," he explained. All that was visible in the darkness was an endless stream of car headlights rushing along the shoreline. I simply could not understand where all those cars came from or went in the middle of the night. "Does this city never sleep?" I asked Mr. Gray. "Dat's Nu York," he answered.

I was simply overwhelmed by the size of New York, the skyscrapers, the traffic, the crowds, the distances. In Jerusalem, when I went to visit someone, I walked there in ten or fifteen minutes, transacted my business, and walked back—all within an hour or so. Here, I had to schedule a half or whole day for a visit, after having with some difficulty mastered the mysteries of the huge subway network. It was difficult at first, but not traumatic. One eventually acclimates to everything, I just had to rethink my working day and schedule. I was very fortunate to have my fellowship with the Viking Fund. They were in New York; they gave me working space and a nice office where I could work and meet people. Of great benefit to me were the fund's Friday evening supper conferences at which I met all the leading American anthropologists. These contacts eventually resulted in invitations for me to give courses at Columbia University and the University of Pennsylvania, on "The Peoples and Cultures of the Middle East."

My original plan in coming to American was to study here, get acquainted with the anthropological methods developed in this country, and, after a year, go back to Jerusalem. But in the spring of 1948, the war between the Arabs and the newly born state of Israel broke out. On the very day after its declaration of independence, six Arab states attacked Israel. For Israel it was a matter of life and death. All civilian institutions, including the Hebrew University, closed their doors. Had I gone back then, I would have no job, no income, no livelihood, and could not have supported my family. In America, on the other hand, I received invitations to several universities to teach the anthropology of the Middle East. I decided to stay a second year, then a third, and so on. The universities helped me arrange for an immigrant's visa to replace the visitor's visa. Later I applied for citizenship papers.

I also had a serious family problem that had arisen in the meantime. When I left Jerusalem, I came to America alone, leaving my wife and two children there. My wife and I had been having differences and the separation added to them, so we decided upon a divorce. She remained in Jerusalem, then moved to Tel Aviv, and later agreed that the two young children should come to live with me. I became responsible for them, and they grew up in my house. It wasn't always easy, but I had great satisfaction doing it. Today, one of my greatest pleasures is having those two daughters—they are wonderful children. One is a doctor, the other a professor, and both are writers with several books to their credit.

But let me get back to my own work. In addition to teaching at various universities, I worked for fifteen years as editor of the Hertzl Press, a Zionist book publishing house in New York. Then, for ten years before my retirement, I taught anthropology at the Fairleigh Dickinson University in New Jersey. However, during all those years, I considered my editorial work and my teaching as a way of making a living. Some of the books that were published under my editorship became classics, and some of my students went on to become recognized anthropologists. But in my heart of hearts I have always felt that for me research was the thing. I have so far written about fifty volumes, and some seven hundred articles. Whatever time was still to be granted to me, this is what I want to go on doing.

When they retired me from Fairleigh Dickinson University, at the age of sixty-five, I was at first quite upset. I felt finished with life. But that feeling quickly passed because research continued to hold fascination for me. In fact, in the past fifteen years, since retirement, I produced more books than in any comparable period before that, because I was able to concentrate solely on writing. No interruptions, no technical or administrative duties, no editing the work of others, no teaching. I believe that my most important books were written during this period, and in the last three or four years I produced at least one book every year. One of these is my autobiography, which covers my life in Budapest—my first twenty-two years. I've just completed the second volume, which covers my fifteen years in Jerusalem.

At present, I'm engaged in a major scholarly undertaking, which will be a history of the participation of the Jews in alchemy. Most people think that alchemy was a fraud, or at best a foolish attempt at making gold, but that is only a small part of it. It's really a philosophy, an attempt to understand the relationship between body and soul, between matter and spirit. Alchemy has been believed in and practiced by some of the greatest minds in the world— Newton was an alchemist, Goethe was an alchemist. If you look up alchemy in any encyclopedia, there will be very little about the Jewish participation in this field. That is nonsense, because they were among the initiators in alchemy. All this is not known, and that is why I'm doing the book.

Way back in the ancient Alexandria period, the second century A.D., there lived a woman known as Maria the Jewess. She was the inventor of all kinds of alchemist implements and procedures. In fact, one of them has become a kitchen utensil used everywhere—it consists of two pots of glass or metal, one inside the other. In the outside pot you put water and in the other you put what you are cooking. Yes, it's a double boiler, and its proper name is "bain-marie." Regrettably, no authentic writing of Maria has survived, but her disciples quote her all the time. In a paper I wrote about her I call her the "founding mother of alchemy."

Religious beliefs had much to do with attributing alchemical mastery to Jews. Many of the biblical figures were considered by alchemists as having been alchemists. For instance, there is the story of the Children of Israel who made a golden calf and worshiped it. When Moses came down from Mount Sinai, we read in the Bible, he broke the Golden Calf in pieces, burnt it in fire, ground it to powder, mixed the gold dust with water, and forced the sinful people to drink of it. And the alchemists of the Middle Ages said this showed clearly that Moses was a master alchemist—he was able to make *aurum potabile*, drinkable gold, one of the great, never-attained aims of alchemists.

Since I've reached my eightieth birthday, I've been

thinking about my life and trying to summarize as to what was it that has kept me going throughout the decades . . . in various countries, in changing circumstances, through personal crises, occupational problems, and the like. I think the answer is quite simple—there was always something that was of great interest to me, a task that had to be accomplished. I don't remember any period in my life in which I wasn't deeply involved in working on some kind of scholarly, historical, cultural problem, in which I did not have the feeling that here is something unknown, that I, and possibly only I, can make known—something that, at least to a small extent, will enrich the totality of human knowledge. And I believe that this is what keeps me going to this very day.

Yes, I am aware—like all of us must be—that my physical strength is ebbing away, that I cannot do all the things I used to do. I cannot even sit at my desk as many hours a day as I used to. But, fortunately, my thinking ability has remained unaffected by the years, and today I am just as much fascinated by scholarly problems, as eager to tackle a new task, as I was when I was half my present age.

What is my advice to people who reach my age, and to all the others? Try to be interested in something. If you have an interest, it will keep you going, it will make you continue your life. If you lose interest, you yourself are lost!

September 30, 1990

HERMAN PERLMAN

He is an artist, and his unusual canvas is glass — *sculptured three-dimensional carvings etched into slabs of clear glass. His work may be found in churches, synagogues, memorials, buildings, private collections, and the White House, and it has been exhibited in many areas of the country.*

Herman Perlman is a deeply religious man. Biblical figures and spiritual subjects are among his favorite themes. His sculptures of well-known personalities, his rhythmic figures, and his large murals have also attracted much attention and critical acclaim. In earlier days, he was also well known for his caricature sketches, and some of that humor occasionally shows up in the sculptures.

Thankfully, our in-person meeting negated the need for me to depend solely upon photographs of his works. Instead, I had the opportunity to look at and touch a number of his glass sculptures — ones he has retained in the living room of his apartment in Rockville, Maryland. They are beautiful.

* * *

LET ME FIRST give you some thoughts about how I feel at this stage of life. Not long ago, I decided to go to Florida to be amongst those of my own generation. Well, it was a mistake and I came back, as you can see. I happen to be a very religious person, and I go to the synagogue wherever I happen to be. Here, in the Baltimore area, there was life! Young people, children, bar mitzvahs, bat mitzvahs, marriages, friends, refreshments, and lots of activities. In Florida, there was none of this kind of active life. At the synagogue, the rabbi would announce who passed away that week and so on. Generally speaking, a number of these people were basically just waiting to die, and that's not something I'm going to worry about. When it comes, it comes. Last year, on my eighty-fifth birthday there were 312 people who attended that celebration—*that's* life!

I'm not saying that the Florida lifestyle isn't good for some people, it's just not for me. Another thing I try to do is to avoid stress. There have been losses in my life that were, and still are, very painful. But even though they may still bother me daily, I try to control it; I sit down and don't continue to think about it. I try thinking about a lot of creative things to do. I plan how to do them even though I may not follow through. It's a way to control yourself. In the synagogue, the three hours I spend there, I concentrate fully on the prayers and singing. Everything else is out of my mind, and it's peaceful.

Now let's begin. My birthplace was a small town in Poland, near the Russian border city of Lutsk. My father was a weaver of materials, and when I was still an infant, he got a job in a Russian city near Kiev. He was a better educated than most of the others—he could read and write Polish and Russian, so they promoted him to the office. My mother, who was the daughter of a rabbi, operated a small grocery store in the neighborhood.

Because both of my parents worked, there was a girl who took care of me and my older brother, Max. My first language was Russian; that's what she taught me. When I was old enough for school, both Max and I went to the Russian school, because my father's boss used his influence to get us there. All the other Jewish children had to attend the Hebrew school. At the Russian school, no one knew we were Jewish, and we had to speak Russian. The school was like a military academy. Even at that age—I was only five—we had to wear uniforms and practice in the forest with wooden rifles. Red shirts and black wool with brass buttons, just like the Russian soldiers.

I remember making some ice skates out of wood and heavy wire. We lived near a river and played a lot there. One time [when] I was skating with Russian friends, the ice broke and we crashed right through it into the icy waters. The three of us were in the water about fifty feet from shore, and thank God, a man came along and dragged us out. Then other people took us into their house, wrapped us in blankets, and put us on top of the brick ovens to get warm. That was an incident I never forgot.

After a few years here, my father was worried about many things in the community. The people were Polish, Ukrainians, Russian, and there was a lot of anti-Semitism, even some pogroms. There also had been a strike at the mills, and some of the workers had been laid off. So when he got a letter from my uncle in America, he decided to go to Columbus, Ohio, and join him. We were to go to Kolk and live with my grandfather until he could send for us. Kolk was a town with about five hundred families, and when it rained, the streets became so muddy you couldn't cross to the grocery store, or to see friends. Our grandfather made us take off the Russian uniforms right away, and we went to the Hebrew school as soon as we got there. My brother and I spoke Russian to each other and that was terrible for my grandfather, so we had to stop that. After all, he was a rabbi and our lives there had to be in a completely Jewish atmosphere. The town of Kolk was a territory owned by Prince Radziwill—I think Jackie Kennedy's sister was married to a Radziwill.

We stayed there only a few years because my father was able to send for us in 1914. From Estonia, where we took the boat, it would take eleven days to arrive in America. We were in third or fourth class, and our first meal was wonderful, the best kind of meat and food. But as soon as the boat started out into the Black Sea, the water was very rough and I got seasick and gave up the whole meal. In fact, I was seasick for the entire eleven days it took to get to Ellis Island. I didn't really enjoy the trip, but there was no alternative.

In those days, there were no immigration quotas, although you had to go through customs at Ellis Island. But boats were coming in from all over the world—once you started out for America, you got in there. At Ellis Island, everyone was checked for diseases. They also searched everyone's belongings for things they didn't want you to bring into America. Because everyone was poor, the most precious things they carried were their beddings, which were tied up in bundles with small pillows inside. Well, the inspectors sometimes slit the rope quickly and the knife would accidentally slash into the bedding, and the feathers would fly into the air all over the place. That's something I remember clearly—the flying feathers.

There was an organization at Ellis Island that would meet the Jewish immigrants. They had a big dining room—a kosher dining room, because most of those who came were very religious and ate kosher foods only. The organization permitted the immigrants to get food and shelter for three days, until their relatives arrived to take them out. Some, of course, were met immediately, and they left. But others had to wait for their families to come from different areas—travel was slow in those days. Well, my father didn't come until the fourth day. In the meantime, we had good meals and a good place to sleep.

On the fourth day, however, my mother was reluctant to go into the kosher dining room to ask for food. So she went around the terminal and came to a concession where they were selling nice, boxed food for fifty cents. You got a sandwich, an orange, and a tomato—no drinks. But there were plenty of water fountains around, and five cents was too much to pay for any other type drink. She bought three boxes, and we started to eat. At that point, a very pious person came over to us and said, "I've seen you in the dining room the last few days, and now I see you're eating this food. It's ham—it isn't kosher." Well, we opened the sandwich and it was a combination, ham and cheese. That combination alone is wrong and since we were religious, we went to the bathroom and got rid of the food.

My father finally came in that evening. There had been problems when he changed trains at Cleveland, and he had to wait four or five hours. By the way, in 1912, when my father came through Ellis Island and they asked him his name, it was Perlmutter. When he tried to spell it for them, the inspector said, "Why don't you spell it Perlman. If you have to go to court to change it, it will cost you a lot of money. Why don't you just change it here." So my father said fine, and he got an American name at no cost. When we arrived, we came in as Perlmans too. He took us all to Columbus, Ohio, and my brother and I were put into school there.

Originally, when my father came to America, he didn't go to Columbus immediately. He stayed in Brooklyn first— you know, you can be a smart man in Russia, but you're dumb as hell in a strange place. He didn't know how to travel properly, and a compatriot who worked in a hospital got him a beginner's job there. Then this friend suggested he should apply immediately for his first citizenship papers. When my father said he would be leaving soon for Columbus, the friend said, "That's okay. For now, you can use my address here. Then you can return in five years and apply for your final papers." This friend was a politician, working for the block leader who was seeking a higher office. The idea was to get a lot of votes, so my father's friend was to collect as many names as he could. When the five years were up, my father came to New York and got his final papers. Okay, that was fine. Now I was also a citizen through my father's papers. But years later, when I was about twenty-five, I was suddenly informed that I was *not* a citizen. That friend of my father's was caught in a number of swindles, crimes, and other illegal schemes. Anybody who became a citizen through him had their papers revoked. And I lost my citizenship too, had to become a cit- izen on my own, with first papers and so on.

Getting back to Columbis, Ohio. That area we lived in was a German neighborhood, and those kids made our life a living hell. They got my brother and I in trouble with the teachers, the principal, and just made everything difficult. And trying to learn a new language wasn't any fun either. Finally, we moved to a Jewish neighborhood, where my father rented a house for fifteen dollars a month. We could mix with our neighbors, and there were many other Jewish kids in the new school.

I was very fortunate with my art and music teacher in the Fulton Street School. She took a special interest and helped greatly to overcome my lack of English. When she mentioned something, she would go to the blackboard and sketch it so I would understand. When I didn't know the English word for something I was trying to say, she would motion me to draw it. She felt I had some artistic talent, and she encouraged me in both my drawing and language abilities. My brother and I wanted to forget our Russian language, and I also didn't speak Hebrew, except at home. So with my teacher's help I started to become better and better with my English.

During the year my father would buy housewares, brooms, dishes, and he would then take his horse and wagon and ride out to the countryside. He would sell the housewares to the farms and smaller villages which were very far from the city of Columbus. He would leave on a Monday morning and return by Friday afternoon so as to be home for the Sabbath. In June, my brother and I would go along with him to help out and to enjoy the country. I liked those trips very much.

In 1918 there was a big flu epidemic, and my brother became very ill and died. He had only been in America for three years and was eighteen when this happened. It was a tragedy for all of us. The Jewish custom after a death in the family is to mourn for a whole year, and that excludes anything in music. When I went back to school, after a month of grief and prayer, the teacher had me practice drawing for the music class in the morning, and continue drawing for the afternoon art class. Because drawing took in two classes, I started clipping pictures of people from the newspaper and sketching them. The teacher liked them and started to hang them in the lobby and the classroom. Later, she entered them in contests that involved all the Ohio schools. There were thousands of entries, and I won two honorable mentions. Only a hundred were exhibited, and I was proud to have my two there. I was eleven or twelve then, and I think that's when I decided I wanted to be an artist.

Even at that age I worked, selling newspapers and as a pin boy in the bowling alley. Later, I worked in a defense plant making electrical equipment, and then some friends and I had our own business installing electric doorbells. I only spent a half year in high school before quitting to work full-time. I was sixteen and looked all over for some job that would relate to art, but there was nothing. The only think I could find was with a butcher, delivering meat from three to eleven in the mornings. So for the rest of the day I kept making electrical things, and when I was nineteen, I became an electrician's helper. I didn't know it then, but all that electrical knowledge was going to help me in the future. In the meantime, my brother's death created a strain between my parents, and after a few years of blaming each other, they decided to part. My mother and I left Columbus and went to the Baltimore area.

I enrolled at a good art school, the Maryland Institute of Art, and studied design, commercial art, and different media. My mother opened a small grocery and I helped out there, but it couldn't support the both of us. So I got a job in a deli in the evening. There were three Jewish people in that store, and that makes for a story. When I left Columbus, you could never tell that I was foreign-born—there was no accent from either the Russian or Jewish languages left. But those three guys in the deli wouldn't speak English, not even to their non-Jewish customers. Well, after working there for three and a half years, I regained my Jewish accent and I still have it to this day—as *you* can easily tell.

This deli was near the theatrical district and lots of customers came in after the theater; that's why we stayed open until midnight. One rainy night there was only one person still there, and he invited me to join him and have a Coke. It turns out he was the art director of the *Washington Post,* so I got my artwork from the back and showed him. He was somewhat impressed and suggested I drop in when I came to Washington. Sometime later I did visit him, and he showed me around. When I asked about a job, he pointed to all the desks and said they were occupied. However, they did need a retoucher. In those days, photographers still used the flash powder guns, and the extent of their knowledge related to using the camera—not making great pictures. So they might go to a ball, and when they photograph a man in a tuxedo against a black background—he's lost. And if he has black hair, it's even worse. Then the retoucher has to lighten the background, touch up his features, and put highlights in the hair to be able to have it reproduced in the paper. In one case, a developer wanted a full-page ad of his project, so I had to paint out all the construction equipment and add trees, shrubs, sidewalks, and whatever around the model house photograph. It was a lot of work.

Now as to salary. In the deli I was getting $38.50 a week, which was pretty good money at the time. At the *Washington Post,* the salary would be $15.00 a week—they never started any apprentice with more than that. It was a hard decision to make because I was now supporting my mother; the grocery store didn't work out. But it was the chance of a lifetime and I took it. We moved to Washington and took a room, not an apartment. We shared a kitchen and a bathroom with others. I only worked the evening shift, five to eleven, and I attended some more art classes during the day. Both the retouching and the school were not very challenging, and I was getting a little bored.

Later, I met someone from the *Saturday Evening Post* and he encouraged me to think of a new approach to drawing—to draw from memory. Well, I started to do that, especially with faces. I made some drawings of the men I worked with, and I tried to emphasize some of the features. They liked them and wanted me to autograph them. They were caricatures, rather than portraits. One day the publisher got to see them, and soon I was doing caricatures for the editorial department, the drama and society departments, and some of the important visitors to Washington. I also went to Philadelphia, for a preview of *Merry Go Round,* with Ginger Rogers and Fred Astaire. The drama editor wanted caricatures for its opening in Washington. In the meantime, I also started doing free-lance work for theater owners—caricatures of the stars in their shows, and so on. It was fun and it was extra money.

In Philadelphia, I visited some relatives and met Sara Schuster, who was only eighteen. I was attracted to her and went back later to see her a few times. After a short while, we wanted to get married, but there was a problem. Sara had two older sisters and two older brothers; none of them were married. Both from a religious and social point of view, the older ones should be married first. Well, we solved that—we eloped! The family wasn't at all happy, they gave us hell, but it was done and I took her back to Washington. Then two weeks after we were married, the *Washington Post* announced a 50 percent layoff in every department, and that included me. That was tough because we had just rented an apartment. So I concentrated on free-lance work and caricatures, and things did work out for a while. I did a press book for MGM's film *Rasputin and the Empress,* which starred all the Barrymores. That gave me some national exposure, and I became well known for the style of my caricatures.

A year or so later, I met Walt Disney in Washington and helped him to make some contacts in the newspaper editorial departments. After lunch one day, he suggested I go out to Hollywood and work for him. Since I had been on and off with the *Post,* I took the family out to California and went to work for Disney. I'm creative, and the animation tracing was just too mechanical for me. It was monotonous, but jobs were scarce and nothing else showed up. I stayed eighteen months, and I don't know how I stood it that long. But food was cheap there. I could buy ten pounds of potatoes for a dime; a dozen oranges for a dime; onions were a penny a pound; and the butcher would throw in a bone with marrow, and so on. I like salty herring and that was three for a dime. In a restaurant, a bowl of cereal was three cents. Even when I was in New York, two slices of bread and a tea was ten cents—I made many a meal out of that when I couldn't afford to buy a sandwich.

The depression did hurt me at various times, especially between jobs when nothing was available. Also, when I made fifteen dollars a week—that was my depression! After leaving Hollywood, I free-lanced in New York and Washington—subway posters, theater posters, and that kind of thing. When I moved the family back to Washington, I worked for the *Post* doing advertising art and illustrations. One day the publisher sent for me, and when I entered his office in shirtsleeves, he said, "You don't expect to come into the publisher's office without a jacket and tie?" As I started to go back, he laughed and pulled me into the conference room, where a number of editors were already seated. "We have a new program," he explained, "called 'New Faces in Congress,' and we want you to do the caricatures of each congressman to go along with the articles. It may take two or three years to complete."

I felt very good about that assignment, and it worked out financially as well. My salary was thirty-five dollars a week and each caricature brought in an additional fifteen dollars. There were three of them each week, so it meant eighty dollars a week, plus the fact that each congressman wanted the original sketch. Although I sent it to them without charge, almost all of them sent fifty dollars for their sketch. I was in the money then, and it lasted for three years. During that time I also did caricatures for the editorial department, as part of my regular job. These usually featured the foreign dignitaries that visited the White House.

At one conference of Jewish leaders in Washington, I made a composite of the group and it was published the next morning, about five columns wide. I received an immediate call from a rabbi who attended the conference, "Mr. Perlman," he said, "you have done a disservice to the Jewish people. The caricature you drew of Mrs. Goldsmith showed a very big nose—the same things the Nazis are doing in Germany to make the Jews have an ugly appearance. You're a disgrace." I apologized and felt very bad about it. In fact, over the years, whenever I attended affairs where Minnie Goldsmith might appear, I made sure to keep out of her way if she showed up. But many years later, I did meet her in the office of a friend, and when we were introduced I said I owed her an apology. I explained about the sketch that had appeared in the paper about thirty years ago. She just laughed and said, "I remember something about that, but I wasn't the one who complained. It was the others, and I did tell them I always had this nose and it was always big." She continued, "But they should have seen my father. He had such a long, hooked nose that in summer or winter he used to wear a shawl around his neck, and when he went out in public he'd wrap it around his face."

In 1939, the *Post* was in trouble again and we parted. Jobs were still hard to get, and the free-lance work wasn't enough to support a wife, two small children, and a mother. A number of our friends had small grocery stores around Washington and they tried to talk me into doing the same—they were making three and four hundred dollars a week, something I never made. Finally, I said okay, but it's like I committed a terrible crime and I'm being sent to prison for five years. So I'll go into the grocery business for five years and no more! I did, and I succeeded very well and made a lot of money. I think one reason for that was a sign I made up—PLEASE DON'T ASK FOR CREDIT, OUR REFUSAL WILL BE MOST POLITE. Too many small stores went under because of their credit load, and I didn't want that. The business prospered and in 1945, after five years, I got out. I sold the store and was able to buy a large building on Connecticut Avenue, which I remodeled completely into an eleven-unit apartment. It's located in what has now become one of the most expensive areas in town. A few years ago we were offered over a million dollars for it, but we turned it down. The building was given to my children. We've had congressmen and professional people as tenants, and Shirley Temple lived there for a year.

After the war, there was a lot of construction going on in Washington, and I began designing various aspects for the architects and builders. A few years later I was introduced to an artist who carved into glass with a sandblasting technique. The equipment was simple, and the frosting effect interested me for my work with the architects. When he offered to sell, I bought it, and the first thing I did was to improve and develop the equipment. My electrical background came in handy, and I developed my technique on glass that went beyond a simple frosting of panels. I pursued more artistic and pictorial effects. Soon my murals went into religious institutions, banks, public buildings, restaurants, even the White House.

For the White House, I was commissioned to design and make glass panels for five bathrooms. On the president's partition I carved a bald eagle holding an olive branch, and in an area that would be sealed against the wall I engraved a message, "In this tub bathes the man whose heart is clean and who serves the public faithfully." You see, that's the way I felt about Harry Truman. By the way, that secret message was how some friends got me on the TV show "I've Got a Secret." It was a national show, and when none of the panel were able to guess what I did, I told the story of that secret message.

Although I kept refining and improving my tools, the etching and sandblasting created lots of glass dust. I used masks, a complete hood over my head, and even developed a cabinet where I stayed on the outside and reached in to work on the etching. One of the largest pieces I ever made was the Virginia War Memorial in Richmond—110 feet wide and 30 feet high. My six helpers and I took a full year to complete it. We engraved eleven thousand names on this glass wall.

It wasn't until the sixties, however, when my work changed into a more three-dimensional sculpture that also embraced the area of fine art. That's a story in itself, and there's a mystery about it which has never been solved. One day a truck driver delivered a large, flat wrapped package to the studio. He said, "A woman gave me this and said she would call later with instructions." Well, no one ever called. So, after a year passed, I opened the wrappings, and I was amazed. It was a huge slab of glass, about an inch thick, and it was the clearest glass I had ever seen. For years I had been thinking about religious sculptures, and this "heavenly gift"—I have to call it that—seemed to indicate the time had arrived. I cut the slab into eighteen pieces, made my sketches, and gradually sculpted eighteen biblical scenes. Because the glass was so thick, I went beyond my usual technique of shallow frosting and achieved instead an intaglio effect—a deep engraving carved into the glass from the back of the slab.

Although I fully intended to keep them for myself, a rabbi I was working with insisted on an exhibition of them at his synagogue library. The library was not a very light room, so I put each sculpture on a wooden base, with a small fluorescent bulb in it. In this way, the light came from below and made the three-dimensional carvings stand out dramatically. The exhibit was a great success, and I was commissioned to do more and more pieces. This, in turn, led to exhibitions all over the country, and my wife accompanied me everywhere. Most of the works were religious in nature, for synagogues and churches . . . *The Joy of Sabbath, Noah's Ark, Rebecca at the Well, Shalom, Scrolls of the Law, Benediction, Sabbath Services, Moses on Mount Sinai,* and many, many others. But I also did a great deal of work for

the Washington architects in the Blair House, the Federal
Reserve Building, the Renwick Gallery, the Walter Reed
Hospital, and others.

When it comes to personalities, I sculpted numerous
"portraits in glass." Some you can see here in the apartment—Lincoln, Churchill, Einstein—but there also were
Jack Kennedy, Golda Meir, Robert Kennedy, Martin Luther
King, Eleanor Roosevelt, Harry Truman, Pope John XXIII,
and so many that I may have forgotten. I guess my caricatures in those early years are still with me, for every once
in a while one of the glass portraits has a good trace of
them. These individual sculptures have also been commissioned by many organizations to be given as awards—
sometimes in the image of the recipient, other times as a
symbol of the organization's annual presentation award.
Speaking of caricatures, a few years ago they had an exhibition of my work in that field and I donated I think it was
sixty of them to the National Portrait Gallery of the Smith-
sonian Institute. That medal you're looking at was the
award I received from the National Gallery for that
contribution.

Now we can come up to date. For forty years, my art has
been in glass, and today, of course, that work has slowed
down. I gave up my studio a while back, but I still have
many friends to go to when I need that extra space. As a
matter of fact, I do have a project now for a Reform temple.
I may not be too enthusiastic about it, but there are many
friends who see that I'm still walking around, and they
want me to do certain projects. But more important, whenever I get a feeling that there's a special challenge—that's
when I jump in! I'm not too interested, at this stage, in
duplicating something. It's a *new challenge* that gets me
going, keeps me interested in my sculpture.

October 8, 1990

A quick one-hour flight to San Diego and a short interview in his high-rise condo in Coronado, California—that was the plan. Unfortunately, the one-hour flight took three hours and I was quite late. But Orville was a gracious host. We talked a bit in his home office, then ate some lunch at the fabulous Hotel del Coronado with Mrs. Redenbacher— and finally had a concluding chat back at the office. His farm upbringing gave him a down-home quality, which was reflected in his sincerity about many of the values he believes in. I enjoyed the hurried hours I spent with him.

Although his popping corn is now the best-selling brand in the world, it was a rough road when he tried to interest others in his special hybrid seed some twenty years ago. But Orville believes firmly in goals and the need to achieve them. He's convinced the one who wins is the one who tries. That same belief has guided him into the winner's circle many times, from early school days to his present fame as the popcorn king.

Although he's an effective salesman via his TV commercials, Orville continues the promotional efforts wherever he is. One of his well-known quotes is, "I provide the hot air, while others produce the popcorn."

*   *   *

IT'S TRUE I've gotten a great deal of recognition because of the television commercials we've made. As far as how I feel about making them, I do feel comfortable and kind of enjoy doing them. About the only thing I don't like is memorizing the lines. So there was a time when we changed all that and we did our lines ad lib—no script at all. I think we did twenty or twenty-four spots that way. Now we're back to doing fifteen-second spots—next week, I guess—and you do need a script for those. Anyway, it seems they take twice as long to do as the thirty-second ones. Although the

ORVILLE REDENBACHER

lines are on a teleprompter, they don't like you to use it unless you really have to, so it's better to memorize the short ones. We make about an average of ten commercials a year, although with the fifteen-second ones there may be more.

People often take TV spots with a bit of skepticism. Is there really an Orville Redenbacher? Is that him in the commercials? Is that really his grandson? The answer to all the questions is a big, unqualified yes! Way back, one of the creators of our commercials said the following, "We could not cast someone to play the part of a character named Orville Redenbacher who would be more perfect than Orville Redenbacher himself."

Another thing some people wonder about—is that my real name? Once again the answer is yes. My father, in addition to being a good farmer, was also a good mechanic, and Orville Wright was his idol, especially after that first flight in 1903. So when I was born in 1907, I was named Orville. To date, I've done about a hundred commercials and Gary, my grandson, is now appearing in a number of them. He was chosen by the advertising agency out of the eight grandsons I have been blessed with. And the funny thing is that one of the other grandsons was studying to be an actor, but he wasn't chosen although I thought he has the greater resemblance to me. Two of my daughters each have four sons; that's where the eight grandsons come in. Someone said that every fifth child born in the world today is a Chinese baby—perhaps that's why each of the daughters stopped at four. [*Chuckles*]

One of our competitors has a commercial running now where they mention our corn—I think we're getting more good out of it than they are. A commercial like that always helps the other brand more—we don't do that. By the way, there have been requests for me to do TV spots for other products, but I told the Actors Guild I didn't want to get involved with anything else. Naturally, I belong to the actor's union because you have to after you make one commercial. I've made guest appearances on programs, though—"What's My Line," "To Tell the Truth," Merv Griffin, "Good Morning America," Pat Boone, Joan Rivers, "Hee Haw," and some others. Those early shows were a lot of fun when the contestants had to guess who you were, or what you did. I don't mind doing the shows because the host always mentions the popcorn aspect a number of times, and that's good publicity, free advertising too.

Brazil, Indiana, was my hometown. It was a small community, maybe eight thousand population in those days. Coal mining was one of its assets until that petered out and then the main thing became clay—for bricks and other products. We lived on a farm there, and I was in a one-room schoolhouse in the lower grades. Yes, I had my farm chores, and I remember telling one magazine writer, "I don't think anything is more miserable than milking cows in freezing weather." For those few who do it today, I'm sure they'd agree. At that time my father ate popcorn every night, and maybe that's where it all started. During the late twenties the bottom fell out of the hog market by 50 percent, and all farm prices were affected. Then it got much, much worse during the depression. In order to salvage some returns of our labor, my father would load up his Buick car with fruits and vegetables, and frying chickens, and we'd drive around selling door-to-door. I was his helper. In the winter, we'd butcher some hogs and sell sausage and hams, tenderloin, and things like that. When I was fourteen, I drove the car and sold the produce myself, once a week. The reason I did it alone was to avoid the two of us being away from the farm—we couldn't afford to have no one working the farm for two days a week, there was just too much to do.

When I was eleven, I joined the 4-H pig club. It was the county agricultural agent who got me into that, and it changed my life. I was very active in the 4-H projects throughout high school. In fact, here's a picture that shows my entire suit covered with 4-H ribbon awards—they're on my shoulders, chest, arms, trouser legs, all the way down to my shoes. I was so busy with those projects, I never had time for the other activities in the high school. One of the interesting things at that time was the senior class charging admission to the auditorium to hear radio programs. It may seem preposterous now, but those were the days when radio was so new and many people didn't own a radio. The students built a crystal set and then charged a modest price for the townspeople and families to hear the popular programs we tuned in. This lasted for two years, and the school benefited from those funds.

When I graduated high school, they gave me an appointment to West Point. But I turned it down because I wanted to go to Purdue University and become a county agriculture agent. I guess I missed out on two or three wars that way. At Purdue, I worked my way through college and earned my degree in agriculture. There were a number of activities I got into there—the university paper, track, and the band. When I went back for an honorary doctor's degree, I told the audience, "The two most important courses I took here were track, which taught me to win and stay out in front, and music—which taught me to toot my own horn." [*Chuckles*] You see, I ran cross-country in the Big Ten competition and I played the sousaphone in the college band. Unfortunately, when I was a senior in college, our home burned down and I lost all my clippings and records. But I still have a fifty-year-old sweater with the sport letter on it, and someone sent me an old clipping reporting I won a cross-country race in record time. Incidentally, the three men behind me in that race were varsity runners, but somehow I won. You always have to keep trying. As far as "tooting my own horn"—well, I'm still doing that.

While at Purdue, I took enough courses to qualify me for a teacher's license. In those days you couldn't go right from college into a county agent's job. So I taught vocational agri-

culture for almost a year and then went to Terre Haute as
an assistant county agent, to the same man who got me
interested in the 4-H clubs when I was eleven. A few years
later I became the county agent in Terre Haute and stayed
on that job for ten years, until 1940. During that time, I was
the first agent in the nation to do daily radio broadcasts
from my desk, and also mobile broadcasts from various
farms. I left the county agent's job to become the farm
manager of Princeton Farms, a large twelve-thousand-acre
operation of cattle, sheep, and agricultural crops. Dent
corn—for cattle and other animals,—was one of their big
crops, but they also sowed the corn variety for popcorn.
That's where I first started breeding hybrid popcorn seed
and continued with that work from 1941 to 1951. During
World War II, forty-two of my employees were drafted into
the armed services, and we eventually contracted with tenant farmers rather than employees. I was exempt because
I was running one of the largest farms in the area.

After twelve years of managing Princeton Farms, where
there was no opportunity for ownership, I joined with a
partner, Charles Bowman, and we purchased a small
hybrid corn seed business in Valparaiso, Indiana. Fortunately, Bowman was still under contract to Purdue University and couldn't physically join me until a year and a half
later. I said it was fortunate because the new business
couldn't support two salaries at the beginning. When he
did join me, he concentrated on the technical side of storage bins and grain elevators, while I continued pioneering
and developing liquid fertilizers and breeding hybrid corn
seeds. Eventually, Chester Hybrids became the world's
largest producer of popcorn seed, which we sold to all the
name-brand popcorn companies. At that time we were not
in competition with them, we were just popcorn seed suppliers. And we didn't own any farmlands—instead, we
supplied our seed to farmers who have their own acreage,
and they grow and harvest the corn for us. We agree on a
price they will be paid before they plant it, and we will take

the entire crop when it's harvested. Wherever necessary, we also supply any required technical know-how. What it all amounts to is that we guarantee them a fixed income, and they guarantee us a fixed, controlled, quality product.

During those years our company was growing, I continued to cross-pollinate and breed a better popcorn seed. In 1965, we made the breakthrough to this "gourmet" variety, which was somewhat more expensive to produce because the yield per acre was smaller. Then I wasted four years of my time trying to convince the processors—Jolly Time, Cracker Jack, Weaver, and all the others—of my idea that they would do better by selling a higher-quality popcorn. All I heard was, "Popcorn is popcorn, Orville. No one is going to pay more for yours." Another was, "It won't work. You can't put a corn up on the shelf that's gonna cost twice as much as what's already up there."

In a way, they were right, because popcorn had always been sold at a price per pound. If you were selling it at eight cents a pound and someone came in with a seven-cents-per-pound bid, that's the one they'd buy. But our new gourmet variety was a better grade, fluffier and tastier, and they popped up bigger. Before we ever had hybrid corn, the popping value of the corn seeds was in the range of nineteen to twenty-four times to one. In other words, if you had a glass tube twenty-four times higher than a glass jar of popcorn kernels and you popped it, the popped corn would fill the glass tube. With the first hybrids, this volume went up to thirty to one. When we made this breakthrough with the gourmet hybrid in 1965, we went to a *forty-four* to one popping volume.

When I couldn't convince the processors, my partner finally said, "If they're so damned wrong, why don't you come out with a brand name and go into Chicago to hire a marketing firm to help you develop a price?" Well, I did go to an advertising firm in Chicago, and the first thing they said was, "Sit down and tell us all you know about popcorn." I did that for about three hours, and then they suggested I return in a week to see what they might have come up with. When I returned, we got together in the conference room and they said, "We've come up with the name Orville Redenbacher's Gourmet Popping Corn." You could have knocked me over. I thought then—that's odd, that's the same name my mother came up with in 1907. And they're charging me thirteen thousand dollars for the idea. [*Chuckles*] But let's get back to the story. I told them having my name on the package might be too funny and besides that, I had a partner named Charles Bowman, so I felt uncomfortable about the idea. Their answers were, "About the name, it may seem funny but that's the point—it will be hard to forget. And about your partner, you'll find many Charlie Bowmans all over the country, but you won't find any other Orville Redenbacher." And in addition, they wanted my picture on the label—I was also uncomfortable with that.

It seemed the best thing to do was to follow their advice and make up some packages to test market. We used glass jars rather than our competitors' cans or bags, and I thought it would hold the desired moisture content better. We thought, at first, we'd have to sell to high-quality and gourmet stores. I sent a case of corn to Marshall Field's gourmet department buyer. After waiting sixty days with no response, I went in to see him and he said, "I've been waiting for you." So he gave me an order right there and okayed the idea for me to come in and autograph the jars of popcorn. They put that notice in all their windows, and for three different days I autographed the labels on the popcorn jars. The first day, Eyewitness News—channel 7 in Chicago—came in and took pictures for an hour. They showed six minutes of it on the six o'clock news and three minutes on the ten o'clock news . . . with big lines waiting for autographs, and other glass jars being signed and wrapped to mail out all over the country. After all, whoever heard of autographing popcorn.

Churchhill's in Toledo, Ohio, got me off to a big start also.

His was the first grocery store our popcorn was in—a real fancy store, very big and all carpeted. There was an organization of these type stores, about thirty-five or forty of them all over the country, and they met twice a year to exchange ideas and work together in that respect. I was introduced to them at their meeting, and later when I called on them, I never failed to make a sale on my first visit. Many times I would deliver the first truckload myself, and I made some long-lasting contacts that way. The first chain we got into was Kroger's in Cincinnati. Then a chain called Blue Plate Foods stepped into the picture. Unbeknown to us, they made a test in Dallas that involved three hundred housewives. As I heard it, "They gave 150 of them your popcorn and the other 150 got Jolly Time popcorn. Then the next week they reversed the popcorns." After that, we were told, "In the third week, they went back to ask if those housewives would be willing to pay twice as much for your corn as they would for Jolly Time." Apparently enough of them said yes, because they came to see us about selling Redenbacher's popcorn in their stores. They were a well-known chain in the Southeast—Texas to Florida— and they were owned by Hunt-Wesson Foods.

In fact, about 1976, Hunt-Wesson bought our popcorn division, Orville Redenbacher's Gourmet Popcorn, from Chester Hybrids, and they also sold the Blue Plate Stores chain. With relation to the gourmet popcorn, I agreed to stay on as a consultant and to do the TV spots for the rest of my life, or as long as I was able. You know, within five years from the introduction of our popcorn in 1971, we went from zero to number one in sales. But it would have taken too much money for two farm kids, Bowman and myself, to market the whole country. In that respect, the sale to Hunt-Wesson made a lot of sense. Today, of course, we're way up there in sales the world over, and we keep trying to improve our product all the time.

You know, if you want a 100 percent pop, that will only come from controlling the exact moisture content in every kernel of corn—about 13½ percent, which means you have to dry it very slowly. When we harvest, we harvest it on the ear. Others harvest with a combine. It's cheaper to harvest with a combine, which goes through the fields, picks off the ears, and shells them—all in one operation. We take it off on the ear, which gives us a chance to ear-sort it, and then we put them in a bin with perforated floors. Warm air is sent up through the floors to dry the ears very slowly—at picking time, the moisture content is 19 or 20 percent. We dry those ears down to 15 percent, and then we shell them through a conventional corn sheller. Then we put the kernels back in the bins and take out the last 1 or 2 percent of moisture very slowly, so that we get every kernel the same. That also helps get rid of "old maids," the trade term used for leftover unpopped kernels. As far as bulk sales of popcorn seed, we only sell that to Disneyland and Disney World. Together they use 500,000 pounds a year, and ours is the only popcorn sold there.

I mentioned earlier the "tooting my own horn" aspect, but it didn't quite work when I was on the "Hee Haw" television program. They had a sousaphone quartet on the show and a special song was written for me, which they wanted me to sit in on and play along with them. Well, they gave me a sousaphone, and while they played and tried to encourage me, I just sat there, reluctant to join in. As they came to the end—voom, voom, v-o-o-o-om-m-m—*that's* when I joined in, on the *last* note! You have to remember, I hadn't played or held one since college days, some sixty years ago. And my lips were all wrong. With a sousaphone, your lips have to be somewhat hardened, and without playing for so many years, my lips were as soft as butter! Another thing, in college the sousaphone was about the only instrument purchased by the band itself, it was too expensive for any student to purchase. That's one reason I didn't keep up with it.

But there were other promotion ideas that worked. I had some fun with our popcorn-shaped hot-air balloon when I took it to the Chicago ballpark on a doubleheader day. In between games, we went up over the ballpark—plenty of promotion there. But that wasn't all. At the start of the games they had me throw out the first ball. Instead of a regular ball, I threw a ball of caramel corn to the catcher, and he took a bite out of it and threw it right back. Another time, I was invited to the Indiana State Fair, where I was to sign my name in the concrete at their Hall of Fame. Earl Butz, the former secretary of agriculture was the other person to be honored. Well, he signed with a wooden stick, like you're supposed to. When it was my turn, I pulled out an ear of corn from under my coat and signed my name with the tip of the ear. Later, they took that ear and mounted it on a plaque, with a few photos of my signing with it. That may still be exhibited at the fairgrounds.

Another thing I get a kick out of are the circular stickers I carry wherever I go. Here's one. It has my photo likeness on it and the phrase "I met Orville Redenbacher, 'The Popcorn King.'" As you noticed, when we went to lunch, a few people said, "Hi, Orville." Well, many times like that, I'll take out a sticker and autograph it "Orville," then peel off the backing and have them put it on their chest. I guess you really have to call that "tooting my own horn." But it's all promotion, and often it's a lot of fun.

I used to travel a lot and have been in ninety-seven countries, all told. Funny thing, when I told people I was born in Brazil and then moved to Valparaiso, they invariably think South America—but it was all Indiana. The reason for some of that travel relates to the People to People program developed by President Eisenhower. Groups of farmers, educators, engineers, and other professions visited the countries behind the Iron Curtain, and they in turn sent groups here. It was an exchange of information relating to farms, factories, schools, and the varied approaches each country may have had. Later the program took in South America, and I even directed the first tours to Africa and the Scandinavian countries. Once I had the first group to travel to China, but their government found out I had made a previous trip to Taiwan and they blackballed me— wouldn't let me into China. The People to People programs were not supported by tax dollars; it was all contributions from corporate givers. It started with Hallmark Cards, which gave a million dollars to begin the program. After that, the program had to develop its own funding. I'm still listed as a director of the program, although I'm not an active one at this time.

However, I'm still chairman of the board for the Chester Company, and my partner, Charles Bowman, is the president and general manager. That company has grown. We pioneered liquid fertilizers, built storage bins, installed corn dryers, built grain elevators, fabricated irrigation systems, and got into the construction business—motels and that type of buildings. We even got into the computer business, originally to sell them to farmers, but strangely enough we sold a ratio of forty-eight out of fifty to nonfarmers. Today, I remain involved in the business from this home office. I do a lot of phone contact, corporate meetings, relate to certain financial affairs, and so on. Plus, of course, the TV spots and some details of the popcorn business.

Actually, I think you have to stay busy all of your life. You set goals, you reach those goals and other goals. It's just a continual movement. You can't just put down your pen and pencil and quit. Oh yes, I think you have to enjoy the work you're doing. You'll enjoy it if you know other people are getting some good out of it. Just like with the popcorn—whether you're four or eighty, you still like popcorn. It's a healthy food and it's a fun food. It has all those attributes.

I wrote something for a book not too long ago and it's still worth saying:

I've followed the classic homespun principles: Never say die. Never be satisfied. Be stubborn. Be persistent.

Integrity is a must. Anything worth having is worth striving for with all your might. Does it sound corny? Honestly, that's all there was to it. There were no magic formulas.

January 4, 1991

Jimmie Reese

We met at the spring training camp of the California Angels in Mesa, Arizona. The Gene Autry Park is a huge complex, with three large fields, numerous batting cages and pitching areas, and lots of other related activities. I observed Jimmie constantly on the move from one area to another, chatting with recruits, other coaches, player-visitors, and die-hard fans—there wasn't anyone he didn't seem to know. Smiles, a pat on the back, or a quick handshake were always included in these warm exchanges.

He put me on hold for our interview because he had to "chart" the upcoming game with the San Diego Padres. It wasn't the A team, but the players of both teams knew their performance was being thoroughly evaluated by their respective coaches. When the game was over, Jimmie reluctantly tore himself away from a visitor, and we found a quiet area near the clubhouse. I offered to get a chair for him, but he just waved that away and started talking. He was on to his most favorite subject, and his facial expressions reflected his enthusiasm. For my part, the interview was much too short.

* * *

YOU KNOW, it's a most unusual experience to be connected with a sport like baseball from 1917 right up to the present day. I've been in the game for more than seventy years, and it's been the most rewarding association a man could ever have. Without doubt I've been extremely fortunate to be involved with something I've always wanted to do—all my life.

I've been with the California Angels baseball club since 1972. In fact, Nolan Ryan and I came to this club at the same time, almost twenty years ago. My association with Nolan has been unusual, and we've become very good friends—one of his children is named after me. It's a won-

derful experience, exciting you might say, to be on these
terms with Nolan Ryan, who is one of the finest men I've
ever met in the game. Yes, you're right, he's also a heck of
a good pitcher. He's one of the best, a future Hall of Famer,
no doubt. He's forty-four years old now and he's still throwing almost as hard as he ever did in his prime. He's come
up with a change of pace and control now that makes him
an even better pitcher. There's talk about adding two or
three years to his present contract, and that's an unusual
thing for anyone at his age. I think he signed this year for
three and a half million dollars. But, then again, Nolan's a
rare man to start with.

I was born in New York way back in 1903. But as a baby
the family moved out to California, and I've been here ever
since. All my schooling was in Los Angeles, but as far as my
studies go I was somewhat handicapped. You see, baseball
was my first love, so the studies and all that goes with it
were second. I finished up with high school and became a
batboy with Frank Chance in 1917.

Frank had been the manager of the Chicago Cubs, but he
came out to join the California Angels because of his
health. His doctors said he had TB and should get out to
California. Uh-huh, you're right, Frank Chance *was* the
same guy of the "Tinkers-to-Evers-to-Chance" famous
double-play trio. He later became manager of the Chicago
Cubs and was known as the "peerless leader." Although
Frank only stayed with the Angels one or two seasons, I
started as mascot and batboy with him and then continued
my training and playing with the Angels until 1924. Then
the Oakland team signed me to play second base. As far as
my own playing days go, I've always played second base.
With Oakland, I practically sat on the bench for a year and
a half until the second baseman got hurt and they put me
in the game. After that I played for over five years with Oakland, and then the Yankees signed me. Actually, they
signed both Lynn Larry, the shortstop, and myself for

$125,000. That was a heck of a lot of money in those days. Of course, we players didn't get any of that.

I stayed with the New York Yankees for two years before going with the St. Louis Cardinals. In those days, the Yankees included Babe Ruth, Lou Gehrig, Bill Dickey, Herb Pennock, Tony Lazzeri, and the other greats. It was pretty tough trying to break into that ball club. I was fortunate to even be there for those two years. While I was there I played in over two hundred games, and during the first year I hit .346. The next year, however, I didn't do so well and that was it—I was gone. They didn't keep you around very long if you didn't do well. Unfortunately, going to the Cardinals wasn't one of the best opportunities. They had the really great Frankie Frisch at second base, so you can easily see I didn't have a chance to do much playing there.

Getting back to the Yankees, I have to tell you a bit about Babe Ruth. In my estimation, there'll never be another like him. He had more drawing appeal and charisma than any player I've ever known. Fortunately, we became quite friendly; I think he kinda liked me a little bit. I spent a lot of time in his home, went to dinner there many times. He was the most generous man I ever met in my life; he wouldn't let me spend a nickel whenever I was with him. I enjoyed the association very much, and we kept up a correspondence over the years, until he passed away.

We were playing Cleveland one day at the Yankee Stadium. I was hitting second in the lineup, just ahead of the Babe. The bases were full and there was only one out. The manager walked up to me and said, "Look, the Babe's up next; whatever you do don't hit into a double play. If you do hit the ball on the ground, make sure you run like hell." Well, I took the first ball pitched and hit it into the bleachers—with the bases full! Babe met me at the plate and carried me to the dugout. On the way there he whispered, "You're only fifty-nine behind me now." When I got to the dugout, nobody said a word. It was so quiet I blurted out, "I guess nobody saw that home run?" Herb Pennock had put them up to it—keeping quiet. But my remark went over so big that they all broke down and congratulated me, lots of guffaws and backslapping. It was the first home run—with bases full—I ever hit, and the only one!

I was Babe's roommate during spring training and on the road. But I've often said I roomed with his *bag* most of the time. He was a very popular man and was out socializing almost every night. Everybody liked him, and with all that going out I didn't see very much of him. He had a lot of strengths and he could go out—spend a great deal of time doing whatever he wanted to do—and then the next day, go out to the field and hit the ball so far you could hardly believe it. He never disappointed anybody. He would put on five-minute exhibitions before each game, and you'd be amazed at the balls he used to hit. People came out hours ahead of time to watch him during practice and warm-ups. At that time he was an outfielder, not a pitcher. And he was one of the best defensive players in the business, although he never got the recognition for that skill, simply because of his prowess as a great hitter.

As far as curfews go, there was a midnight one, and they finally caught up with Babe one day. Miller Huggins, who was the manager, never checked the rooms, and he decided to wait up for Babe one night, in the hotel lobby. It was a few minutes after twelve when Huggins saw him, but he didn't say a word. The next day at the ballpark he said, "Babe, don't take off your clothes, you're suspended—indefinitely." When Babe asked what for, Huggins replied, "You know what for. It isn't only for the few minutes last night, not by a long shot. It's all those other nights!" Well, the fine was five thousand dollars and an indefinite suspension. That was pretty stiff, but as Huggins said, it was for all the other times Babe had taken advantage of the curfew.

Babe Ruth spent money like it was never going out of style, but in any kind of game of chance he didn't want to lose. Lou Gehrig and I were playing bridge against Ruth and another player. This was during spring training and we were on a train at the time. We had them beat for a dollar and a quarter. It was nearing midnight and Gehrig, who was a stickler on conditioning and training, said, "Well, guys, I'm gonna turn in at twelve. We have an exhibition game tomorrow and I want to keep in shape." Ruth laughed. "Hell, it's only a game with a college team. They won't give us any trouble." But Lou shook his head. "I don't care who they are, I still keep in shape. So we'll play one more rubber and then it's quits for me." We continued the play and we beat them again, so now they were down by two and a half dollars. It was just past midnight and Gehrig said he was going to bed. Babe was unhappy and threatened to tear up the score sheet, and when Gehrig still insisted the game was over, the Babe did tear it up. Well, to this day the Babe still owes me two and a half dollars—he never did pay either of us, he just didn't like to lose. And yet he was the most generous guy around. The next day he'd spend hundreds of dollars like it was nothing, and wouldn't let anyone else pay. That's just the kind of man he was.

Lou Gehrig was a different kind of guy; he was just the opposite. I spent a lot of time with him too. Went over to his home often. I remember the time he said he was in a slump—he went zero for four in one game. When I went to his home that night, he said, "Jimmie, we're going out to the park first thing in the morning and we're going to find out what's wrong with me. I've got to get out of this slump." In my own mind I was thinking, *one* day with no hit and he's in a slump? Well, anyway, the next day we got a few kids to shag the balls and I pitched to Gehrig a while. He was hitting for about ten minutes—the balls were flying all over the park. He stopped and said, "Okay, I think I've got it." That afternoon, in the game, he got four hits for four times at bat—four for four!

Lou Gehrig was a very fine man, quiet and unassuming, and always interested in keeping in perfect condition. He and Babe were completely different types, but both were great ball players. The tragedy with Lou was that he died in his prime; he was only thirty-seven years old. That disease came on so suddenly and for an athlete who always kept in tip-top condition, it was ironic and a double tragedy. For a few days Lou had been having trouble with his playing, and then one day he went up to Joe McCarthy, the manager, and said, "Joe, I can't lift the bat anymore. It's got awful heavy for me. I can't do anything." Joe was shocked, but he said, "Well, I'll have to take you out of the game then." And that was the last game Gehrig ever played; I think it was 1939. They discovered he had amyotrophic lateral sclerosis (ALS), and to this day that disease is often called Lou Gehrig's disease.

It was only a few years later that he died. I remember one time when he was over at the house during his illness and one of the guests who had come over to see him said to his wife, "I'd like to get Lou Gehrig's autograph." Eleanor shook her head and advised him not to ask, for Lou couldn't hold a pen in his hand anymore—that's how weak he had gotten.

As far as my own career goes, I never was one of the greats in the game. But I did play second base for the various clubs close to twenty years. I was pretty lucky. Of course, in those days things weren't as good as they are today, especially for these young players you see around here. We had nothing then, there wasn't anything like a minimum salary, or any guaranteed contracts, or even the training we have today. There were players in the big leagues who only made two or three hundred dollars a month. Even at that time, it wasn't much money. Remember, there were only sixteen major-league teams then, and breaking into the big leagues was tough! Today, in the major-league ball clubs, there's a minimum contract of $100,000 for anyone who joins that club. Now our young players are living in the best time of their careers.

We used to get five dollars a day for meals then; now we get fifty-seven a day during season. Of course, in my early playing days you could actually eat on that five dollars. At that time, all our travel was on trains; there weren't any planes crisscrossing the country. We stayed in hotels, though, not boarding houses. I roomed with Lefty Gomez one time and we stayed in the Edison Hotel in New York, a good hotel. We paid two dollars a night. Maybe things weren't all that bad with those salaries and the contracts — or I should say lack of contracts. With only sixteen major-league clubs, you really did well if you made it with them. They were all good clubs and it was very competitive. If you had one bad year, there were forty people ready to take your job. Today, of course, there are guaranteed contracts, if only for one season. It's a new era, which is fine—more power to them. It's still a great business.

When my playing years were done, I began my career as a coach—that was 1942. I've been coaching over forty-five years and loving every minute of it. Most of that time was spent in the Coast League, until I joined the California Angels in '72. A great deal of my coaching duties related to hitting fungoes—you know, batting out fly balls to outfielders. It takes a lot of time and practice to hit those balls just slightly out of the reach of those fielders—to get them running a little more each time, stretching their abilities bit by bit. Yes, you're right, it also takes a good degree of skill on my part to place those fly balls just where they'll do some good. It's the same when you're hitting ground balls to the infielders, getting them to reach out that extra bit. When a ground ball gets out of the infield, it's a hit, so if you can trap it before—you have a good chance for an out.

Once when I was in Seattle with one of the Angels' organizations, the manager there was watching me hit fungoes. He pointed to a flagpole about two hundred feet away. "I'll tell you what I'll do, Jimmie. If you can hit that flagpole, dinner is on me tonight. You can have ten shots at it." Well, you might not believe this, but with the *first* ball I hit the pole—and quit right there! He said, "Hey, aren't you going to give me a chance to get even?" I shook my head. "Not on your life. I couldn't do that in a hundred tries. It was pure luck." I guess it wasn't *all* luck. After all, I still had to have the aim, the correct trajectory, and just the right amount of power. But I sure wouldn't want to put that to the test again.

Sometime last season I had a bit of a coronary. They worked on me and put a lot of tubes down my chest, and I was hospitalized for three or four weeks. That kept me out of the game for the rest of the season. Off season I recuperated and I'm okay now, feel pretty good. Our manager, who's one of the nicest guys in the game, told me, "You do only what you think you can do—then get your fanny out of here after that. I don't want you to overdo it. You're not exactly eighteen anymore." He's really a very kind and thoughtful man.

Gene Autry is also one of the finest men in baseball. Everybody loves him, and if ever a man deserves to win a pennant—he's the one. A few years ago we came within one pitch of accomplishing that. But in the ninth inning, with two out, the opposing batter hit a home run, and we didn't go to the World Series. I hope we can make it this year.

Most of my coaching activities over the years have included hitting fungoes; it's an art in itself. I still do some of that. If I couldn't, I think I'd give up. It's one of the things I'd rather do than anything else. Of course, at my age now I don't do it constantly. Yes, I do "charting," as you saw while having to wait a few hours for me. I and some of the other coaches sat some distance behind the plate—there's a wire screen to protect us—and I was keeping a record of balls, strikes, steals, hits, bunts, sacrifices, runs, steals, and whatever. Then I usually give those records to the pitching coach, and he goes over all the listings and tries to figure what has to be done to improve that player's performance.

As far as what keeps me going—that's pretty easy to figure out. As I said before, baseball was my first love, and it still is. After all these years it means more to me than anything else. I've been lucky to have had all these years and to still be a part of it. Not many people have the good fortune to be totally involved, all their life, with something they always wanted to do. That's enough to keep anyone going. If you're doing what you like to do, anything you're interested in, well, I guess that's got to keep you in the game. And, like I've said many times before, when the time comes, I hope to die with my boots on.

March 14, 1991

CESAR ROMERO

Two of his major career efforts — his dance routines and his film portrayals — involved the entertainment field. At the height of his film career, Cesar was most often categorized as a dashing, suave, handsome, Latin-type leading man. And there were many producers who deliberately fit him in that characterization. Fortunately, there were some others who saw more than the surface aspect and gave him the opportunity to play a wider range — light comedy, strong characterizations, even comic villainy.

Today, his maturity has taken over. He's still quite handsome, with a graciousness and easy confidence about him. From the moment I entered his home in Los Angeles, he put me at ease with his own relaxed air. And the interview session reflected that feeling throughout. His recollections were always on the positive side, no downbeat comments about anyone. He expressed a genuine thankfulness for his profession and his present ability to continue in it.

* * *

BY THE WAY, I'm a Junior and my middle name is Julius— Cesar Julius Romero. My father's father named all his sons after famous men—*backwards.* So he named my father Cesar Julius and my uncles Franklin Benjamin, Nelson Horatio, and Oliver Simon. That's a pretty interesting idea.

Well, I was born in my grandmother's house on West Sixty-fifth Street, in New York City. Through the years we lived all over various parts of the city, with most of my teenage years spent on West Seventy-fourth Street. I went to numerous boarding schools from the time I was eight years old, and I graduated from the Collegiate School on Seventy-seventh Street and West End Avenue. Douglas Fairbanks, Jr., went there and so did the Hearst boys. More recently John John Kennedy was a student. Bill Hearst was a classmate of mine. It was a wonderful, wonderful school.

I graduated from Collegiate in 1926. While studying there, the first summer job I ever had was as a wrapper for the dry-goods section of Steinbach's, a department store in Atlantic City, New Jersey.

The next summer I was in their floor covering department, and I even went out with a linoleum layer a few times and laid some of the linoleum in people's kitchens. The last two summers I worked for Steinbach's, I was a truck driver and drove one of their delivery trucks all the way down the Jersey shore. These were summer jobs, you see, because we had a summer home down at Bradley Beach, New Jersey, and working there was pretty darn convenient. My father was the president of an exporting house on Wall Street, and he exported sugar machinery and hardware to all the plantations in Cuba. Unfortunately, the silver market crashed in 1922 and that ruined my father, so by the time I graduated from prep school there was no father's business to go into.

However, he did get me a job at the National City Bank in Wall Street because one of the vice presidents in the bank had been an associate of his. I hated it! I was starting at the bottom and I was a runner, going all over New York City with a satchel handcuffed to my wrist. It was filled with securities and money, and I thought any day now somebody's going to hold me up and chop my hand off— and there I go. In the meantime, I was on the list for all those New York debutante parties, and one of my friends was a young debutante named Lizbeth Higgins. Her father was Charles M. Higgins, and he was the Higgins India Ink king—Liz was the ink heiress of New York. She was a beautiful dancer and we used to dance well together because I was a hell of a good dancer when I was young. We got a lot of publicity dancing together. One day Liz said, "Let's you and I be a dance team and we can work all the wonderful supper clubs that are in New York." There certainly were many of them at that time, and I thought being a part of a dance team would be great fun—dancing to me was just not work. She had her family's approval, so we got together after I finished working at the bank and went over to a dance school where one of the instructors specialized in creating routines for dance teams.

One day Lizbeth asked, "How much money are you making at the bank?" Well, I was making $17.50 a week, and I was on my own in New York. The family lived all year round now in the summer home in New Jersey and didn't know what I was doing at the time. [*Laughs*] I paid $7.50 a week for my room and I had to live on the other ten bucks, but I didn't want Liz to know I was only making $17.50 a week. So I said I was making $25.00 a week. Then Liz said, "Well, if you quit your job, I'll pay you the salary you're making now and then we can rehearse all day long and go out to give auditions." That was okay with me, so I quit my job and got a big raise right away. We did our auditions, and we got a job in a musical comedy called *Lady Do*. It was a Busby Berkeley show, and that's how I got started in show business. I danced for the next four years with Lizbeth and other partners in nightclubs, vaudeville, and other musical comedies. There was also another Busby Berkeley show called *The Street Singer* with Queenie Smith as the star.

It's hard to think back, but I do remember a vaudeville show when I was working with a girl by the name of Jeanette Hackett. She had a big "flash act" that she and her husband did at one time. They were big headliners, Hackett and Delmar, and when they split up, she needed somebody to replace him and I got the job. But it was her act and we were playing different dates in New York, breaking it in. This flash act had two big scenes. In the first, the curtain went up and there was a big sort of an urn thing, with a lot of smoke coming out of it. I was standing at the back edge, dressed like the devil, with two big poles and all this chiffon that looked like flames. As I'm standing there, Jeanette would come out from in between my legs—as if coming out of the pot—and she would do this wild dance. Then there was an in-between act, the Reis Brothers doing their dance routine.

For the next scene, the curtain would go up and there was a big flight of stairs in center stage. Jeanette would be on a chaise lounge in a filmy negligee, drinking champagne—the playgirl, you know—and at the top of the stairs I would appear. I was dressed in a top hat, tails, white tie, and a black cape. I had a death mask made to fit my face, and over the skeleton mask I had a wig that covered the thing and a black mask covering everything. I could hardly see through the two things, and when I started walking down the stairs—I always forgot to count them, you know—I'd get to the bottom and either stumble a bit or fall, every damn time. Anyway, at that point I'd take off the hat, peel off the cape, take her into my arms, and sweep her off into a dance routine. The dance of death, you see. At the end, with her in my arms, she takes off the black mask and the wig, and the death mask is revealed! She screams and runs around the stage and I'd grab her, carry her up to the top of the stairs, and as I lean over and kiss her on the chest, she rolls down the whole flight of stairs, pulling the drapes with her. As I said, it was a big flash act. We were going to play the Palace, the mecca of all vaudevillians, but something intervened.

I was in bed early one night and this buddy comes in and says, "Hey, put on your top hat, put on your tails and white tie, we're going to the Cholly Knickerbocker Ball." I asked if he was nuts, because that Knickerbocker Ball was fifty bucks, and that was good money in those days. He said, "Don't worry, I know how we can get in. Just make sure you follow me when we get there." So I got all white-tie-and-tailed up, and off we went to the Plaza Hotel. We walked into the lobby, checked our things, and then I followed him through a door in front of the inside fire escapes, up a couple of flights, through another door, and we come out behind the bar. There the waiters are serving water and mixed drinks for people who brought their own liquor, because it was still Prohibition. Nobody said anything to us as we walked around the bar and out into the main entrance of the ballroom.

The first person I bumped into was Maury Paul, who was the Cholly Knickerbocker—the society editor—of the Hearst papers. All the young debutantes in New York used to quiver in their boots because Cholly used to rate them A, B, C. [*Laughs*] She was an A debutante, or a B debutante, or a C debutante. Anyway, we meet and, of all things, Maury says, "Oh, Cesar, how are you? Tony Biddle and I were talking about you the other day. You know, we are opening the St. Regis Roof as a private club, calling it the Club St. Regis, and we were talking about you to open the club for us." I said that would be great, but I haven't got a partner right now because I was doing the vaudeville act. He said, "That's okay, because we're not going to be opening for three or four months, so keep in touch." Well, I told Jeanette if I could get a partner to open at the Club St. Regis, I would be leaving the act. She understood, and I later did find a partner, Florence Coca, who was beautiful, tall, slim, and lovely. We worked out some routines of ballroom dancing, and I called Maury and said we were ready if he was. We opened at the Club St. Regis with Vincent Lopez and His Orchestra, and that's how I got the job, by crashing his ball—which he never knew and I never told him.

Then one day I got a call from an agent who handled all the big theatrical stars in the business, and he asked, "Do you think you could play the lead in *Strictly Dishonorable*? Well, I had seen the play. The star was an Italian actor by the name of Julio Cominardi, I think, and it was Preston Sturges's first big hit in the theater. So, of course, I said yes—I said yes to everything in those days—and he made an appointment for me to see the producer. The woman that directed all his plays was Antoinette Perry, the famous Tony Perry for whom the Tony Awards are named. They asked me to return the next day and read for the part. I had seen the play, but I decided to go see it again and study the way Julio played it. It was at the Avon Theatre in New York, and I never took my eyes off him throughout the play. The next day I went to the audition and gave the best imitation of him as I possibly could. It must have been okay, because they gave me the part and signed me to a run-of-the-play contract, and I played it on the road for a solid year.

So the first stage part I ever played was the leading man. My leading lady was the lovely, charming Elizabeth Love. Her understudy was a young girl just starting out on her theatrical career, and she later became a big star in the theater and motion pictures—Margaret Sullavan. Well, she was always talking about her boyfriend, Hank, and one day in Philadelphia she said, "My boyfriend, Hank, is coming to see me today." So we all waited to see Maggie's boyfriend and sure enough in he walked, long and lanky, the way we all got to know him later. He was Henry Fonda. [*Laughs*]

It's fun to look back on those days when we were all young and striving. The height of the depression was 1932. But I was lucky because in that year I was in a play called *Dinner at Eight* and we ran for a year, from '32 to '33. It wasn't all easy going after that; in fact, it was the worst time of my life. I had been out of work for some time and when I returned to my hotel and put the key into the lock—nothing happened! They had changed the lock because I owed them four weeks' rent, and when I went and talked to the manager, it was no dice. I couldn't even get in to get my toothbrush; everything was locked in there. So I'm out in the street, saying, now what? By luck, I bumped into this friend of mine who was the managing director of a swank apartment hotel on the West Side. After I explained my predicament he said, "I have an extra bedroom in my apartment and you're welcome to come there until you get back on your feet." More importantly, he loaned me the money to pay my back rent and get all my belongings out of the hotel.

I was there only a week when my agent called. "Pack

your bags for California, MGM is signing you to a contract."
I was really flabbergasted, but then I remembered a screen
test that I did months before but had never heard anything
about it. At that time, we had been trying out a play called
All Points West, produced by John Golden. It never got to
New York, but John had brought the casting director from
MGM out to see the play, and that's when he had asked me
to do a screen test. So on Friday, April 13, 1934, I arrived in
Hollywood.

The contract was only for one picture, with an option for
another picture, an option of six months, and so on. Three
days after my arrival I went to work in the film *The Thin
Man.* It was the first of the Thin Man series with William
Powell and Myrna Loy. I had a small part, I played
someone's gigolo husband, but they picked up the option
for another film. They loaned me to Warner Brothers for a
very good part in the film *British Agent,* with Leslie Howard
and Kay Francis. So everybody said, "Oh, that's a good sign.
They've loaned you out and the studio is making money on
you and this is only the beginning." Unfortunately, when I
reported back to MGM, there was a pink slip waiting for
me. [*Laughs*] Well, that's it, I thought, I'll be going back to
New York a failure.

But my agent took me out to Universal, where they were
looking for a new face to play opposite Claudette Colbert in
Imitation of Life. The director made a test with me, and he
told Universal, "This chap is not right for the film because
he comes across too young. He's too young, but I think you
ought to sign him." So Universal signed me and I was there
for the next three years, but during those years Darryl Zanuck kept borrowing me for one picture after another. I did
Clive of India with Ronald Colman and Loretta Young, and
then I played opposite Maureen O'Sullivan in *Cardinal
Richelieu,* with George Arliss. When Zanuck went over to
Fox, I did the first picture to be filmed on that lot, called
Show Them No Mercy. No big names in it, just Bruce Cabot
and myself and a lot of great character people. It's one of

my favorite pictures, and it was a "sleeper." It was booked into the Roxy Theatre in New York for a week, but it played for three or four weeks—it was a big, solid picture. Then Zanuck borrowed me again for *Wee Willie Winkie* with Shirley Temple. About that time my option came up with Universal, which was on shaky grounds in those days. They said, "We'd like to keep you. Like you to stay on at the same salary but we can't give you . . ." I said no! If I could get out of the contract then Zanuck would sign me, because I'd been working for him all the time. And that's the way it went. Zanuck did sign me, and I stayed with him for the next fourteen years.

I went off to war in '42, '43. I enlisted in the coast guard because I had some friends that were in the guard and they seemed to be going up and down the coast in little yachts and stuff. I thought that's for me, and besides I didn't want to be drafted in the army. So I enlisted in the guard and went to boot camp. Then I was shipped out to the Pacific so fast it made my head swim. I went through two invasions on my ship—Saipan and Tinian. After Tinian, we came back to Pearl Harbor, where the ship had to go into dry dock. There, my orders came through to go back to the States.

I was attached to the Industrial Incentive Office of the navy, and I went all over the country making speeches at shipyards and munitions plants, for the workers of the war. Talking about how important their work was to the war effort. It was a lousy job. I hated it. It made a nervous wreck out of me, talking about it all the time, but you do what you have to do. [*Sighs*] When I got out of the service, I reported back to Twentieth Century-Fox and picked up my contract where I left off. My friend Tyrone Power got out of the Marine Corps at the same time. We were very close friends and also neighbors in the Brentwood section of Los Angeles. Then the studio decided to send us both on a good-will tour. Ty was a pilot in the Marine Corps, and they supplied us with a little twin-engine Beechcraft. Ty was a good pilot, so he did all the flying, although we also had a copilot. A secretary, a chap from the publicity department, and myself, that made five of us in the plane.

We flew down through Mexico, and we hit every country in Central America. We circled all of South America . . . down the west coast to Santiago, Chile; through the pass to Buenos Aires; up to Brazil, the Guianas, the West Indies, Havana, Miami, New York, and California. We were on this trip for ten weeks in this little plane, and we had no trouble at all. We met all the presidents of every country we went to, because it was all arranged by our American ambassadors—a meeting, or cocktails, or luncheon, or whatever. The most interesting pair we met was at the luncheon with Juan Perón and his wife, Evita. She was a charming hostess, I must say.

She didn't speak English and neither did he, so I interpreted for Tyrone and the others. I was seated next to her at the luncheon and she'd say, "Why do people in your country call my husband a dictator? He's not a dictator. He's a patriot." And she'd turn to him and say, "Isn't that right, Juan, you're not a dictator. You are a patriot, aren't you?" and Perón would say, "Sí, sí." Later, she commented, "You're so fortunate in your country because the people love and respect their artists. Here in my country, they spit at them. I know, because I was an artist." But she was charming, she was really charming. Bright, bright woman. When Tyrone and I left, it was drizzling outside and the limousine was waiting for us. We got in and turned to look out—there was Juan and Evita, standing in the rain, waving good-bye to us. [*Laughs*] It was very interesting, just a goodwill tour, you know. I look back on it because that is something you do only once in a lifetime. And poor Ty died at the age of forty-four.

Well, I finished my contract at Fox in 1950, and of course, I felt like an orphan because this had been like my second home. But by this time everything had changed. Television was coming in and some of the studios were going out. Everybody was an independent producer, and now the studios weren't functioning in the usual ways. But that gave me a new opportunity to do a number of films in other countries. I made pictures in England, France, Spain, Portugal, India, Japan, South America, and the Hawaiian Islands. I traveled to numerous places I would never have been able to go to on my own as an independent free-lance actor.

I only made one picture in the Spanish language, and I had a hell of a job doing it. I wasn't used to working in Spanish, although I've spoken Spanish all my life and was brought up with both languages. My grandmother's house in New York was a gathering place for people from Cuba, and South America, and all that. My maternal grandfather was one of the great men of the Latin Americas—José Martí. He is the George Washington of Cuba, the liberator of Cuba. You've read his name a million times . . . Radio Martí, TV Martí, and if you go to Havana, you will land in the José Martí airport. We spoke Spanish all the time at home, but through the years of not speaking it in the entertainment world, I've gotten very rusty. I can carry on a casual conversation, but I couldn't give an interview in Spanish because I've lost my vocabulary.

Yes, I did the "Batman" TV series and the motion picture in the sixties. And I had a lot of fun doing it, I must add. It was a gas playing it, very different from the film Jack Nicholson did when he played the Joker. What we did was a great big spoof; it was fun. The new *Batman* was a pretty grim picture; you can't compare the two at all. The TV series only ran two and a half seasons, and I did about twenty or so episodes as the Joker. When we did the film, the other three villains were Burgess Meredith as the Penguin, Lee Meriwether as the Cat Woman, and Frank Gorshin as the Riddler. The makeup for the Joker was pretty way out—the green wig, white face, and big red lips. I had told them I wouldn't shave off my mustache, so they had to pile on the white stuff to cover it. Then we'd go out there and whoop and howl and laugh, and it was a ball.

You know something—in all the films I ever did there was only one time I shaved my mustache off, and that film was never released. It was a shame because it was a darn good film called *The Runaway,* an independent production about a priest, a little boy, and a dog. The producer thought he had made another *Gone With the Wind* and he wanted to put it out in the top bracket, up there with the best. The distributors wanted it for the lower bracket; it was a delightful picture but only a small one. So the producer went to Italy and bought one of those big *Hercules*-type extravaganzas so that he could release them with *The Runaway* as the top film and the other as a companion one. It didn't work and our little film was never in general release, even though it got a few good reviews. I played the priest and I had to shave the mustache off, but I had told them I was only going to shave it that once and not again. Luckily we finished my scenes in two weeks, just as it started to grow back again.

At that moment I had to pencil the mustache in more, because I was just starting in on *Oceans Eleven.* Everybody was in that one and yes, it was fun. The nice thing about it was that Frank Sinatra didn't like working early in the morning, so we never started shooting until noon, or afternoon. It was some group—Frank Sinatra, Dean Martin, Sammy Davis, Peter Lawford, Joey Bishop—and the Rat Pack was the fun name they adopted. I'd kid a few of them about the little bars in their dressing rooms and how they sometimes came on the stage to rehearse with a glass in their hand. But it was a great crowd, and the picture turned out to be pretty good—"lightweight but pleasant" was one review that I remember.

When I started in films there was no television, and there was a definite motion picture colony in this town. Within that colony there was a very elegant society, and when you attended the social functions, every big star would be there—Norma Shearer, Clark Gable, Mary Pickford, Douglas Fairbanks, Charlie Chaplin, Carole Lombard, Gary Cooper, and all the rest. That has completely disappeared; there is no such thing in this town anymore. It's a shame because in those days it was very glamorous. There was glamour and excitement in Hollywood then; today it's all commercial. And the money the top stars make today— four, five, six million on a film. That was unheard of years ago. Why, Clark Gable at the height of his career was making $7,500 a week, and although that's good money, it's nothing compared to what the top stars make today. Oh, I know things have changed; it's just a little bit of history I'm sort of reporting.

It's the same with the old-line producers; they don't exist. They're gone. Louis B. Mayer, Darryl Zanuck, Jack Warner, Samuel Goldwyn, and all those others, they started the business. Heck, Goldwyn was a glove salesman and Louis B. Mayer was a junk man, but guys like them made this business. They were kings, oh yes. They were kings of their lots, believe me. But they also took care of their stars. The greatest gripes were at Warner Brothers, where they all hated Jack Warner. Everybody, but everybody, complained about him. Bette Davis and James Cagney had no love for him. I made a few pictures there, and I kinda got along with him. Actually, I liked him; he was a funny man and should have been a stand-up comedian. I was invited to a dinner at the White House when Nixon was president and bumped into Jack Warner there, so we got together. Along the way there was a minor incident with one of our society ladies, and all Jack could say was, "What did I do, what did I do?" He was a bit out of his element there.

I've been invited to the White House a few times, but I only went back once. Reagan invited me twice, but I was working both times and didn't go. I've seen him a couple of times since he's been back here; we go to the same barber. But I used to know Ronnie when he was married to Jane

[Wyman], for God's sake. Even before that we'd go out together. I remember one night, Virginia Bruce and I and Ronnie and Jane ended up in a little nightclub in the valley called Charlie Foy's. There was a little stage where people would just get up and do little impromptu things, and this one night Ronnie and Jane got up there and did a little song-and-strut thing they used to do together. Little did I realize then that I was looking at not only the future governor of California, but also the future President of the United States. [*Laughs*] I never got over it. Well, he got away with eight years as president and came out smelling like a rose.

Anyway, I've worked with a lot of wonderful people in films, and Betty Grable was one of them. A lot of people didn't like her, but I loved her and found her a joy to work with. She had no great talent and she wasn't the best singer in the world, but she knew how to use what she had. She had that wonderful figure, those beautiful legs, and she had a charisma that came across on the screen and made her a tremendous star. The musicals with Alice Faye and Sonja Henie were such great fun, and so were they. And one of the loveliest ladies I every worked with was Greer Garson. Most of the films she had worked in were dramatic, like *Mrs. Miniver, Blossoms in the Dust,* and *Madame Curie.* This one, *Julia Misbehaves,* gave her a wonderful opportunity to play comedy, and she really enjoyed it.

My role in it, believe it or not, was to play a *cockney* acrobat! I was a member of a cockney acrobatic troupe and the only one of the group to have any dialogue. But I had a coach, a cockney coach, and he taught me so I was able to do it. I did all my acrobatic stuff—worked like a dog and I was the *bottom* man! No trapeze action, just acrobatics. You know, where one jumps on the springboard, does a somersault, and lands on someone's shoulders. *I* was the shoulders they landed on! And they lifted Greer Garson up on wires and she was to land on top of all of us. Boy, that was really something, great fun too. Walter Pidgeon was in it and Elizabeth Taylor took the part of Greer's daughter, with Peter Lawford playing her boyfriend. Elizabeth had her seventeenth birthday while we were shooting, and we had a big birthday cake for her. What a beautiful young lady she was.

The following year I went to England on the *Queen Mary* to do a picture in London, with David Niven and Vera-Ellen, called *Happy Go Lovely*. Also on board the *Queen* were Elizabeth Taylor and Nicky Hilton, on their honeymoon. She was eighteen years old. A few other passengers were Richard Rodgers and his wife, both friends of mine, and the Duke and Duchess of Windsor. The duke was a great fan of Richard Rodgers's music, so one night we all got together in one of the small music rooms on the *Queen Mary*. Dick sat at the piano, playing a number of tunes from his Broadway shows, and the duke stood by and sang. He couldn't sing, but he knew the lyrics to all the Rodgers songs. He was a very charming man and easy to talk to. The duchess wasn't, but she was very elegant about the whole thing, you know. All in all, it was an interesting evening. [*Laughs*]

By the way, it wasn't all motion pictures. I played a lot of theaters, dinner theaters all over the country, for several years. Then, in between, I'd come back here and do television things. "Falcon Crest" was a successful series, and it was good to work with Jane Wyman. I knew Jane for many years and it was like old home week, we had plenty to talk about. She's very professional and wonderful to work with. We'd get there early in the morning and most of my scenes were done then, so I'd be finished by twelve or one o'clock. It was a very pleasant way of working because it was only two or three days a week. After that I did a pilot for a new series, with Connie Sellecca, but CBS didn't pick it up—guess there were problems with it.

My agent called today and said Tommy Tune wants me to play the doctor in *Grand Hotel* for the national tour. I said no thank you, going on tour on the road is hard work and

I'm getting a little old for that now. I don't need to do it, so I'm taking life a little easy now. Retire? I'd be bored stiff! If a good script came along, I'm ready. And I'll still do television. I'm going to be doing a stint on "Golden Girls" next month and whatever else comes along. That's fine, but going on the road is too much of a hassle.

As far as I'm concerned, I've been fortunate in my life, really. I had no training for this profession, what I did I just did naturally, and one thing led to another. After my father lost everything, he kept me going to private school until I finished prep school, and I don't know how he did it, but he did. So it's been constantly on my mind to take care of my family, and I brought them all out here—my parents, two sisters, and younger brother. I had my parents under my roof until they passed away; they weren't going to any nursing home if I could help it. They did so much for me and the other children that I was only too glad to be able to take care of them. Life has been good to me and I did what I wanted to do, which was take care of my family. I was able to do it because I was an actor and I had the good luck of being successful in it. So I have always been grateful and believe me, I count my blessings.

September 4, 1990

Leo Rossman

Over the years, the legal profession has undergone many changes. In Leo Rossman's day, for example, you could go straight from high school into law school—no college degree required beforehand. Although that change was for the better, he feels strongly about many of the others that have taken place in today's society. At the same time, Leo doesn't want to be considered an "old fuddy-duddy" who only longs for the good old days.

Our discussions in his home, in the Cleveland area, did include many reflections on the past, but his present profession as an arbitrator doesn't really allow him many backward glances—the problems to be solved all take place in today's arena. Fortunately, he's retained an ongoing sense of humor, and his stock of one-liners is well received by his associates. He tossed a few of them my way and they've been dutifully recorded, but his dry, deadpan delivery is missing.

✻   ✻   ✻

IT'S TRUE, I often refer to the past. I guess there were a lot of values in those days that we could use in our lives today. In the earlier times I had fun, more fun in a less affluent society than people do now. You appreciated it more. We had no television but we went on picnics, visited each other more often; people didn't lock their doors, and you knew everybody in your area. The storekeeper and his workers were your neighbors, and all the kids knew each other. Oh, there were problems, but nowhere near the kind of things you put up with today. Now you have special locks on doors, bars on windows, signs that say NO TRESPASSING, NO SOLICITING, BEWARE OF VICIOUS DOG, and KEEP OUT. It's a different world. I once asked my wife, who's eighty-one, whether or not she would like to come back and start living now, and she said no. Perhaps that's the philosophy of many older people.

Oh yes, I had a Model A Ford then. If you didn't set the timer right, you'd break your arm when you went to crank it to get it started. As far as color goes, there was only one— black. But, then again, the price was right, about six hundred dollars. Today, one fender costs that much. If you went to check the gas, you had to get out of the car, take the front seat off, and then put a ruler into the tank to check what was left. The first car that had a self-starter was the Star. It became very popular because, as I mentioned before, it was a terrible thing to crank the car to get it started. I also remember a salesman who came in and was selling a stoplight for the back of the car. It would signal when you were stopping, and that was a real revelation because you never knew what the car in front of you was going to do. Of course, things haven't changed that much today; you still don't know. We also had those isinglass shades for the side windows, which made it difficult to stick your hand out for a turn. The rumble seat was fun, though. Everybody piled in and we'd take off for a picnic or the old swimming hole. All in all, I think there was a closer relationship amongst people. But we can't look back, except to remember. What was then, was then. It's gone.

I was born in Brooklyn, and we moved to Cleveland when I was a kid of six. I've been in this area ever since. My father had a delicatessen store in Brooklyn, and when we relocated to Cleveland, he opened a small grocery store. That's a lost art today, a small grocery in this age of specialization and supermarkets. Now the individual, unless he's in a small neighborhood, really has only very little chance to succeed.

My schooling was in the area, both grade school and high. The neighborhood was predominantly Polish, and there were only a few Jewish families living there. Yes, there was discrimination, and I had many fights defending myself. In fact, it was so bad that if one Polish guy was fighting another Polish guy, he'd call the other one a dirty Jew. But the neighborhood people would patronize my father's store. I guess they didn't have much choice; there weren't any chain stores around then. But my father was fair and treated them well, so I guess that had something to do with it also.

While going to high school, I worked in a radio store, and I noticed that one of the managers was taking up law. When I asked where, he said it was in night school. So I inquired, and after I graduated high school I enrolled in the night law school. It was difficult! It was a four-year course—I worked in the radio store days and attended classes at night. I worked until five and had to be in school by six, with supper squeezed in between. Three nights a week were for the law classes and two nights were for study. In the store, I was a salesman—nothing technical, because technically I knew nothing much about radios. I concentrated on the accessories that people could use and hadn't thought about. In fact, I made more money on commissions and extras than the manager did, but I never sold anybody anything just to make a sale. It had to be needed. Like when they first came out with radios that had the headphones, I'd suggest to the customer, "Why don't you buy another set of headphones and then the both of you can listen to the programs." They thought that was a very practical idea, and they bought the second set. Of course, that was before they had speaker systems in the radios and everybody could listen.

Anyway, I finished the law courses and became a lawyer. As I said, it wasn't easy but we did it; we had some incentives. The unfortunate part of anyone being in a profession today—especially law or medicine—is that when I went to law school at night, the whole four years didn't amount as much in cost as it does now for a single quarter. And that's too bad. For the young and poor, even if there are opportunities for subsidies, they're not all able to obtain them. Fortunately for me, when I was in night law school, that happened to be the last year you could get in without any college. After that, you had to have a year of college before you could graduate law school. Then they changed it to where you needed a year of college before you could even enroll in law school. Now you have to have a four-year college degree before you can even enter law studies.

When I got out of law school, it was difficult getting a job. I remember in one law office a fellow there said to me, "What did you want to become a lawyer for?" Well, I thought that was quite out of line. I can recall an incident when a man came into my office to sell me insurance. I told him I really don't want it, I don't need it, I'm not married, but I'll be glad to listen to you. A few days later, I got a call from one of the judges, who said, "I want to thank you, you were the only one who was courteous to my son-in-law when he was trying to sell insurance. You listened to him after everyone else sloughed him off. He had become very discouraged and after he spoke to you, he felt a little better." Well, when I finally got a job, it was for seventy-five dollars a month. Today, lawyers start off with eighty or ninety thousand a year. But they do work them to death, like eighty hours a week, and they're worn out before they get the chance to do anything. By the way, did you hear about the lawyer who spent all night trying to break a widow's will? [Chuckles]

I'm not envious of the lawyers today and I don't think anybody should be, because the law firms in the big cities work twenty-four hours a day. They have three shifts of lawyers and you've got to produce, or you're out. In the law office where I got seventy-five dollars a month, I brought them in a case, a good referral. Usually, a lawyer got a fee of one or two thousand dollars for that kind of business, and although I worked hard on the case—going all over the county seeing people—I had a devil of a time trying to get a hundred dollars out of them for my referral. Well, I needed the job, and I wasn't that proud not to take it. But then I left and went out for myself in my own practice.

When I did start, however, I was with two other lawyers in a little room for which we paid fifteen dollars a month rent. When one of us had a client, the other two would get out of the office. Now, of course, you have fancy offices, secretaries, paralegals, and to practice law today is a little like practicing medicine. There's a lot of technical equipment involved—computers, printers, fax machines, libraries, telephone systems, and all that. Even though I felt I was a pretty good lawyer, if a client came in from out of town wanting to set up a corporation and he was having labor problems, I would have to call up five or six different offices to have their lawyers come in to discuss the different aspects. In the big firms, though, they now just push a few buttons and the labor man comes in, the tax man comes in, the corporation man comes in, and it's all handled in one office. So when a client or anyone says to me that their lawyer knows everything, I want to laugh in their face. It's impossible for one man to keep up with everything today.

Naturally, during those yesterdays, lawyer's fees were a lot different. We got $150 for a divorce case, and we were very happy about it. Now it's more like five or ten thousand dollars. But, you know, those were also the days when a postcard was a penny, the telephone was a nickel, and the ice-cream cone was a nickel. Incidentally, did you know the Jewish people were boycotting Eskimo pies? Why? Because they're putting the Cohens (cones) out of business [*chuckles*]. Anyway, when we used to go to the amusement park, money had some value then. Now you go to Disney World and it'll cost you nearly a hundred dollars for a small family to go.

As I said, I started to practice law, but later I had an idea of preparing and putting out legal forms. I formed a corporation and we supplied the lawyers with all kinds of forms required in their practice. Since I was the only lawyer in that field, business was very good. The young lawyers would come in and ask what kind of forms they should use, and I always gave them the right advice and information.

My reputation was tops because I didn't try to sell them forms they didn't need. But I did have to quit practicing *adversary law,* because it was unfair to ask lawyers to deal with me on legal forms and then appear against them on a case. So I stuck to law that didn't involve the adversary aspect—things like wills, probates, real estate transactions, and so on.

During the depression, it was tough on everyone. We would sometimes handle cases for just the court costs. On top of that, the banks failed and you lost your money. One good thing about that era was if lawyers gave you their word, or a handshake, it meant something. Today, unfortunately, the legal profession has changed. Everything has to be in writing and even if it is in writing, there are those who don't always abide by it. If any of us advertised in those days, he would have been disbarred. Now in our local paper we have pages of lawyers advertising, and I think it demeans the profession. To round it all out, we now have dentists, doctors, and even their commercials on TV, as part of this whole fiasco. If there were those who held the legal profession in low esteem before, this hasn't helped. Personally, as far as I'm concerned, I think it's a very bad idea.

Anyway, getting back to things, I kept the legal form business for about eighteen years, but I stayed in the same downtown building for forty-eight years. You know, I still see lawyers who are sorry I'm out of the legal forms business, because there's only one company in town supplying them and they don't have any professional people on staff to help and guide the young lawyers. It's nice to have a good reputation, and it pleases me that so many remember and wish I could still help those who need it.

I've been very active in clubs; at one time I think I belonged to eighteen of them. As a lawyer, I guess it was good for business to be known in as wide a circle as possible. I've even formed a number of the clubs myself. Once I started a singles club, but then all the members eventually married and I was the only single one left. I didn't get married until I was about thirty-four. By the way, did I tell you about one of the clients who was a weatherman? He said he could look into a girl's eyes and tell whether. [*Chuckle*] But about the clubs, I started a few new ones later; unfortunately, all the people who were in those new clubs have gone to their eternal rest.

Before I went to law school, I didn't really know what I wanted to be. And when my son was ready for a career, people came to me and said, "Why doesn't your son become a lawyer? Why should he become an auto mechanic and dirty his hands?" Well, he was always interested in mechanical things; he'd even go into ash cans to pick out broken motors, and then he'd repair them. He went to a trade school and got first prize there. Today, he owns a service station, he's an entrepreneur, and he's on radio and TV as the "Motor Doctor." In fact, one of the judges came to me a while back and said, "Your son appeared before me as a witness and I want to tell you that he was very articulate in his answers, and he knew his subject very well."

Incidentally, he had a very tough case not too long ago. One of my son's customers came to him when his son was killed in an automobile accident. He paid him a substantial sum to go up to Massachusetts and check on the accident car, in order to determine if it was the car's fault or the son's fault. When he returned, my son said it was the hardest thing in his whole career and life to tell the father it was the boy's fault. The car was a five-gear-shift thing and the last party who drove it left it in gear, and the minute the son put the key in the ignition, the car went forward and plunged into a wall, killing him. My son said he had to be honest and report it the way he saw it. He's known for that and so am I. I told him when he went into business to be honest, don't take advantage of people, tell the truth and people will respect you. Nevertheless, it was a difficult report for him to make.

The funny thing is that some of the same people who

belittled him when he went into the automotive field, they're now coming to me and, because they're having problems with their kids, want to know what I did to encourage my son. I think it's very wrong for parents these days to push and want their kids to get all A's and they're not up to it, or be a doctor and they're not qualified, or don't want to. So the kids are under stress and they can't stand it, or they take the easy way out. That's why the suicide figures amongst the young, or at least a portion of them, are a result of these and other pressures. The parents ought to let them choose, if it's an honorable profession, what they want to be. They'll all be a lot happier.

Anyway, as far as I'm concerned, I've always been healthy, and thank goodness I still am. I'm still playing golf and still walk the track—I used to walk four miles and now I walk two, but still do some exercise. As far as anecdotes go, it reminds me of the woman who knocked on the door and when I said what is it, she said, "Would you like to be a Jehovah Witness?" I said, my God, I didn't even see the accident! Or how about the time my wife went the wrong way on a one-way street? The policeman was giving her a ticket and he said, "Didn't you see the arrow?" She said, "Oh no, I didn't even see the Indians!"

Okay, let's get back to the law. You know, years ago, the lawyers used to yell and scream and pound in court. I once told a client if you want a lawyer who's gonna scream and pound, you don't want me, because if everyone does that, no one will know what's going on. The lawyers that used to be like Clarence Darrow are no more. Today, it's very quiet in court. Law is too complicated for that hollering and yelling of those times. On the other hand, it's not like "Matlock" or "L.A. Law" on TV either. Those shows are done for dramatic purposes. They're not realistic, but there are people who get the idea their lawyers ought to be that way—but it's all put on.

I find in the judiciary, in the old days of the Supreme Court, we had Holmes, we had Cardozo, we had Brandeis, we had people who were deep thinkers. Today, it's become a political thing. One president appoints someone from his side, another appoints someone from the other side. No thought of whether or not they are deep thinkers. They come around with this abortion issue, which beclouds the issue entirely. Even in our courts here, if a judge resigns or dies, they're already down at the governor's office trying to get their side appointed. We do have some good judges, but unfortunately people vote by name and not by intellect. It becomes a political issue; he or she is elected as a Republican or Democrat and may be beholden to those people.

I was a lawyer for over sixty years. Then I became an arbitrator in the common pleas court, where I'm chairman of an arbitration panel, with two other lawyers who sit with me. We aren't the only panel; there are a large number of them. The one I chair hears civil cases only, up to twenty thousand dollars. As far as what type of cases we get involved with, most of them are contract cases and personal injury ones. Unfortunately, in many of those injury cases, both parties claim they came under the green light at the same time. And, like King Solomon, we have to decide who's right and who's wrong. It makes it very difficult. As a matter of fact, sometimes these lawyers get into an argument with each other and I tell them, "Gentlemen, I want to tell you something. I'm eighty-five and if you two are going to keep this up, you'll never reach that age." So they cut it out, they stop it and get back to business. Some lawyers are too zealous and they're too anxious—they lose the perspective of the case.

It's a regular trial, but it's a little more liberal. There are two types of arbitration. One is the regular arbitration, which they can appeal. The second type is a binding one, and that's more serious. We have to give it careful consideration, because they can't appeal—the decision is binding. Because of that aspect, it's somewhat stricter. It's a newer concept and it's needed. Today, the worst part of it is that there's so much litigation, everyone is litigation-minded. When people go into the hospital, they wonder why there are so many tests from the doctors and the hospital. Well, the reason is fairly obvious: There are so many malpractice cases, the doctors have to be sure of what they're doing. If they are in court, on cross-examination they'll be asked why they didn't take an X ray, or why didn't you do this or that. So, right away, if they left out something, the jury may think that was a malpractice, which it is not. It also builds up the costs, and that's why people complain about all the high medical expenses they have to pay.

When I sold my business in 1977, I became more active in arbitration. You don't have to be elected. We have a commissioner who appoints you and then, with the other two arbitrators, he takes one from letters *A* to *L*, and the other from *M* to *Z*. I guess that helps balance it out. As far as how old the other arbitrators are, I really don't know. But I don't think there are many in the age of eighty-five and up who are active mentally—with sound mind and memory. And yes, as far as being active at present, you can say I'm very active. In addition to being an arbitrator, I keep fit, and I still keep up with some of those many organizations I belong to. I'm past president of the Cleveland-Marshall Law Alumni, and for forty-five years I was treasurer. This is also my fiftieth year as an usher at the temple, and I'm vice president of the local Red Cross of Israel. At the Men's Club, I'm the oldest director. So you can easily say I'm still on the go.

Incidentally, while I was waiting for a hearing in arbitration to chair, I was sitting in the courtroom and one of the judges called me up. "Mr. Rossman, would you approach the bench please." I asked His Honor what seems to be the problem. He said, "No problem, I just want to know what the latest story is."

When I was practicing law, I used to tell my clients, why don't you take a vacation? And they would say they'll wait until they retire. The unfortunate part is that when that time came, they were too old and they passed on. And now some of their widows come and say, "Mr. Rossman, you know, you were right, we should have taken those vacations." Personally, I've always had the philosophy of vacations. Before I married I took vacations, after we married we took vacations, and now we still take vacations. You've got to take them while you can, you can't wait till *mañana*—because there'll always be something that presents itself that's beyond your control.

When people say to me they want to retire, they say they're going to play golf, and read, and so on. You can't just retire! You have to have something to retire to—something to do. No matter what it is, you just can't retire. You'll go downhill. You've got to belong to something, you must have some interest. I don't have the interests I had when I was younger, but I still retain enough activities. Don't ever retire without having some specific thing to do!

September 19, 1990

FATHER WILLIAM SCHUMACHER

FATHER WILLIAM SCHUMACHER [82]

On his way to the priesthood, William Schumacher went through a half dozen or more careers before his final vocation. On the personal level, he achieved marriage, six children, a golden anniversary, twelve grandchildren, and three great-grandchildren. Unusual for a Catholic priest? It sure is, but that's only part of it.

Father Schumacher attained the mantle of priesthood at an age when the great majority of the population has given up any thought of working or starting a new career. And his present duties do not consist of any short schedule or reduced responsibilities—they are full-time.

Our interview in his parish office was an unusually lengthy one—I found it somewhat difficult to interrupt a priest. It did, however, give me the opportunity to witness an energy and vigor that belied his calendar years. His memory of yesteryear details and events was amazing.

* * *

AT THIS advanced age, I have to think back to the story told me by my mother, when there was great doubt that I would be born at all. It seems Mother had been visiting at my grandmother's house and suddenly it started to rain. Mother picked up the wash basket and ran upstairs to take in the clothes from the outside line. In going back down the stairs, she tripped and tumbled down two flights of stairs. She was pregnant and it was only twenty-five days before I was due. Luckily, my father's sister, who was a midwife, was home, and she took Mother into the bedroom, tore some sheets into strips, and bound her legs together, in an effort to have the womb readjust itself. They didn't think Mother or I would live. Fortunately, we both survived.

My dad was a master plumber, and a few months after I was born he managed to purchase a cottage just outside the northwest section of Chicago. There were open fields and pastures, and only a few houses at the time. Today, it isn't very far from O'Hare Airport. We were the only family of German extraction; the others were mostly Scandinavians, and they were my playmates. As a result I attended the Lutheran Sunday school with my friends. There was no Catholic church anywhere in the vicinity. The public school we all went to was about two miles away, and we walked through the farms and cattle to get there.

When I was eight years old, Mother had to spend a few months in the hospital to take care of her back, which had been hurt in that fall down the stairs. In addition, she would recuperate at one of the relatives' homes. So I went to live with an aunt in the South Side of Chicago. Every Sunday my uncle would drive me in his Pierce-Arrow limo to a Catholic church. I had been baptized as a Catholic, but this was the first time I was able to go to Sunday mass. At nine years old, I was back home and discovered they had now built a Catholic church and parochial school about a mile and a half from our home. When I asked my parents if I could attend the school, they pointed out that the public school was free and there was some tuition at the parochial one. But they agreed, and I enrolled in the fifth grade and continued to graduation. In De Paul Academy, which also had a tuition, some of my friends worked at a movie house to help with these costs. I also applied, but the manager said there were no openings at the time.

The next week a neighbor asked if I would try to fix his radio, because he knew I had fooled around with making the old oatmeal-box crystal sets. Well, I took it over, tightened some connections, put a drop of solder here and there, and it sounded great. When I returned it, he pulled out a five-dollar bill and said, "You know, this would have cost me three or four times that if I went to an electrical shop, and maybe they couldn't even fix it." I said I didn't want his money as he was a neighbor, but he could do me a favor in return. Would he introduce and vouch for me to the theater manager, since they knew each other fairly well? He agreed, and that weekend we went over. The manager remembered me and said this time they had a really big picture playing, could I start working that afternoon?

After alerting my mother, I worked the afternoon show, stayed for the evening show, and then he put me on for the Sunday afternoon and evening shows. Before that was all over, he asked if I could come in all the next week and thereafter. Well, it became a regular job, after school. I even made extra money changing the panels in the lobby; this was in addition to the ushering. It was a big theater, with six aisles and three ushers to each aisle. Many months later, our head usher announced he had been accepted at Annapolis and would have to leave. The manager called me into his office and said, "The head usher has recommended you to take over his job. It will mean a few more hours of your time at work and, of course, there'll be an increase in pay." But he also warned, "This must not interfere with your schoolwork; if it does, we'll have to call it off and do something else."

I was very proud to be able to have that job and help pay my way through school. I was busy all the time anyway, and I did keep up with my studies because I did want a good education. It's true I didn't have time to play with the other kids, or football and other sports, but I didn't mind that. As head usher and fire guard, I now had twenty-six employees under my direction, and a number of them were my seniors. There were the ushers, the cashiers, and the fire guards, and I was only seventeen at the time. My dad was unhappy because he was concerned that I wouldn't be able to keep up with my schoolwork. What none of us realized, however, was that Dad had just been hurt on a construction job and as a result of those injuries, he would die in three or four months.

The theater job lasted a few years, and then I became interested in working on a lake steamer during the summer of my junior year. I left the theater and became a busboy and assistant waiter on one of the steamers. I had five tables, which included one for the president of the line and his guests. It didn't pay much, just ten dollars a week and a white uniform. But I was also a bellhop, for when the people came aboard and when they left the ship. As I did that, helping passengers on and off the ship, there were plenty of tips. In addition, the guests of the line's president were quite generous, with a five- or ten-dollar gratuity. So I was earning sixty to seventy dollars a week, and in 1926 that was good money. The job lasted one summer, but I was able to take a side trip with the other crew members to Niagara Falls, and it was my first chance to see something so grand.

After that and just before the school year, I got a job as salesman in one of the first Sears Roebuck retail stores. This was the time Lindbergh was flying across the Atlantic, and I remember constantly running out each day to the newsstand guy, who had a radio, and asking "Where is he now? What's the latest? Did he get there yet?" That was really an exciting time. I worked in the paint and wallpaper departments, commission only, but I did okay after school and Saturdays. There were a number of commercial customers who waited until I was available, and their orders were larger. In fact, they told me to connect with the hardware department and I could serve them there. It wasn't bad at all.

I graduated high school and enrolled in De Paul University, with the intention of taking prelaw courses. The president of the university asked to see me and mentioned that my senior teachers had suggested the possibility of my studying for the priesthood. "The recommendations are good and if there's some way you could take care of your widowed mother, I'll have you go into the seminary." I told him there was no one I could turn to for that and I have been able to support her, and will just have to continue doing it myself. He agreed. "I know you have. You've been working after school, you've been working all the time. Sometimes you've even held two jobs. But if you can find some way, my offer is still open." I was disappointed, but there was no way that could be done.

Anyway, I continued at Sears and kept bugging a friend of mine to watch out for a law clerk's job, and finally, one opened up. I worked in that office for two years. I not only filed suits, I also checked up on five trial lawyers, made court calls, dictated letters, and even did some investigating. I also did some skip-tracing on my own time in the evenings. If I could find an old case where nothing had been paid for more than a year, then if I could get some payments, I would get a percentage added to my paycheck. I continued in school but started my own collection service, which included collections, process serving, and investigations for personal injury cases, or anything else. Of course, all this had to be in the realm of what I could, as a layperson, correctly handle. My office consisted of desk space in a lawyer's office, and secretarial or phone services as needed. One of my paychecks went for stationery and business cards.

By this time I had enough school credits to enter John Marshall Law School in 1930. Since it was a continuous curriculum, I would be able to graduate in three years if everything went okay. In the last year of school, there was an election coming up for the city council. It was nonpartisan and I decided to try for it by printing up petition forms and visiting people in my ward, talking to them and hoping they would sign it. I reminded them the present alderman had never introduced any legislation in his two terms, except for one. That one had stated male dogs should not use the fireplugs. [*Laughs*] That was for real, I had researched it! Well, I got a lot of signatures in my ward, and even the newspapers noted my name as being right up there in the possible choices. However, that little item backfired on me at the law school. The dean saw it and called me in. "How come you're two months behind in your tuition? You know we don't give anyone permission for that. You either pay your tuition for the year, or at the first of the month for monthly payments." He continued, "You've slipped by for two months; you don't have it because you spent it on political activity." I told him I only spent twenty-five dollars on petition forms and business cards. He said, "If you can pay up all your tuition by next week, you can continue. If not, come back next year." He was firm about it, and that ended my legal schooling.

I had married in '31 and [we] had our first child in '32. This was '33, and everything was pretty tight. My original intention had been to get on the city council, get my law degree, and because my name would be known politically, I'd get lots of exposure for clients. But that didn't come to fruition, for more reasons than the dean of the law school. My father-in-law was working for the big Democratic boss, and he honestly didn't know I had been running for the city council. I never had discussed politics in either of our homes, with my wife or with him. His regular job was in the probate court as a recorder of deeds. The political boss, who wanted his own man in, called my father-in-law in and said, "John, you're not playing fair with me. We've worked together for over twenty years, and you never told me your son-in-law was running for alderman." When John denied it, the boss pointed out my name and address and all that. Then the boss said, "If you can't control the votes in your own family, then you're no use to me or the party, and you might as well stay home." Well, that really meant his job—so I had to quit the campaign. In the meantime, more problems. My criminal law teacher asked me over and mentioned he was concerned I might be overstepping and giving legal advice in my collection services business. Although I denied this, his advice was to sell the business and "keep my shirt clean" in the event I ever came up for the bar exam. I took his advice and sold the business a short time later.

After all that, there was a short stint as a law clerk, but the pay was not very good. Then I took the insurance broker exam and of the 415 candidates who took it, I was among the 15 percent that passed. I became an independent broker in my own office. While that business was going on, I also took the real estate exam and became a real estate broker. In this way I could handle the property sales, as well as the insurance aspect. But when a number of real estate deals I set up flew out the window and into the hands of some associates, that was it for me. Without doubt, there were a lot smarter people in the real estate game than I could ever be.

That was 1938, and from those heights I took a jolt downward. I went to work for Montgomery Ward as a collection and sales correspondent, dictating letters at twenty-five dollars a week. I had two children now, and it was a steady job in a still-depressed economy. It wasn't easy there. You had two five-minute breaks a day to go to the washroom, a half hour or forty minutes for lunch, and you worked until five o'clock. There were quotas for the number of letters to dictate a day, the number of dictation cylinders to use, and the number of account ledgers to handle. One associate across the way was laughing at a letter he received from one of the accounts, and he handed it over to me. The next thing I knew he was in the supervisor's office, then the manager's office, and finally he returned—tears in his eyes. He packed his briefcase and turned to me. "I'm through—for taking time out to laugh!"

That very afternoon, after work, I went to an employment agency and told the interviewer what happened, and how bad I felt. He checked my background and thought I'd make a good credit manager—"Come back tomorrow, I'll send you up to Socony Vacuum, a big oil company that needs a district credit manager." I went there and was hired at considerably more pay. This went on quite well for almost two years when an unfortunate thing happened. There was an antitrust trial against the oil companies for price-fixing, and Socony was hit the hardest. The New York office sent a telegram to Chicago asking them to immediately lay off the last fifty people hired. They called me in, read me the telegram, and said they were sorry but I was one of the ones to go.

From there I got a collection job with Spiegel's. They sent me out of town to collect past due accounts, but locating the people in that town proved difficult and nonproductive. During the second week, in another town, I went on my knees and begged for some kind of inspiration. It took a while, but it came. In this town we had a good list of addresses and the factories in the community were busy. I went to the telegraph office and sent *collect* telegrams to everyone, asking them to meet the Spiegel representative at the hotel to discuss their past due accounts, a way to reestablish their credit, and the opportunity to start buying again. I told the telegraph office I would pay for any telegrams that were not accepted. Well, it was great! People came in every evening, and I was able to return to Chicago with $2,600 in cash and judgment notes for $1,200. What I didn't know was that the telegraph office manager had called Chicago and spoken to my boss, telling him what I was doing, and was it okay? The boss had told him, "That's fine. Don't take any money from him, our office will back it up." The upshot of the whole thing was to bring me into the office area to train others, set up procedures for all types of problems, and so on. Finally, a good job, frequent raises, and upward promotions.

A few years later, when I was out of town setting up regional collection offices, to be managed by women—our home office staffs had been depleted of manpower by the war—my wife called. She was in tears and said, "You have a new job. Uncle Sam wants you. You have to report Monday." We had two children, but she knew one of our neighbors who had a lot more and he was already in service. I rushed back, went to the draft board, and luckily got the manager instead of one of the interviewers. He was impressed with my background. "You don't belong in Uncle Sam's uniform," he said. "You belong in an industry that's engaged in supplies to the war effort, but it isn't your present mail-order. I'll give you thirty days to get into that type job. If you haven't by then, your time will be up."

Through my credit connections, I managed an interview with American Hospital Supply, who was then shipping 50 percent of their output to the army and navy. Their president couldn't hire me away from another company, but if I resigned from my present job, I could work for him immediately. Spiegel told me to go ahead and there would always be a job waiting for me if I came back. I stayed with American Hospital Supply until General MacArthur and Emperor Hirohito signed the papers on the *U.S.S. Missouri.* But that action was not the reason I left them. No, it all goes back to another time—like when I didn't tell my wife I was running for the city council. You see, American Hospital wanted me to take over the sales office for the whole state of Oklahoma. I was enthused about it. The company would pay all expenses of our trip out there to look for a home, and would help us to buy a house. I hadn't told my wife yet because I thought I'm the head of the family, I've got to do the things that keep the family going, and I have a right to make the decisions. So I said okay to the deal, and the announcement was made to the others at a staff meeting. Then I went home glowing to tell my wife what we were going to do. She said, "*You* move and go, but the children and I are staying!" Well, two weeks of pleading didn't change her mind, and I finally had to resign.

Needless to say, we stayed in Chicago. Over the next half dozen years I worked at two smaller companies as assistant to the president. I used all my background knowledge from the larger companies to streamline their operations and increase the scope of their business. In one, the sons returning from military service were a sign they would be taking over in the future, so I gradually eased out. In the other, there was a clash of personalities, and after a few years it was also time to move on. By that time, job interviews simply meant hearing phrases and turndowns like "Gee, you should have my job"; "You're really overqualified"; "Well, we're looking for someone who can stay with us for many years"; "I just don't think we have anything to match your vast experience"; and so on. One chap finally pointed the way. "You could easily have my job in a few months," he said. "Why don't you try to get a state or federal job—it may be less money, but you may not be competing."

I decided on that, and soon I was able to take a state exam which resulted in a job in the personnel placement area. A later exam got me into a supervisory position. Some years down the road, the governor threatened to dismiss fifteen hundred employees who hadn't been in their jobs for at least fifteen years. There was an economic crunch and this was one of his suggestions. Well, the union got all hipped up, called a big meeting, and became involved with a lot of rabble-rousing. They also wanted pickets out, and I was supposed to be a picket come Monday morning. I said never—we work for all the people and not for our personal satisfaction. That's the way I felt. It was a principle with me. They insisted that I was a union member and to that I said, I resign here and now. That weekend, precipitated by all the union stress, I had a mild heart attack and was in the hospital for a week or so, with all kinds of attachments and electrodes. For the next few weeks I was home, and visiting the doctor for EKGs and other tests. He couldn't get my blood pressure down and finally asked my wife about it. She said, "Our house is like Grand Central Station. People who know him in industry call and come over. His people at work call and tell him what's going on and what's not going on. It's a mess." So they both got me to visit friends in Florida, and when we got back, things were more normalized. Even all that threatened firing by the governor never took place.

I went back to my job and thought perhaps a leave of absence might be the thing to do. But I found out that if you're over sixty-five, you couldn't take a leave. In other words, I could either retire or keep on working. I decided to work until June and then retire, after thirteen years on that job. In anticipation of that I was going to school to become a travel agent—I certainly wasn't going to retire and do nothing! During the evenings and Saturday, I began working in an agency to get started on this new career. I became my own boss in the two agencies I worked with, and we split the commissions according to our agreements. The last agency was close to my home, and that's why I stayed there. My wife suffered a stroke in 1981. I had an LPN daytime nurse with her, but during the evenings, weekends, and holidays, I was the nurse.

Four years later, my wife was back in the hospital for a gallbladder operation. She had further strokes and went into a comatose state. For four days she was on all kinds of apparatus: IVs, respirators pumping air and food into her, excreting it through pumps again—what a horrible sight to see. That body heaving up and down, up and down, up and down. I could only take fifteen minutes of it and I'd have to leave the room. My children all came, and it was the same thing with them.

Then one day, I begged the Lord to take her and if he did, he could have me for anything! I repeated that a number of times. That was my real prayer, my real petition. That same morning, the children and I were all together at the hospital. I had already been in to see her, and she was still in the same condition. We were off to a room on the side and I was talking to my sons, when we heard the nurse give a slight scream. She came out and said, "Your wife has passed away." I went in—that was it, she had stopped breathing. And I said, "Thank you, God, now you will have me, ever after."

There was an article, "Never Too Late for God's Call," that told about a seminary in Cromwell, Connecticut, which had worked with older men, second or delayed vocations—doctors, lawyers, you name it. When I read it, I said this is for me, and I wrote to them. Previously I had written to other seminaries, ones we had even donated to over the years, but had never gotten a favorable response. The Holy

Apostle Seminary in Connecticut did respond and sent me
an application, along with a request for certain papers.
Later, they invited me to come and see them over the
Christmas vacation. I went in January of 1985 and was
interviewed, but because of my age they couldn't take me
in. I was seventy-five then. If I were ten years younger, they
would have been happy to take me in. But they did say,
"Should you get a bishop yourself who would sponsor you
in his diocese, then we want you back here." They mentioned that the bishop in Dallas had taken in two older
men. Why not write to him.

I wrote to Bishop Tschoepe of Dallas and *forty-nine* others. The letters also mentioned I would pay my own way
through the seminary, and with my independent income I
would be of no cost to the diocese. Thirty-two said in one
way or another I was too old; the others didn't reply. A
month or two later, Bishop Tschoepe called and asked me
to come down and see him. We talked and then he introduced me to the others in the chancery. At that point, he
asked for the phone number of the seminary in Connecticut. He spoke to the director and asked, what did a spon-
sorship entail? They said a letter from you, indicating you
feel he has the qualifications and when he finishes his studies, you will have him in your diocese. "Oh," the bishop
responded. "You'll have that in the mail tonight!" We
shook hands and I went home.

I went back to De Paul University and took a philosophy
course until the new term would start at the seminary. The
day before I left for the seminary, I said good-bye to the
travel agency personnel, left my typewriter and all the
other stuff that just accumulates after eleven years of travel
agenting. The seminary course is four years, but I completed it in three, because I went to classes morning, afternoon, and nights. On Saturdays, I also taught sixth and sev-
enth grades at one of the churches. On Friday afternoons,
during my last year, I took off and went to Somers, to the
prison where I would regularly visit a few maximum-secu-

rity prisoners, individually. It was about eighty miles each way. I drove it and then would have a class that evening. [*Laughs*] I've been a workhorse, to some extent, all my life.

I was ordained at my home parish in Chicago, June 4, 1988. The Bishop Tschoepe ordained me, but I really didn't know where I was going until he announced it at the reception. He got up and said, "Well, I guess you all want to know what's going to happen to your friend, Bill Schumacher? I'll tell you—I'm sending him to St. Patrick's Church in Dallas. They will be his melting pot. They will be the place to see what he really has in him."

And I've been here now for two and a half years. I keep very busy, and the interesting thing is that I've been through all the problems my parishioners have, whether it concerns children, family disagreements, marriage, finances, or anything else. People will come to me because they know I've been through those phases of life, and I know what they entail. I also know the religious and spiritual side and how we have to come together with it. In fact, many parents whose children are getting married ask if I will talk to them, get them prepared, and handle the wedding—simply because I went through it myself.

By the way, I'm sure you wondered why I asked you to bring along some other things you've written and had published. Here's the story. When I first came to St. Patrick's, a writer like yourself called and wanted to do an article on me and my background. After I had given him a lot of information, I asked where it would appear. He said, "Oh, I write for the *London Mail.* I'm writing an article about older people and it will be in the Sunday edition of the *London Mail.*" He promised I would see it and took off. Well, I never received any copy of the *London Mail,* and I'm still waiting. Then, one day, a parishioner called the pastor and asked, "What is our Father Schumacher doing in the *National Enquirer* newspaper?" And that was it, it was that same writer. [*Laughs*]

But to get back to my activities here. I'm the assistant pastor at St. Patrick's, and also the chaplain of a nursing home in the vicinity. This is a very large parish and there are about 6,000 parishioners from 3,500 families. Sunday masses usually total about 4,000 or so. As far as my own schedule—I have a mass to conduct every morning, and on Sunday I handle at least two services. There will usually be a wedding on Saturday afternoon or evening. I also visit six hospitals in our area, when and if there are any sick parishioners there. Additionally, there are those occasions for funerals, sick calls in the homes, and consultations. As I said earlier, it keeps me busy.

And I also have to say this—regardless of age, anyone can do anything if they have a mind to. Secondly, they're never too old to start something new.

September 12, 1990

ZAKA and MILTON SLAWSKY [80]

Facing 160 years of activities is beyond the usual norm, and, at the same time, it could prove to be somewhat formidable. But Zak and Mitch Slawsky, who are eighty-year-old twins, have a tendency to put one at ease quickly. It's a lifelong characteristic that has been especially helpful to their many students at the University of Maryland at College Park.

The Slawsky Physics Clinic at the univeristy has been the twins' "retirement" activity for the past fifteen years, and they have no immediate intention of a second retirement there. To this news, their students are in total agreement. The clinic is no part-time effort, not with a five-day schedule from 10:00 A.M to 3:00 P.M.

Our interview didn't get started until Zak and Mitch were certain their classes were organized and the graduate students who help them with tutoring were ready to take over. I decided against separate interviews and asked them to help one another with their recollections.

* * *

ZAK: We were born in Brooklyn and when we were almost a year old, our parents took us to Russia, where our grandfather lived. He had wanted my father to visit him, and since he was somewhat prosperous, we were fairly well situated there. Then, after three or four years, we were caught by the First World War breaking out. In 1917 we went to Moscow, where my father was doing some work for Grandfather, who had a leather business. While in Moscow, the Russian Revolution started—we were seven years old then. We were holed up in a hotel and it was dangerous to go out because of all the shooting going on. As I recall it, the only reason we were able to get food was because we had a very attractive housekeeper. The soldiers used to loot the area and bring some back to her.

243

ZAKA and MILTON SLAWSKY

Mitch: I remember a few incidents in Moscow. During that summer we had been in the Crimean area, when Dad told us to come back home to Moscow. When we got there, he showed us a movie projector that he had brought to let us see some movies. Unfortunately, the night we arrived the power went out and we never did see any movies. [*Laughs*] One of the other nights we were there, Dad decided to go to the opera, and that evening he didn't come back. There had been plenty of shooting outside and we were all worried. So Mother, Zak, and I went looking for him, and that was an experience that was hard to forget. There were many dead bodies that had been dragged from the streets to the nearest houses, and we had to go among them to see if Dad was one of them. That really was an experience! But, thank God, he did get home when we went back to the hotel. Then, after that, we were trapped in the hotel because the Bolsheviks had a machine-gun crew up on the second floor of the hotel and we had to stay inside.

Zak: As history noted, Moscow was isolated, and pretty soon there was no food. Somehow or other, Mother and Dad were able to take us to Kiev. There was food in Kiev, but we also picked up all the rest of the fighting between the Whites and the Bolsheviks (the Reds).

Mitch: That fighting between the Reds and the Whites was centered in Kiev. We lived in an apartment, a high-rise apartment, and across the way was a park in which the Bolsheviks had put a gun battery. The Whites were down the street, in a marketplace, and they were shooting at each other. For a while we stayed in the apartment, and we used to sleep in the stairwell. One time a shell came into the top floor but never exploded. Later, we'd go out on the balcony to watch. The Bolsheviks were entrenched in the street in front of our building, and we watched and listened to the bullets flying. Once when we were eating in the dining room, one of the bullets actually came into the room and hit the grandfather clock behind my father. Then when the Whites did come into our area, they rounded up the

Jews and took them away to be executed. They came to our apartment and took my dad. Fortunately, there was a White general across the hall from us and he was able to talk them out of it. I think it was three or four times they came for him. Anyway, we finally got out of that.

Zak: You know, as children, the shooting wasn't frightening at all. As Mitch pointed out, we used to stay out on the balcony and listen to the bullets go whoosh. Kids aren't really aware of the dangers—except, of course, when they were trying to take our father away; then we realized things could be bad. That's when we took off from Kiev, for the Polish border. At that time we were ten years old, in the fall of 1920. How we got there was best shown in the film *Doctor Zhivago*—by walking, by cart, and in an unheated boxcar on the railroad. We finally got to a town near the border. It was near Christmas, and we waited for a stormy night. There was a lot of snow, and a peasant had been paid to take us across the border in a horse-drawn sled. Actually, there were two sleds, and they wanted to put Mitch in one and me in the other so we would keep warm. There were two families trying to escape and we objected to being separated— we wanted to be together. Well, finally, our family all went into one sled and we went across. The other sled never got through.

In getting to the border, a Russian sentry leveled his gun at us and wanted to know where we were going. My dad pulled out a piece of paper that looked official and said we were just going to the next town. We got to the border crossing very late at night. The peasant, a Russian, would not go across, but he pointed out some lights on the other side of the border and said there was a factory there. So the four of us, with packs, got to the factory, and someone there said we couldn't stay because the Polish patrol goes by regularly. He pointed out where the town was, and we started walking for a mile or two. It was about midnight and when we went knocking on the doors of some of the houses, they wouldn't let us in. Finally, a Jewish family did, and we stayed there underground for about five or six days until my mother's sister could be contacted. She lived in Poland.

Mitch: Once we got to my aunt's house, we made arrangements to go to Warsaw, where there was an American consulate. My dad, in the meantime, had to hide because he was of military age. In Warsaw, it was established that Zak and I were citizens by birth, but Mother and Dad had never got through the naturalization process before they left the United States. But they were allowed to come as our guardians. Zak was the older by about five minutes and my mother's decree. She said, "The doctor had to pull the first baby out with pincers and because I could see the marks of the pincers on Zak, that's how I knew he was the oldest." Being the older, he was able to take us all into the States. We did have our birth certificates with us always, so there wasn't any problem in proving our citizenship. From then on, it was all gravy. We went on the train to Cherbourg, where we stayed in quarantine for thirty days, and finally on the boat to the United States.

Zak: In all the years in Russia, we had very little schooling due to the war and the revolution. There was some private tutoring and Dad did some teaching, but nothing in formal education. We didn't know much English, but we did have a few months before school started in Brooklyn to try and pick up some of the language. We did learn that the big thing in America was baseball and that there were two leagues . . . the American and the National. Of course, we had to go American—we were 110 percent Americans because of the way we were treated in Warsaw. So we rooted for the Yankees instead of the Brooklyn Dodgers. Meanwhile, we went to school in the fourth grade and when we heard they were going to put us in separate classes the next year, we transferred to another school where we would be together. And from then on, we stayed together . . . elementary, high school, Rensselaer Polytechnic Institute for our bachelor's degree, Cal Tech for our master's, and the University of Michigan for our doctorates, always in the same class. Along the way, there were many awards, especially in math.

Mitch: When we came to Brooklyn, the relatives got together and established a place for my parents, and there they ran a small laundry. Zak and I both worked in that laundry, and when we were sixteen, we were able to drive the truck for my dad. No, we didn't get paid, but our parents never denied us anything.

Zak: Our family philosophy was apparently unusual because we never had an allowance. My mother always said, "There's the cash box over there and if you need something, that's it." As far as the depression went, it certainly did affect us. I think we had a total income of probably fifty dollars a week. That's why they worked sixteen-hour days in the laundry. When we finally went away to college, I think half the family income went for those expenses. Mitch had a full scholarship—I didn't—but we both worked in the dining hall, or should I say kitchen. You see, they thought we were too short to be waiters, and eventually we worked in the kitchen. We became champion dishwashers—four years' worth. That's when we decided that we hated eggs for breakfast. We hated them because we used to judge the meal, not by the way it tasted, but how easy it was to wash—and eggs are hard to wash! [*Laughs*]

We always had a little car, a 1927 Ford Model A roadster with a rumble seat. After our bachelor's degree, we signed up for Cal Tech and decided to drive out to California. We bought a tent to camp out and did okay until Chicago, where the World's Fair was going on and we had to go to a rooming house. The landlady said, "What a coincidence, a pair of twins just left here and they were going to California too." She gave us the name and when we did get to Cal Tech, we found the other twins were also enrolled there.

I remember our stopping at Yellowstone Park and meeting two other guys who also had a Ford roadster. When we were washing our clothes, one of them came over and said, "We hear there are bears in this place." Although he might be trying to kid us, I said it was true and since we had a tent that could sleep four, they were welcome to join us. Milt, that was his name, said no, he was okay because he had a cot and would sleep outdoors. Well, that night he came bursting into the tent, "Somebody started pushing me and I thought it was you," he said. "I was going to swat you, but it wasn't you—it was a bear!" Well, we all howled. Thereafter he was more careful. Since they were from California, we teamed up and drove our Model A's to Pasadena.

We spent a year at Cal Tech and got our master's degrees there. No one offered us any fellowships there, so we decided to take our doctorate degrees at the University of Michigan. It was the best thing we ever did because it was a marvelous school. While there, the university established the first full summer physics symposium, and there we met practically every great physicist—including Enrico Fermi and Robert Oppenheimer. It took three and a half years to get our doctorates, but then we weren't in any hurry. You see, it was warmer inside than outside in 1934 to 1938. I think it was Bob Hope who said at a graduation, "Don't go out there, it's cold outside."

Mitch: We had teaching assistantships at Michigan, so we lived on that. When we graduated, we went back to Brooklyn. There were no jobs available; the depression was still lingering on. Zak did get a job at night, teaching a graduate course at Brooklyn College. I got one later, a part-time job as an inspector for the summer with the Civil Aeronautics Authority. But, in the meantime, during the day, we were working in the laundry. We decided that it took a bachelor's degree to work normally in the laundry; a master's degree to handle the slightly soiled laundry; and a doctorate degree to handle the whole thing, no matter what was there. [*Laughs*] We worked almost two years in the laundry and then the war started to warm up, in 1940, and there were openings for a lot of physicists, so we got offers. Zak and I got offers from the navy—the Bureau of Ordnance. I also received an offer from the Naval Ordnance Laboratory in Washington and, at the same time, one from Union College. I decided on the laboratory job in Washington.

It turned out that the director of the Naval Ordnance Laboratory was also on the board of trustees at Union College, and he withdrew his offer from the Naval Laboratory. When I asked why, he said, "The college is short of professors and I would rather see you in a teaching job there. That's where you're really needed." But I didn't like the idea at all—the college pay was fourteen hundred dollars a year, and Washington was three thousand dollars a year. So I went to Union College to talk to them about it, and Zak came along with me.

During our discussion, I said I preferred to go for the Washington job, but my equally qualified brother was available and I assured them they wouldn't know the difference. With that I walked out, and sometime later I let Zak go back to the department head's office. Upon seeing Zak, the department head said, "Well, Dr. Slawsky, I'm glad you decided to come back and join us." At that, I walked in and said, "See, I told you—you would never know the difference." [*Laughs*] So Zak bailed me out, and he took the job for six months and then joined me at the Naval Ordnance Lab in Washington. It was the one time when we really took advantage of our twinship.

Zak: As a matter of fact, that six months was the first time we were separated. And it caused a big fight because we only had the one car. I told Mitch I thought he should take it to Washington and he said no, I should take it with me to Schenectady, I'll need it at the college. Then he said, and I said, and he won—I got the car. It turned out to be very useful because soon I was getting little notices from the draft board to appear. When Mitch told the commander they were after me, the Naval Ordnance Lab sent me a contract to start work there immediately. It was March and I decided to put some time in at the lab before school ended. So on Thursday I drove the car from Schenectady to New

York; took the night train to Washington; worked Friday and Saturday; and went back to the college on Sunday. I did that until the end of the term.

Mitch: I stayed at the Naval Ordnance Lab for eight years, until 1948, and then went to the Bureau of Standards, where I also worked for eight years. After I went to the air force, in their Office of Scientific Research, which was sponsoring basic research at the various universities. Zak stayed on at the Naval Ordnance Lab and started teaching off-campus at NOL for the University of Maryland in 1947. When I was working at the Bureau of Standards, I also taught off-campus classes at the bureau. All these students were people working at NOL or the bureau, and they were attending classes to get graduate degrees. When I went to the air force, however, the job involved traveling and I couldn't continue the teaching. My job was to select researchers and follow their programs and accomplishments. Sometimes the travel was extensive, both in air force and commercial planes. I've been to Israel three times, to Sweden, Norway, England, France, Germany, Greece, even Japan. In some cases, my family accompanied me. This went on for eighteen years, until I retired.

Zak: I'd like to say that I'm the stable one, for while Mitch was changing jobs I stayed at the Naval Ordnance Lab. The navy gave me permission to teach for the university and we had classes from four to six o'clock, at NOL premises for the people of NOL. Initially, I was an instructor, then assistant professor part-time, then associate professor part-time, and finally a full professor part-time. By doing that I was able to direct programs for master and doctorate degrees.

In 1949 I was invited to spend a year in Holland as a visiting professor. I started doing research on my own and when I returned, I was able to get funding for establishing a molecular physics laboratory at the University of Maryland. When I went to Holland, it was with a professor who was one of the world's experts on high-pressure gases, and I helped to establish a similar setup here. It was sponsored by the Office of Naval Research.

In 1974, Mitch had a heart attack and decided to retire from the air force. He was quite high up by that time—had a three-star protocol rank. That reminds me of an incident that must have made a pretty amusing picture. We had a meeting set for the University of Oklahoma, and Mitch asked me for a jet to fly us out there. For a three-star rank, the airport had the red carpet out, and when we got there, I'm sure many of the crew were thinking, who are these butterballs and what are they doing here? After all, our heights of five feet and five feet and one inch were not very imposing and to add to that, we were very heavy at the time. I have a picture taken near this jet and I'm sure they might have been puzzled, but we did get the royal treatment. [*Laughs*] My rank, by the way, was the equivalent of a two-star, and I did okay when I got out. I received the top navy award for civilians and I retired at sixty-five, about a half year later than Mitch.

Then I told the university that I couldn't continue teaching courses at NOL, but I would like to help. They responded, "Hey, Zak, our professors are convinced that the difficulties the students have with physics is because of their lack of mathematics. We have a workshop, a math workshop. Would you be willing to take it on?" Well, Mitch was already on campus taking an accounting course, and I said between the two of us, we'll do it. So we took it on and in two or three weeks we realized that math wasn't the problem, not really. The students didn't know how to write the equation in the first place, let alone work on it. And that's when we suggested we should try to teach them how to express an idea in mathematical form. I think it was Mitch's suggestion that kids are paranoid about physics and we should call it a clinic—the Clinic for Physics Therapy.

Mitch: Today, it's the Slawsky Physics Clinic, named in

memory of our parents, Mollie and Simon Slawsky. Let me go back a bit and tell you a little more about them. The reason Dad took the family to Russia was because my grandfather knew dad had become twenty-one years old. Under the czar, when you become of age, you have to register for military service. If you don't register, then you can never come back to Russia. So my grandfather begged Dad to return and register. Dad really wasn't eligible for the military because he was very nearsighted; he wouldn't have been able to recognize an officer from a nonofficer. But the army didn't believe that and they were ready to take him in.

My mother, who was four feet and nine inches tall and redheaded, was the dynamo of the family. I understand she went all the way up to the chief of staff and got Dad out of the army. That's the way she was; if she had to go up to the president here, she would. When we had the laundry, she was the spark plug that ran it. Dad did deliveries and he was an expert shirt presser. Mother was also the one who really got us out of Russia. They deserve more than having their names in the clinic title; therefore we set up a memorial fund in their names to give the clinic financial support. The clinic is really a volunteer effort. It is staffed by volunteers who are given faculty status as lecturers. They are paid a small sum, mainly to cover travel expenses. The students who attend the clinic pay nothing, it's free! The cost to the university consists of providing the facilities and the travel expenses. In return, the university gets about a hundred hours of tutoring every week during the academic year.

Zak: We don't teach a physics course. Those courses are taught by the professors in regular classes. Our students have trouble in following the regular course materials, so we try to explain more to them. There are three parts to teaching physics. One is telling them what physics is like, some examples of how you figure things out, and what the laws of physics are. In the second, there's a laboratory where you get some idea of how to solve these problems with your hands. Those two aspects, the professors teach. The third part is what we relate to—analysis with a pencil and paper. We teach them how to look at a problem, how to set it up, and how to come out with results. In no sense are we competing with the professors.

Mitch: We practice physics like the coaches do. If you want to play tennis, I can give you the best equipment you'll need, all the books you can use, and all the lectures that will help—now go out and play. But that may not be enough! What you really need is someone on the tennis court with you . . . watching you, telling you when you're doing something right and when it's wrong—that's about what we do with the students. They don't have the skill of reading words and converting them into letters—or the skill of saying things in an equation form. We're increasing their skill and not really teaching them anything. We give the students a lot of individual attention and get them to write in algebra, not in English.

Students will never let the professor know that they are ignorant of something. They think, I'm stupid and he'll grade me. So we tell them we *don't* grade you here! Ignorance is what we *credit* you with. If you weren't ignorant, there would be no purpose in you being here. Stupidity is a different thing. Stupidity is when you don't do something you know you should do, and do something you shouldn't do. That's stupid! And if you don't come to the clinic— that's stupid.

Zak: Mitch, did you tell him why we teach here? Our wisecracks? Well, someone asked Mitch why he does teach here and Mitch said, "You know, there are over thirty thousand students on this campus—and half of them are women." [*Laughs*] I also had a similar situation. The chairman of our department was walking along the hallway and I thought I'd be a wise guy—Brooklyn people are wise guys, there's no question about that. So I said, Alex, I think I'm going to quit. He was quite upset and asked why would I do that. I replied, "Well, I can't take all this hugging and kissing from the girls." Hey, do you think maybe that's what really keeps us so young, after all.

But seriously, you ask what keeps us going. Well, many years ago—about the second year of the clinic—there was a young man who had a bachelor's degree in social services and couldn't get a job. He decided to go into engineering, but his math was nonexistent and he'd forgotten whatever science he ever had. He was about twenty-five and in the middle of his first semester in physics for engineers. He told me, "I'm not going to make it." I assured him he would. He looked at me and said, "You've got infinite patience." I said no—compassion.

Well, he got a B in his course, then another B and an A, and he's a good engineer. That's the reward! You know, when they come and tell you they got an A—what else?

Mitch: One thing I can say about this is something I heard way back when we were at the University of Michigan. One of our professors, who was a very good physicist, also helped the police department in their analysis of specific situations. Well, I asked him why he spent so much time on that. He replied, "The thing you can do best, you do for a living. The thing you like to do best, you do as a hobby, and it's fortunate if what you do best and your hobby are the same." And with Zak and me, it is. Teaching is a hobby with us, and we're lucky because physics is what we do best. We behave almost like grandparents, and this arrangement is ideal. I once read an article about the "bridge" that's between the grandchildren and the grandparents. That relationship is always pleasant. The relationship between parents and children is not always pleasant, there can be problems. One of my friends in Italy has a lot of grandchildren—he calls them his avengers.

Once someone picked up a statement I must have made. He asked what was I going to do when I retired, because he had heard I was going to do that. My problem, I've pointed out, is that if someone comes up to me and explains what retirement means, then I'll be able to tell you when I'm going to retire. I'm not going to go home and knit sweaters—that's for sure!

One of the other things Zak says about retirement is that you begin to feel you're not needed. There's no such feeling here. You can just look at the clinic over there, and to say we're not needed is stretching the truth quite a bit.

September 18, 1990

I located Tempia with the help of a friend who writes for the Arizona Senior World *newspaper. I'm glad I did, for it turned out to be a wonderful visit with a very special person. Our meeting took place in her lovely home in the northeast area of Tucson.*

She was born in an era when feminists were almost unknown, and her early years personify what their struggles are all about. Buttressed by her own determination to make something out of her life, Tempia Strobhardt succeeded by making every decision a positive one. Although she didn't suffer the discrimination so prevalent in the South in those early days, she did have to make her own way—one step at a time. She attributes many of her successful moves to a lot of help from the powers above.

Her present retirement involves remaining active in one of the most satisfying accomplishments of her life.

* * *

I DON'T KNOW too much about living in the South because my parents moved from Philadelphia to New Jersey when I was nine months old . . . northern New Jersey in the town of East Orange. My mother was educated in Boston—in Cambridge—and she spoke with a "Down East" accent, you know, "cahn't" and "shan't," and things like that. When I was small, I thought she was from a foreign country. She sounded like she came from London. As I grew older, that accent was lessened—because of me, I guess.

My grandfather was a bootmaker, and he had places in Cambridge and Boston at one time, so that's where my mother grew up. My own upbringing was also primarily in a northern atmosphere. In East Orange we went to school together, blacks and whites, and my next-door neighbor whom I played with was Margaret, and she was Irish. She and I grew up together. Although there were fences and

TEMPIA STROBHARDT

gates in front of the houses, the backyards were open and we had no problem going from one yard to another. The school was only about five blocks away, and our town was a very settled and very nice community.

I know very little of my father because my parents separated when I was about six years old, and he moved to Chicago. My mother worked at whatever jobs she could find, but most of the time she worked with infants—taking care óf newborn babies, some without parents. She liked that kind of work the most, whether it was in hospitals or homes.

My school years were pretty normal except when the depression years came along. That '29 crash tied up the money and I lost my college education. I attended college for two years—that's all I was able to get because then the money went up in smoke. College wasn't expensive like it is today, but there wasn't any money, scholarships, or government loans around in those years. I had been attending a college in New York which specialized in music education. I played the piano well, also a little bit of violin, and I was taking up voice studies because I sang very well. I had to give it all up—I couldn't pursue a music career because there was nothing to pursue it with. After the money dried up in the depression you had to get out and do whatever you could.

You know, at that time doctors were driving cabs—I mean medical doctors! Me, with just two years in college, I had to get anything I could get. So the first thing I got was factory work, a dress factory in New York City—just across the river. It paid better than I could get anywhere else at that time. I was lucky enough to get a very good boss who liked my work, so I did very well at that. You see, my mother also went to Pratt Institute and she could take a piece of material and cut out whatever you or I have on, and run it up one, two, three. Because of her, when I was young, I was one of the best dressed girls in my crowd. Seeing her do that kind of thing all those years must have rubbed off on me, and in the garment industry I felt quite at home. My boss was very fond of me and he gave me a lot of work, a lot of extra work too so that I could earn more money on Saturdays. All in all, I did very well there.

Then later on I found myself getting married. My husband worked for the Pennsylvania Railroad, and I kept working in the dress factory for a short time. We moved to a nice, small apartment way uptown in New York City, and that was the first time I was ever in an apartment—never in my life did I know what it was to pay rent. I had always lived in a house—my grandmother's or my mother's. My husband didn't want me to work at all so I stayed home. After a year or so I wanted to get back to work. You see, I always had it in my brain that you should stand for something on this earth—and if you don't do it when you're young, you certainly can't do it when you're old. That was my idea.

Well, that wasn't my husband's idea; he wanted me to stay home. But I didn't want to stay home. And my former boss in the dress factory kept calling me because he couldn't get anybody who could sew or do the work as well as I did. So one day I said to my husband, "I'm going back to work because I can't see people going around without jobs and here's someone almost begging me to come to work. Someone who's willing to pay me for my work and willing to pay me overtime for my work. So I just can't see sitting home all day in this apartment."

Of course, that didn't suit him so well but he tolerated it and I went back to work. Once again, I did very well. Then, later on, I tried to get my husband to buy a home but he just didn't want to buy any house. He said, "I'm not gonna go out and buy a house, then lie down and die, and then let some other man come in and take it up." He was nine years older than me but that still didn't make any sense. Anyway, those were the wrong words to say to me. I decided that if he didn't want anything in life—*I did*, and I was going to have it!

Since I was working, I decided to separate his money from mine and put my money into a savings account for myself. As the years went by, I bought five pieces of property in New Jersey—rentable property. They were bought gradually and I didn't borrow any money because these properties were picked up at bargain prices—some required lots of repairs, some were foreclosed, and so on. I did it without my husband because he didn't want any responsibilities—just like he never wanted children.

On one of our many visits to my mother in East Orange, she mentioned there was a need for a nursing home in that community, for there was no place for the sick and elderly to go. She knew where there was a big house for sale— twenty-one rooms and five baths. It was on a main street with a bus stop on the corner, an ideal location. The house needed a lot of repairs; it was in such bad condition, it was almost condemned. Well, with her help—she was in New Jersey while I was in New York—we negotiated a sale and I purchased the house. This was all also done without my husband, because he didn't want involvement and I didn't want interruptions. Anyway, I wasn't using his money.

He had gotten in with a bunch of cronies and they enjoyed smoking, drinking beer, and playing cards. I didn't enjoy them much but I occasionally did sit in and learned to play pinochle—but they weren't my cup of tea. Anyway, things weren't going so hot with us but we managed somehow. My mother never gave advice unless I asked for it. She said, "I never put you together and I'm not going to take you apart." But she did believe if you want something out of life, then you should get it.

I had gone to school in East Orange, and I knew practically all the people who were now in politics because most of them had gone to kindergarten with me and graduated with me—the mayor, judges, lawyers, and so on. Getting a nursing home license from city hall wasn't a problem, but getting the house fixed up was a big job, and I decided to do a few rooms at a time. Our apartment in New York was small—one bedroom, one bath, one living room, and a kitchenette—not even a kitchen for me to go in. I had always been raised in a house, and those small quarters had always been a little much for me. I told my husband, "Now we've been in this apartment for fourteen years—if you're happy with it, I'm not!" So I told my mother we were going to move to New Jersey, whether he was coming or not.

She told me about a house only one block away from the nursing home, which would really be very convenient. It had eight bedrooms. We certainly didn't need that many, but I decided to buy it. When I told my husband about all this and the moving, he said, "Tempia, you've always had your head in the clouds, but I'm not getting involved." I said right. I didn't dispute him. But if he wasn't going, I was. Well, when I moved, he moved. We lived together, slept in the same bedroom and all, but he never helped with the nursing home. He still had his buddies and beer drinking across the river in New York.

At that time my mother had adopted a three-month-old boy from the hospital where she worked—he was an abandoned baby, a three-pound preemie. While taking care of him, she kinda fell in love with him. He was one of the best brothers I could ever have had. So my mother, my husband, my little brother, and I moved into this eight-bedroom house. It felt like God got in there and helped out.

Anyway, I went into the nursing home business. But first I had to get it fixed up—it was a mess. I shut off one whole floor and started to work only on the first-floor rooms. I went around and got workers and friends who weren't too busy and would work reasonably. Then I went to the secondhand stores to buy furniture and furnishings, and I fixed up what I could without going into debt. As I got each room ready, I put a patient into it. This was a gradual process until all the rooms were remodeled, and finally I had a full house—forty-five patients. Before that was all finished, my husband had moved back to New York and his buddies. I guess living in East Orange was a bit too mild for him.

I never had problems getting patients because I knew who was who at the city hall, and my reputation at the home was a good one. Regarding patients, I always wanted people who were on city or state aid—no private patients. You know, when you go into business, you don't go into it for your health—you go into it to make a profit. And when the patients are on a government program, those checks come in on the first of the month. Now, if *your* mother was a private patient and you lost your job, you would come to me and say, "I lost my job and can't pay for her board. Could you take care of her for a few months until I find something?" Well, the government isn't going to lose its job—is it? So that's what I believed in, and I didn't want to take any private patients. Everyone thought I was a fool— but in the end, well, you see where I am today, don't you?

What convinced me about all this was something which happened on the first rental property I bought. I went over to New Jersey to work on an empty apartment in that building. I had it painted, put new linoleum on the floor, and fixed it up all nice. The new tenant gave me the first month's rent and then she said, "You painted the whole apartment beige, but my decor is blue." So I had it repainted blue. They were in there only one month when the husband lost his job! That was a lesson for me, and I made preparations where that wouldn't happen to me again. And it didn't! Now do you see where I'm coming from?

When we moved over to East Orange, we didn't have a car. In New York there was always a bus or the subway. Here I had a problem, especially when shopping for supplies for the home. I'd take a bus to where I was going, but had to take a taxi back with the supplies. After a long while of doing this I just felt that was enough of this kind of riding around. So one day, I took off my flat shoes which I used for shopping, put on my high heels, and went down to the car dealer and got a new Lincoln Continental. And I've been riding in a Continental ever since 1952. That's the only kind of car I ever had and there's one out in the garage today—it's the fifth one I ever had, all of them brand-new.

About six or eight months after my husband moved out, he called me from a hospital. I checked with the nurses and found that he had lung cancer—he was a heavy smoker. I kinda think he must have known this when he left New Jersey, but he didn't want to burden me at that time. His condition got worse over the next few months and he kept sinking. He died in 1957. That was his undoing—poor fellow. No, I never married again.

At the nursing home, once everything was in good order, we always had a full house. My mother helped, until she died at fifty-seven. My brother grew up and helped, and there were many other wonderful people who were on my staff. I ran that home for thirty-three years. You know, as I went along, God was really with me because I couldn't have done the things I did without his help. He was in front of me all the time. After all those years and all that work, it was time to retire. So I sold the nursing home—I placed all the patients wherever it was best for them. I sold all the other rental properties. All in all, I had done very well, really well.

You see, for two winters before I retired I had developed an asthmatic condition, and the doctor said New Jersey was no place for me. One of those attacks sent me to the hospital, where I was unconscious for quite a while. The doctor said, "See, I told you to move to Arizona—or do you want to be the richest woman in the cemetery?" Well, I knew there was a state named Arizona someplace in the United States but I didn't know where. Fortunately, my friend Viola—from my bridge club—really surprised me one day. She said, "I've got to go to Arizona to see if I want to get married." Just like that—right out of the blue.

Well, to make a long story short, this man in Arizona originally lived in New Jersey and they had met a few times on his last visit back here. He wanted Vi to come out and look things over—his house, the town—go out together, and maybe see about the possibility of marriage. Later they did get married and that's when I had an advanatage—I actually knew somebody in Arizona.

After another winter's attack of asthma and a hospital stay, the doctor said, "I've already told you all I intend to tell you. Now it's up to you to do something about this condition." So I wrote to Vi and said I would be out to visit. My brother, my adopted daughter Pamela—who was now ten years old—and I went out to Tucson, and we stayed in a suite in a brand-new hotel. Vi's real estate broker took us around, and later I settled on a new house way out in the northeast part of Tucson. I wanted no pool, no garage door to lift, nothing that required work—I was retiring! There were three bedrooms, one for each of us, as well as a large patio and backyard. The schools for my daughter were nearby and there was a bus to take her to the university when she was ready for it. That was then—now I'm the only one here. My brother passed on and my daughter is married and has a little girl—my granddaughter.

You know, I never did get back to my music; I really had been too busy working. Anyway, music as a career at the time was not making any big bucks, not unless you were a real headliner. And with my business, I *was* making big bucks, so I guess it wasn't too bad in the long run.

As far as discrimination goes, I never really had any major problems with that. I was brought up in an area that was integrated. My work in New York and at the nursing home involved whites and blacks—both with my patients and my staff. Lots of times I think people look at you like you look at them. People treat you like you treat them. Here in Tucson I've been teaching bridge at Pima Community College, and very rarely do I have a black pupil. Most all are white. I play bridge with them, I go into their homes, we have lunch together, they come into my home, and we are all the best of friends.

You know, a lot of my own people stay within themselves, they discriminate unto themselves. To me, people are people. This is the color of my skin, that's the color of yours. It takes nine months for your mother to bring you into the world, it takes nine months for mine. I guess I look at these things a little different from everybody else.

Of course, there was discrimination in those early years, and it also plainly exists *today* . . . that certainly isn't anything to be proud of. I remember going to President Truman's inauguration festivities in Washington. When I went into a store and was looking to try on a hat, the saleslady said, "You know, if you try it on, you've bought it." Well, I didn't get excited, I just walked out because I knew in New York, I could try on any hat.

What I'd rather remember is what happened in Italy when I was on a bus tour with my three-year-old daughter. Someone had lost a passport and we were stuck for a long while in this big square. There was a fountain in the square and lots of kids were playing in the water. I sent Pamela to join them because it was a hot day. Well, those kids played and played in that fountain—really keeping cool. When it was time to go, my daughter came running and she yelled back, "Good-bye, Guiseppe," And he shouted, "*Arrivederci,* Pamela." There was no black or white thing there, just a couple of human beings. I wish we adults could relate that way to each other.

There's also something else. In the old days people lived a lot different than they do now. In my neigborhood where I grew up, everybody had a front porch, and it was fashionable for everyone to sit out there and wave or talk to all the people who came along. Also, if my neighbor up the street was ill, my mother would send one of us up to get the dirty clothes. Then she'd wash them, put them in the basket, and send them back clean. If there was someone who needed sitting with all night, my mother would go up and sit tonight and the neighbor next door would do it the next night and so on. Like a nurse for the night, but with no charge. Then if Mother was cooking a stew or some soup, she'd just make a bigger pot and send half up to that sick neighbor. That's the kind of way we lived then.

At that time if a girl became pregnant without being married, the two fathers would get together and the boy had to marry her. They always said, "If you're big enough to make a baby, then you're big enough to take care of it." That's a philosophy they used around my neighborhood, so those kids were doomed to get married. But at the same time, both families pitched in to help the kids get settled.

You asked earlier about all those bridge trophies, so I'll tell you how it all got started many years ago—when I learned to play pinochle with my husband's buddies. You see, my mother's home was a very religious one, and there were no cards, no cards at all in the house. Naturally, when I grew up, I wanted to do all those things that were forbidden in my youth. Playing with those buddies gave me some card sense, but I never really enjoyed who I was playing with, especially because of the beer drinking.

Later on I met a lady whose husband was a bridge teacher, and she invited me to her house to play a game with some of her friends. I really enjoyed the game and the people, so I took lessons from her husband and joined a bridge club. I found that I felt comfortable with the people who played bridge. After a while I was helping the husband teach some of his pupils. Then when I was running the nursing home, I got into bridge playing in a very big way, and I seemed to be very good at it. Finally, I got into some bridge tournaments, and then I started traveling over half the world playing bridge and seeing everything. I even had two seminars with Charles Goren in Chicago—he was the tops in the game.

I've been to Paris, London, Austria, Italy, the Netherlands, the Ivory Coast, Bermuda, Puerto Rico, Monrovia, Nigeria, Ghana, Jamaica, and more—and everywhere I'm going I'm playing bridge and winning trophies. Yes, there's about fifteen trophies on that table, and there's just as many or more in the closets. I'm a Life Master at bridge, and to get that rating you have to win so many tournaments. For each tournament you get a number of points and you keep going until you achieve one hundred or more. That isn't so easy, and it takes you forever to do it in the United States, where there aren't as many tournaments going. I was lucky enough to be in business, making some money and able to afford to make those overseas trips.

When I came to Tucson, my friend Vi told someone at the Y about my bridge skills, and so they asked if I would start a class there. Well, I did, and it went over very well. Before six months had passed someone recommended me to Pima Community College, and I started classes there. It's been *seventeen years* at Pima and I'm still teaching—eighty-three years old and still going strong. I have arthritis in this knee, in my hip, and in the bottom of my spine. I have to walk with this cane but I still teach. When I drive to the college, it's my good knee that takes care of the gas and the brake. The kids are always waiting for me, and they help unload and carry all the supplies in my folding shopping cart. Then all I have to do is walk in and start teaching the day's lesson. When we're finished, they put everything back in the trunk of the car.

You know, it's all in the hands of the Lord; I don't think I could ever have done it without him. I'm going to keep on teaching as long as I can. I'm not about to quit. You know you can't quit—you might just as well sound your own death warrant if you do. You have to stay active; it's the only way I can see anyone living. I'm happy teaching; you'd be surprised at the happiness I get from helping my students. I keep reading in the papers about this one or that one who is ninety or a hundred and they're still going strong. So why should I stop in my eighties? I'm still a youngster compared to them—right?

April 15, 1992

STROM THURMOND [89]

I missed a few earlier opportunities to meet with the senator, but this time the Senate was not in session and I was pleased to meet him in his office. Belying his age, there was the distinct trace of an athlete's body . . . slim, trim, fit, and brimming with vitality. He seemed ready to take off at any moment. The office was impressive, with ceilings that seemed twenty feet high. Each of the walls was covered with a veritable tapestry of photos, awards, plaques, and special commendations. They created a remarkable record of events encompassed in his thirty-eight years as U.S. senator from South Carolina.

During World War II he received numerous decorations, including the Legion of Merit with Oak Leaf Clusters, the Bronze Star for Valor, Purple Heart, Belgian Order of the Crown, and the French Croix de Guerre.

Prior to his seat in the Senate, there were many years of government service in his home state, including a four-year term as governor of South Carolina. All in all, his career reflects a deep commitment to civic purpose and public service.

* * *

IN THE EARLY 1900s when I was growing up, segregation was a part of life. *Everything* was separate . . . churches, schools, theater-sitting and so on. It was a custom of the times. At the same time, though, I did work in the fields with blacks. Where a black man was cutting grain, I'd come along to pick the grain up and bundle it. And we worked together in all the field operations—hoeing, plowing, cutting, and all that. Before I went to college I also worked in a garage and clerked in a store during a few summers. Of course I still had to carry on the work at home too. Even when I went to college I worked in a textile mill in between years. So, all of that was a pretty varied form of working . . . on the farm,

STROM THURMOND

in the garage, in a store, and in the textile mill. You know this thing of not letting children work is a great mistake. So long as they work in a safe place and are old enough to do the work without harm, I think it's well to encourage them to work.

I was born in Edgefield, South Carolina, and in our early years my father bought a house out in the rural area because, as he said, "So the boys could work on the farm and that will keep them out of any devilment." During that period we raised pigs and calves and furnished our own meat. We had cows to produce our milk, an orchard for fruit, and a garden for vegetables. Self-sustaining and we didn't have to buy anything like that.

So I grew up in that atmosphere. I worked in the fields harvesting grain, chopping cotton, and plowing in the fields. I rode bulls and broke ponies, and even rode them without a saddle or bridle. I remember one time when we had a skittish pony with a two-wheel cart. My brother, who was two years older and who later became a doctor, told me, "Look, I'll go around in front to try and hold him because he's really kinda wild." Well, somehow he didn't get around there in time and the pony took off and jumped a couple of fences, all the while dragging that cart along [*chuckles*]. Yeah, we got a lot of fun out of that but it did do some pretty good damage to the cart.

In 1918, the year my neighbor went to war in World War I, he wanted somebody to buy his crop. So I bought his crop, worked that and did almost all the plowing myself. Boy, it was hot then! We put peach leaves in our straw hats to keep the sun out. The kids today don't even wear hats—guess they want to get their tans instead. At any rate, that's the kind of things we were doing when we grew up. Two or three years before I went to college I was still milking two to four cows every morning before going to school. Didn't have any automatic milkers then, not in those days. We walked about a mile and a half to a regular public school—

not a one-room schoolhouse. We only lived about a mile out of town and the school was a half mile further.

I believe, though, for the first two years of schooling we went to a private school—Miss Mary Butler's. I learned more geography then I've ever learned since. There was a special geography class every day—name the countries of the world and their capitals. I often wonder why they don't do that more today in schools. And spelling, we had spelling every day. So I got a pretty good little foundation in those two years and from there went into about third grade in the public school. I stayed in the public schools from then on and went on to college after finishing tenth grade. Both in high school and college, I loved sports—running, boxing, wrestling, and so on. Later on when I became a teacher, I was also an athletic coach.

My four years at Clemson College involved agriculture and horticulture majors. I also took a special course in writing; they didn't call it journalism then. After graduation I was teaching school and coaching athletics for about six years. Sometime during those years there was the idea that maybe I might go into politics someday, so I was kind of watching my step. Well, anyway, I started a program to take needy farm boys to summer schools and camps. We taught them health, character, English, and a lot of other things that were good for them besides farming. Half of them couldn't afford to go and I got churches and clubs to furnish scholarships and some expenses. This went on for four years in the summers and it was a great experience for me. It was also a tough challenge to raise the money, get teachers, and transport all of them to the colleges and camps that were cooperating. We had a school bus and some old Model T Fords—half the tires would blow out on the way or coming back [*chuckles*]. In one of those summers all we had to eat were apples, almost three times a day. Those apples were mighty good though.

In 1928 I ran for Superintendent of Education in the county and was elected. The man who had been in there for eighteen years was a good man, but he concentrated more on finances and he did like to go hunting as much as possible. When I was elected (at age twenty-five), I got out to supervise those schools more and during the next few years managed some changes. Got the school board to stay within their budgets, challenged the doctors and dentists to give free health exams, and got the educators to include courses in health and character. While I was doing this I also decided to get my law degree. My father was a better teacher than anyone in the law school and I learned a lot from him. He was Judge J. William Thurmond and he could answer questions just like that—it saved me worlds of time. I read a three-year course in about a year and half—working late at night and getting up early in the morning. I studied for the bar and, not boasting, I tied for first place.

Well, in 1933 I became a state senator and spent most of my five years in office trying to promote education more than anything else. As Superintendent of Education previously, I knew some of the problems there . . . low salaries for teachers, textbook shortages, inadequate buildings at colleges, a need for a school attendance law, and so on. I also did a lot of work on the protection of the soil and water resources of our state, as well as coauthoring the first rural electrification act in the United States.

Was I a strong Democrat then? Everybody in the South was a Democrat then! I wouldn't have thought about running on any other ticket. Anyway, in 1938 the legislature elected me a circuit judge—that's the highest trial court in the state. I served for eight years with a big time-out for World War II. The day Roosevelt declared war against Germany, I wanted to volunteer. They called me in a little later and when I first went in it was as a basic ROTC infantry officer. After a while when we were ready to go overseas, Headquarters noticed I was a lawyer and a judge so they put me into the intelligence section G2. I was to work on exclusion cases with the FBI—that related to Germans who might be dangerous. Later I went overseas with the First Army and while there I went to London to a staff college.

Then the First Army called for three volunteers to go with the Eighty-Second Airborne Division on D-Day. I volunteered for that, along with another major and a captain. We went in on D-Day by glider. I would have preferred a parachute jump but they said, "Hey, you haven't had any training for parachute jumping, so you go by glider." I was mad at that because I was in good physical condition and if they had taught me in one day what was needed, I could have done it. You know, the gliders were tremendous targets; they could be hit a lot easier than a chute. The division's mission was to land between the German lines, those defending the beaches and those in reserve, ready to be called up. So those reserves had to be cut off and that was accomplished—with a lot of losses on both sides.

Anyway, in three or four weeks I went back to the First Army and we continued on into St. Lo, Paris, all through France, Belgium, and into the Battle of the Bulge. That was a tough one and we had to pull back to Liege. It was cold there, the ice must have been four to six feet thick. It was the coldest I've ever been in my life; I haven't been as cold since. After the Battle of the Bulge, we went into Germany, across the Rhine, and on through. We uncovered the concentration camp at Buchenwald.

The things I saw there I will never forget. The commander of the camp was a cruel fellow and his wife must have been too. Anytime an inmate died there, if he had a tattoo anywhere on the body, she would have it skinned off and brought to her to make lampshades. They fed those inmates a bowl of thin pea soup every day and that's all the food they got there—starved them to death. Another method was for some of the guards to pretend they were not looking and as soon as any of the inmates tried to climb over the fence, he would be shot. The guards encouraged that deception. They also made use of a box, kind of like a telephone booth—the inmate would be ordered in there and told to look out the front. A big SS guard would then use a large mallet to hit him on the head and kill him.

There were bodies stacked up like cordwood and you couldn't tell if some of them were alive or dead. The doctors got in and saved some but the prisoners may have died later because they had been starved so long. It was just a terrible, terrible situation. We got after the people who lived in the nearby town of Weimar and asked them why they permitted such a thing, or did they know about it. They claimed they heard about it but didn't know all that was going on there. Anyway, we made them come out and see what had gone on there and also had them clean up some of the carnage.

Later I returned to the States for a while and then was shipped out to the Pacific Theater. I was there when the war ended and was finally sent back to a camp in the U.S. The chief justice of South Carolina said the war was over and they needed me back on the bench. So I asked for permission to return to my job and it was granted. I went back in '45 and served until the next year when I decided to resign and run for governor. I was elected and served from 1947 to 1951. As governor, there were many reforms that I was able to get through. A few of them included—adopting a central purchasing system, removing the poll tax for voting, setting up a pardon board with sole power to act, establishing a Trade School System, adding twelfth grade to the high school curriculum, and encouraging more women and blacks to serve in public offices. There were improvements in schools, a new teaching hospital and clinic, incentives to new industries, the use of voting machines, and a host of other needed changes. During that same period I became a candidate for the presidency of the United States, as a States Rights Democratic candidate.

We only campaigned in the South. We were trying to beat Harry Truman because he was campaigning to centralize more power in Washington. That meant taking it away from the states. Well, in the election we carried South

Carolina, Mississippi, Louisiana, and Alabama—four
states with thirty-nine electoral votes. You know something that's never been published? A change of 20,000 votes
in two of the other states would have thrown that presiden-
tial race to the House. That's what Ross Perot is trying to do,
evidently—throw the race into the House.

If my race had gone to the House, you can't tell what
would have happened. The feeling was that the Republicans would not have voted for Truman and I think the
Southerners would have voted for me—because the South
hadn't had a President in one hundred years. The whole
South, I mean, not just those four states. So we did have a
chance. The good thing that race accomplished was that
for the first time in a century we pulled four states away
from the Democratic party. Ever since the South was put
under military rule in 1866, it hated the Republicans and
no one there would ever run, or ever be elected on any
ticket except the Democrats. So when we pulled those four
states away from the national Democrat party, the sky
didn't fall and they were now independent and able to vote
as they saw fit. And they've done that ever since.

Here's a Truman story for you. After I ran against him in
1948, my first wife, Jean Crouch Thurmond, and I went up
to his inauguration in 1949. We were in the parade, as gov-
ernors, going down Pennsylvania Avenue and passing by
the White House. As we approached the White House area,
I stood up, bowed, took off my hat, and my wife smiled
beautifully. Vice President Barkley raised his hand to wave
and smile at us and Truman turned around, caught his
hand, and put it down. He said, "Put your hand down, here
comes that S.O.B. now!" [chuckles]

After the governorship, I practiced law in Aiken, South
Carolina. There was a lot of litigation there because the
Savannah River Bomb Plant was going to be built in that
area. The landowners were taking a beating because the
government's representative felt he had to offer the lowest
price he could get away with. I think I represented about 75

percent of the landowners who had a case against the government trying to acquire their land at unfair prices. We were able to increase some of those prices by as much as 100 to 150 percent, which was indicative of the unfairness of the initial offers.

Senator Maybank was in Congress at the time and he died in September of 1954. The Democratic party always holds a primary to select the nominee. Edgar Brown was one of the most popular politicians in the state and he really wanted to be a senator. The rumor was that he got those members of the executive committee to go from the Maybank funeral directly to a hotel in Columbus. There they connived to nominate Brown without a vote of the people. When that was announced, the governor said he favored the president of the university as a candidate instead. Well, although many people wanted me to run, I told the governor I'd step aside. But then neither one of them announced! And shortly thereafter it was too late to get on the ticket and they would have to be elected on a write-in. Many people came to me and wanted me to run, and although we didn't know if I had a chance, we made the decision to go for it. You see, we felt strongly that it was wrong for the executive committee to pick a nominee without the public being able to vote.

I was elected on the write-in and carried the vote almost two to one. When I initially ran, I told the voters they were previously denied the right to vote and that was wrong. So I promised that if elected, I would resign and put the office of senator back into the first primary after this general election. In 1956, two years later, I did resign and put the office back into the primary. I was then reelected without opposition. Since then, I've been reelected in 1960, 1966, 1972, 1978, 1984, and 1990. You'll have to check the records to see what I've accomplished in the Senate and on the various committees . . . Judiciary, Armed Services, Veterans Affairs, Labor and Human Resources.

In 1964 I switched from the Democratic party to the

Republican party. That all started when I first became senator with that write-in victory and told my constituents I would vote Democratic in all matters. But from the day I came to Washington, I soon saw that the Democrats up here were a completely different breed from those in South Carolina. My conservatism and the conservatism of the people in my state was more in line with the Republicans, but I had to wait until I felt I could survive. So, ten years after I came here I switched parties—even though my friends and advisers said it would be political suicide to switch from Democrat to Republican.

Oh, I know there are people who think I'm ultraconservative and won't change my ways. But let me tell you something—a person who can't respond to changes can't last. And if you don't respond to changes, you can't best represent your people. We had segregation in South Carolina and the whole South. But when the Supreme Court handed down the decision, the South obeyed it, and we've had less trouble than even states in the North. They're still throwing bricks at school children in Massachusetts and Ohio and other places. We all have to respond to change because change is inevitable. Take my support of the fetal-tissue bill, for example. That surprises many people. Everybody knows I'm a strong opponent of abortion. However, this isn't an abortion issue—it's a *research* issue, and there's a great promise of new treatments for Alzheimer's, Parkinson's, and other diseases. If I felt this bill would in any way encourage abortions, I would not support it!

I've always believed in being fair to black people because down South we grew up with black people. I helped educate a great number of blacks when I was in education, as a state senator, as governor, and since. We've organized the Strom Thurmond Foundation, which today is helping to educate about eighty people a year, and about a third are black students. In the high school named after me in Edgefield County, I established funding from my honorariums which now totals fifty or sixty thousand dollars. They use the income from that to establish about four scholar-ships—two of them go to white students, two of them go to black students.

You asked where is this country going—will it go the way of the Roman Empire? Well, I think there's a certain amount of moral decay in this country and that's a bad sign. The Roman Empire fell from within, not without. That's a danger we suffer from here. No nation in the world could beat us if we stand together and carry on like we did in the past. What we need to do is elect people to office who are interested in the welfare of the country and not in the next election. And some of them may have to run knowing they may get beat for doing what they've got to do.

For instance, we've got a debt of almost four trillion dol-lars. We haven't balanced a budget but once in twenty-one years. Now, nobody can stay in business with an operation like that. No government can either! These big spenders ought to be gotten rid of and in my judgment it's going to take such as that to do it. Steps have got to be taken to turn this country around. Part of the problem is that so many special interest groups, both in and out of government, are so used to being on the receiving end, they don't want to make the tough decisions, so everyone just goes along. And that's another part of the reason there's a big deficit, poli-ticians trying to placate everyone so they can get reelected. I think you've got to get some people running for office who have no fear of getting defeated!

About retirement—I don't think anyone who is in good mental and physical health should retire. I wouldn't stay here if I were not in good health mentally and physically. And keeping involved is also important. I'm interested in the future of this country and trying to preserve it, espe-cially for the young people. I've got four children, but even if I had none I'd still be interested so they can live in a land of freedom, a land of justice, and a land of hope.

You know, I still do twenty minutes of calisthenics and twenty minutes on the bicycle every morning. I also try to get in some swimming three or four times a week. I stopped jogging somewhere in my seventies because the doctor said it might damage my knees. The only ones happy to hear that were some of my aides, who ran along with me occasionally. But the secrets of good health, other than the genes you inherit, are reasonable exercise, a good diet, vitamins, and an optimistic attitude towards life.

May 22, 1992

His slightly bent, extra-lean, taller-than-average figure is a standout in any crowd. From a lectern, his voice is firm and strong, As he left the podium, I caught his attention, and we agreed to a later meeting for our interview in the hotel's conference room. I was fortunate he would be able to spend an hour or two with me.

Lecterns are no novelty in Pat Weaver's career. From them he has addressed many an audience on communications—and received numerous awards. He's been the recipient of an Emmy, a Peabody award, a Sylvania award, a Look award, and a Variety award, among others. He was named to the TV Hall of Fame in 1985. In 1990 he received a National Association of Broadcasters award, among others. At that time his wife whispered, "This is the last one; there's no more room on any of the walls."

* * *

BOTH MY PARENTS were brought to California as little children. Actually, they later ran away from Los Angeles to Santa Barbara to get married. I never got into why that was. I was born in Los Angeles, and it was a great place to grow up for somebody who was going to do the kind of things that I was—although I didn't know what I was going to do at the time.

I was a great reader and the minute movies got started I added to that reading—going to the movies all the time, and going out to watch them shoot movies. In those days, silent movies of course, the cameraman would turn the handle and grind away, and all around the scene they would have reflectors for lighting. The crew would see us kids around and they would get us to hold up the reflectors as we watched the scenes being done. These movies were just shorts.

But at the beach, some of the big pictures were shot, par-

SYLVESTER "PAT" WEAVER

ticularly of desert scenes. After all, we had the sand, the dunes, and there was hardly anything built up in those days. I can't remember which pictures I watched them make, but I never missed a movie while I was growing up.

The minute I got to be fourteen, I started going out with the girls I went to school with. Some of them later became famous, under the different names the studios gave them. We'd all go to the Coconut Grove every Friday, all through my teen years, and dance with these girls, who would later become famous. Joan Crawford was one, and my main girl's younger sister, Gretchen, became Loretta Young. Carole Lombard was originally Jane Peters . . . her brother Stu is a good friend of mine. Anyway, it was a lot of fun and excitement at that time.

As I got to be a little older, I worked in my father's manufacturing business—first in the factory, to learn what work was really like (according to Dad), then in the sales department, and so on. He manufactured roofing and waterproofing materials. He later sold it to Johns Manville when I told him I wouldn't be going into the business—I wanted to be a writer.

All my friends were set on going to Stanford, but I decided on Dartmouth because it was in an area of the country which I never had seen. In those days, in Los Angeles, we would drive out all over—the desert, Tahoe, Yosemite, Del Monte, and lots of other places, all of them terrific. People really did go out for drives . . . the roads weren't very good, the traffic wasn't bad, and it was just great fun. But at seventeen, going east and seeing all the things I had just read about—Niagara Falls, New York, and the grand tour just getting there—it was wonderful.

At Dartmouth, they had a new movie every day and I don't think I ever missed one while I was there, unless I was sick or out of town. Because New York was the main thing and my father shortly had an office there, I would go to the big city a great deal. There I met the *real* stage. I had seen a lot of stage productions in Los Angeles, but it was nothing compared to movies for me. However, when I went to Broadway to see Fred Allen, Jack Donahue, and all the others, it was so fabulous, it absolutely seized me. And the summer after my freshman year when I was in London, the British stage was better than the American—it was just unbelievable! I saw everything I could there.

So now I had both the stage and movies, and was still reading like a fiend. At that time, I used to read a book a day. I still do read, and today I also have the whole Modern Library series of books—practically everything ever written of stature. You may not have the discipline, as you get older, to make yourself reread some of the more complex parts, but you don't lose the joy of reading, that's for sure.

After Dartmouth, I had the admission papers to go to the Harvard Business School, but I didn't go. After all, if I was going to be a writer what good would that do? It probably would have been a wise thing to do, careerwise, because anyone who went there was considered to be an expert in financial affairs.

I intended to stay in New York, was even on the list of writers for *The March of Time,* but I got sick and went back to California. Shortly thereafter I got a job in the radio business, which was just starting. It was with CBS. I was a writer, but within a week or two, as happened in those days, I was a reporter, writer, announcer, a comic, you name it—everything except a musician or technician, which were unionized.

We had a big staff, with Raymond Paige and a forty-piece orchestra, and about twenty performing artists on the payroll. This was because in those days, no records were allowed and there were no tapes, so everything was live. Live repeats cost too much in the first days of radio for the advertisers to pay for them. Within two or three years, however, radio exploded so powerfully that live repeats took the place of the nighttime programming we had to do for the Western network. Eastern programming ended at ten in the evening, which was only seven here, so we had to fill those three hours with live repeats.

In the depression years, I was hardly affected because I was just beginning in the radio business. And radio was going through the roof . . . '32, '33, '34 were really boom years in that field. In any other field I would surely have taken a beating, along with everyone else.

A great experiences, as I used to tell the guys later at NBC, was that we did every form of material that I was ever to see again—even in TV many years later. We were doing all that in radio in the early thirties. Part of that, of course, was the news. I covered the Long Beach earthquake of '33 as the first major event of that type. So you could understand why radio was so explosive. A simple thing that many in the business still don't quite dope out—radio didn't become terribly important just from the famous names, like Amos and Andy and others. The most important aspect for people was that never before had they been able to sit at home and be at the place of their choice . . . the theater, the sports event, political events, the comedy or story hours, and so on. The news, a great deal of it in the early days was a summary from AP or UPI, which we would just read—an announcer, rather than a specialized guy.

In fact, later at San Francisco, where I was the program director, we had a very good newsman named Ed Fitzgerald, who had been a war correspondent and was well known. He became even more famous later, because he and Pegeen Fitzgerald did a show in New York forever. When Ed left for New York and I was looking around for another newsman, I did the news myself for six or eight weeks. There was nothing to it in those days, I'd just tear the yellow sheets off the Teletype machine and read it until my watch said it was time to close. I never enjoyed it much, but I did it.

You know, even when I started in radio in '32, we knew television was coming. We had an experimental television station on the roof in Los Angeles and I'd go up and look at it once in a while—at the old movies they were playing. Movies showed what you could do if you weren't stuck in one location. But as I learned in the theater, it's one thing to do a marvelous story or comedy in movies, but it's another thing to get the "element x," which is *performance*. That's where you get the audience in the palm of your hand. And most of our radio shows were just that. In other words, when we had the big orchestras and the Merrymakers in Los Angeles, or the Blue Money Jamboree in San Francisco (a two-hour show with Meredith Wilson as conductor), we would have an audience of five hundred people. We were performing for *that* audience—the show was good if they liked it, it wasn't good if they didn't. It was *never* played for the home. That's something some people still don't understand.

Later, I was offered a marvelous job in Honolulu, to do the news there at more money than I was making as station manager in San Francisco. Well, I resigned and then went down to the shipping office, where I bought a ticket to *New York* instead. Eventually, I joined the Young and Rubicam advertising agency, where my first big show was the Fred Allen show. He was my god and my favorite—as he was on the stage. He was my friend all his life and it was great fun. At Y&R, I became program manager, and after a few years there I went over to one of our clients, American Tobacco Company.

It was an opportunity to do things that would further advance my knowledge and career. Seeing things from the client side made me a more knowledgeable ad man, with an understanding of what really works. It gave me confidence for what I was to do in the future at NBC. While at American Tobacco, the war years intervened and I was involved for four and a half years. But before Pearl Harbor I went to run all the radio in the Western Hemisphere for Nelson Rockefeller, who had been a classmate in Dartmouth. Incidentally, I ran all four of his campaigns for governor and was even his consultant for vice president.

After Pearl Harbor, although I was deferred, I said the hell with that and I went to join the navy. I was a sailor, had a fifty-six-foot yawl—*Glory Days.* I was a bachelor, and doing very well in my career. In the navy, I had a ship as an exec, and then as captain for three years in the South Atlantic—Fourth Fleet, Destroyer Squadron Nine. It was the best job I ever had, I just loved it. You know, there's nothing like being captain of a ship, nothing—not even being general of the army. But I came back to get a bigger ship and was transferred, instead, to what we called the Y and Army. This was the Armed Forces Radio Service in California. I knew most of the guys who were there, some having worked for me, and these were the top writers for Bob Hope, Jack Benny, Burns and Allen, Fred Allen, and all the guys who were Y&R stars. So this was home for me and I was back into production again, with a stopwatch in my hand. We were doing the "Command Performance" shows, then the VE-day show, the VJ-day show, and all that. But as soon as the war was over, I went right back to my old job at American Tobacco and then, a few years later, to the Y&R ad agency.

Of course, my time at NBC is the most well known because of creating those different shows. I created "The Today Show," with Dave Garroway; "The Home Show," with Hugh Downs and Arlene Francis; and also "The Tonight Show," with Steve Allen. The first show I really got going in '49 was "Broadway Open House," with Jerry Lester and Morey Amsterdam. It was a runaway hit and proved we could get nighttime ratings, even at midnight.

When that show started to slow down and fall apart, I set "The Tonight Show" as a different format. I wanted to make the "magazine concept" more and more available to smaller advertisers so they could feel the power of the TV medium and give us the support to make it grow faster.

Actually, the thing that really made this plan work was the "Show of Shows." Everyone was against the plan . . . the clients were against it; the agencies were against it; the networks were against it; and the lawyers were against it. I sold that program in *minutes,* something that had never been done before! In the early days we had bought spot radio in minutes, but that hadn't ever been done in television. Programs like Jack Benny and Milton Berle were single-sponsor shows.

I had asked Max Liebman to do all of Saturday night for NBC—the whole thing—and we ended up with a ninety-minute program, the "Show of Shows." We bought a theater and reestablished it as a studio—but it was still a theater! We presented a Broadway revue every Saturday night. It was better than most of the shows on Broadway, and it was for nothing! Big orchestra, dancers, Robert Merrill and Marguerite Piazza from the Met, and other popular singers. And, of course, Sid Caesar, Imogene Coca, Carl Reiner, Howard Morris, and a great list of writers. It was a fabulous show.

Because it was such a runaway hit, the advertisers suddenly started to say, "Hold on, maybe this idea of selling program time in minutes isn't such a bad idea after all." But I was already ahead of them with the new format of "The Tonight Show," to be sold in minutes. The "Show of Shows" was an expensive one but as soon as it became a hit, we resold it for thirty-nine weeks—and the summer show also.

With that money, I went out and hired all the guys for the "Comedy Hour" . . . that was Bob Hope, Fred Allen, Eddie Cantor, and Martin and Lewis, who were really hot then. The "Comedy Hour" was sold to General Motors and Colgate. After that sale, I set up the "All Star Revue," which was the same show exactly—but on a Wednesday night. That one had Jimmy Durante as the big hit, Ed Wynn, Jack Carson, and Danny Thomas.

These were big, explosive, successful shows, and it just

skyrocketed the medium far beyond. But most of all, it also meant that my war was over, as far as persuading people that we could change the form and it would work. Comedy, every night, was at eight o'clock—after the news—because the adults would fight the kids for the set. And since the kids wouldn't mind comedy, that was the time for the "Comedy Hour," the "All Star Revue," Groucho Marx, and other comedy presentations. It was very, very successful.

I always had difficulty with General Sarnoff, who was a "hardware man" and knew nothing about broadcasting. He didn't like it and thought advertising was childish. He'd say, "What kind of a living is that?" Bobby, his son, was a close friend of mine and the reason I really went to NBC. All my friends told me I would never be able to work with him, he's an egomaniac, and they said I shouldn't go there. Some of the Wall Street guys had a saying, "If General Sarnoff drops dead tonight, RCA hits a hundred in the morning." (RCA was ten dollars a share then.) And the reason was that his labs in Princeton, all through the war, had been doing advanced work on solid state, radar, communications, satellites, cybernetics, and all the things that were going to come along in the next twenty years. They had a big lead but lost it. Instead, the General bought a stove company and an icebox company—he didn't quite see it, in spite of the fact that his name became synonymous with inventing.

His main thrust was the hardware . . . he used to say "the pipes through which everything will flow." He didn't want to get into the troubles of show business, he hated show business. He never quite understood . . . thought it was awful that guys like Jack Benny and Fred Allen would make more money than he did.

I brought Dave Garroway in from Chicago to do "The Today Show" and I also brought in Hugh Downs from Chicago to do "The Home Show." The best show, really, of all of them was "Wide Wide World." I had developed that for AT&T, mainly to make them work hard on what I knew we could get quickly—the satellite transmission. A friend, Arthur Clark, invented it in '47 and told me about it. So we knew we were going to have the recorder, the satellite, and all the hardware developments. We knew they were coming but couldn't tell how fast they would get there. General Motors bought "Wide Wide World." If AT&T had bought it instead, it would have made a difference. In those days, the way it was set up at AT&T, there were sixteen vice presidents and if fifteen said yes and one said no, that was it.

On the first "Wide Wide World" show we picked up from Havana, shooting by microwave to an airplane and then back down to Miami, and sent it on. We picked up that marvelous Mexican comic, Cantinflas, during the comedy bullfight in Tijuana. Then we had a Canadian pickup and then American pickups of all kinds. It was to use the TV medium to take the American people out to see the wonderlands of the world . . . the badlands, the unusual places, the highest, the lowest, the human interest, and all that. Now, of course, we can go everywhere and we really do.

As far as the stars at that time, there were two groups. One was the entertainers from the stage, the great Broadway and vaudeville performers—like Milton Berle, who was already at NBC with Texaco. It was the guys who had been performing all those years and knew how to control an audience—make it do what they wanted. Guys like Bob Hope, George Burns, Jack Benny, and Fred Allen. For radio, of course, we had to change some things, but they were still working to an audience, just like they had been doing all their life. In radio, they always, always had an audience. There were a few story shows that didn't need an audience, but "Amos 'n' Andy" was the only comedy show that worked well without one. And, of course, we followed the same format when I used them all in television—the audience came along with them.

The next group of emerging entertainers were new, but not brand-new. For example, there was Sid Caesar, who had been in *Make Mine Manhattan* on the Broadway state.

And Martin and Lewis, who were working at the Copaca-
bana Club. It's funny, though, all of them that I used in TV
had been fired in radio. The only one who was working was
Bob Hope. Bob on our "Comedy Hour" did six or seven
shows a year, while most of the others were scheduled once
a month—that was the plan. Hope shared his time with
Bobby Clark, a Broadway performer who didn't quite make
it.

With news, on radio, there was interconnection so we
could go to London, Paris, Mexico City . . . we couldn't do
that on television. But with TV we had all night, so we
could do on our morning show "The Today Show"—anything that happened the night before. Everyone would be
watching "The Today Show" because they knew we would
cover it . . . that was our main job. In the meantime, however, on the day when nothing happens—what's the show?
Well, we got Jack Lescoulie to be funny, did some sports,
we set up certain news forums that could work every day
whether the news was good, bad, or nonexistent. In a sense
it was a morning magazine. And "The Home Show" did
things that would interest women, competing with the
women's magazines.

Then there were the "spectaculars." I called them that
although many of the critics and the people at NBC had no
idea that *spectacular* was an adjective. Later, when I left,
they dropped that name and called them "specials." Actually, it was Max Liebman who said, "Look, I understand
what you're saying, but I'm not going to call my shows
'spectaculars' because I know every critic will say, well, it
wasn't *that* spectacular." And many of them did.

But the spectaculars let us do other things. Seeing the
news of Rex Harrison dying yesterday brought this to
mind. He had, back then, a good movie made by Alexander
Korda. And I made a deal with Korda to put it on "Producer's Showcase"—which might save all the advertising
money needed for its opening. The "Showcase" represented the best of everything . . . drama, ballet, opera, and

movies. No matter how big a rating the movie got, three-fourths of the country wouldn't have seen it, and if everybody talks about it, then the ad money is saved. Well, it worked, and we did two or three more for him.

And there were other projects that went the same way. Humphrey Bogart, with Henry Fonda and Lauren Bacall, in *The Petrified Forest*. Mary Martin did *Peter Pan* . . . it set records that weren't broken for twenty years, in terms of size of audience for Broadway shows. But in selling "Producer's Showcase," I also said Margot Fonteyn is going to be dancing *Sleeping Beauty* with the Royal Ballet for ninety minutes and we'd have the great stars from the Met via Sol Hurok's "Night at the Met," as well as other serious events. Well, the clients almost jumped out of their skins, particularly the agency men, who were more cowardly than their clients. "We'll buy the top shows," they said. "We'll buy *Lady in the Dark* with Ann Sothern, but we don't want the ballet."

I said, "You don't have to buy 'Producer's Showcase,' but if you want the series, these are the shows. You buy it or you don't buy it." So they bought it! And the Royal Ballet danced *The Sleeping Beauty* for ninety minutes . . . no drop in the Nielsen minute-by-minute audience. The audience count was *thirty million* in 1955—thirty million!

It made obvious the cultural revolution we were going through—it made it very, very clear. And I've been working with Lou Harris ever since on that, in trying to make people understand that we can really make television cover *all* of the performing arts and theater, as well as the movies and so on.

Well, anyway, "Producer's Showcase" was one series that did use some of the spectaculars I came up with. There was another series for Oldsmobile that featured a big ballet from England, and then there was Dave Garroway, with a huge cast, doing *Babes in Toyland*—people still talk about that one. Once again, it was the idea of letting people see the arts at their best, and the artists worked even harder than usual because television was so new. It was great! It's still the best part of TV when they do this type of show—they don't do it as much as I did, but they still do some of it today.

After leaving NBC, I went back to the agency field and was responsible for everything outside the U.S. for McCann Erickson. I traveled overseas a great deal and loved it. We already had offices in many countries and clients like Coca-Cola, Standard Oil, and General Motors who were operating internationally. And it was also nice to get away from the radio and TV groups for a while, even though I ran those areas for the McCann agencies in the U.S. as well. We did some good things throughout those years, especially the monthly spectaculars for Westinghouse.

After about five years of that, we formed Subscription Television, Inc., in 1963, and I went in as chief executive. In actuality, this was the beginning of pay-TV. Although sports and movies were the main ingredients, it was important to come up with an overall plan. So I laid out a program which offered three services . . . three channels, two-way. One channel was new movies and pop stuff; the second was coverage of the opera, the concert hall, the ballet, and the performing arts; and the third channel would be sports and special-interest things, like the world of bridge, and so on. Our initial limited market consisted of two areas in California, with 100,000 homes. Fifty percent of the people that we approached in the first year sent in the money to get the service. But the movie theater owners and the broadcasters put up a lot of money and ran an awful campaign against us. I believed it was illegal, and I wasn't worried about it initially. I was sure the Supreme Court would throw it off the California ballot. As it happened this time, they didn't, and I'm not going to go into all the reasons and political fears that were responsible for that decision.

The legal battles went on from '63 to '77. And it wasn't because we didn't try to make it go faster, it was because the "evil ones" were able to legal maneuver their way onto a

different course. And we did win! It *was* illegal to do what
they did. But the 300 million in damages? They didn't have
to pay it because of some Superior Court decision in 1918
between the truckers and the railroads—or some such rul-
ing. Pretty awful, that's what it was! You know, they all
knew pay-TV would eventually happen, but if they could
stop us for ten or fifteen years, then it would stop everyone.
So although we had gotten such a great response from the
public way back then, we were still put out of business.

After struggling to have Subscription TV, I also went
back into the programming business . . . sold a few programs and almost began a fourth network with our Prime
Network idea, but the time-slot availability was a problem.
Rather than going back to the agency field, I did a lot of
part-time consulting. As far as new ideas and innovative
programs, it seemed a hard sell because people were generally afraid to put their necks out.

One of my great faults, which I admit, is that I keep
thinking of something new that is so exciting I kind of forget about the getting-it-to-work part. I think everyone will
understand how wonderful this is and I won't have any
trouble with it. Wrong, wrong! The idea is really only the
beginning.

I remember when I first came back to New York, after a
year in Europe. I must have read a paperback everywhere
I went, including North Africa. I got my dad to introduce
me to a couple of top publishers in New York. We got
together and I told them about my travels and how I was
absolutely convinced of one thing . . . that what this country needed, with the depression starting, was a quarter
paperback book. Well, they sat me down and told me how
the book business was set up and why the quarter book
would never, ever, ever work in the United States. What
they meant, of course, was that the one way the book business was set up, *it* would not work with a quarter book. But
if you took it the other way around . . . would the public
buy a quarter book if it was offered to them? I tried to

explain that but they just shrugged and said I didn't understand the publishing business.

Another thing I did after Europe was to go up to a paper company where I knew the head man because of Dad's business. I told him about a new product (based on my travels) that could be very desirable in many parts of the country . . . a paper toilet seat cover! He said it wouldn't work.

Of course, both those ideas did work later. I spent a lot of my life coming up with new ideas that I was sure would work but nobody would agree to. It's a case of going out and doing it yourself! But only if you have the power to do it yourself and if you really believe in it will it work. Perhaps that's how it was as head honcho at NBC and the ad agencies, where some of my ideas really worked out.

You know, because of my stature in communications over the years, I kept getting requests all the time . . . come to this; send money to this; can we use your name; and this and that, and so on. Somewhere along the line I decided you need *one cause*, and try to work hard enough in that cause so you could say no to everybody. That may be a bit selfish, but nonetheless I decided that was a good idea.

The American Heart Association, at that time, changed from being a scientific society into being a cause as well. It was already a big operation, and I went with them because I could get many of the stars to plug the association and to say things about diet, fitness, and overall health. I could actually sell the public on changing habits that would benefit each and every one of them. I worked with them for fifteen years and was chairman of the board the last three years.

Later on I met Jerry Lewis, just when he had decided that the telethon should really be pursued. This was twenty-five years ago and I went with the Muscular Dystrophy Association at that time. It was not the same as the Heart Association . . . it was more of a managment position rather than a writing one. And I must say we've had great success. Over those many years I've been first vice president, then president of MDA; the chairman of the executive committee for ten years, and now, vice chairman of the committee. This year will be the twenty-fifth anniversary of the telethons and there's also plenty of progress on the research front, with some exciting breakthroughs that were announced at today's meeting.

I've stayed with MDA all these years because it's been a wonderful and satisfying experience. It's important for people to realize that if they have one thing they really devote time to and it's a very valuable cause which contributes to others, it will always be better for *them* in their own lives.

You may have heard people congratulating me today on our newest grandchild—that's Sigourney's first and we're very excited about it. Our son, Trajan, has four children and we enjoy them all. A lot of people have mentioned Sigourney and her work; she certainly has had some good ones in recent years—*Ghostbusters II, Aliens, Working Girl,* and *Gorillas in the Mist.* We are proud of her.

Although she's had some exposure to the entertainment business, she also comes by this through her mother. Liz (Elizabeth Inglin) was with the Royal Academy, back in the days of Vivien Leigh and a lot of the other well-knowns. She was a big star on the London stage and came over to New York to do *Angel Street (Gaslight).* It was the beginning of the war and there was some mix-up, so she did a couple of other theatrical shows. Warner Brothers hired her and she did a few things in California, but didn't like it very much. She returned to New York and did some more shows. By this time we were married and I was off to war.

By the way, I remain an idea man. In the world of ideas, the fact that you get older doesn't hurt . . . in fact, you start to think better and better all the time. I should know, I'm still doing it.

June 3, 1990

"Writing is what I most wanted to do." A simple state-ment—a difficult task—but Phyllis Whitney kept at it and won big. Her seventy-second book has been completed, and she can't wait to start the research for her seventy-third. Over 50 million copies of her books have been issued in the United States and eighteen foreign countries. Thirty-four are adult novels of mystery suspense, and not one has gone out of print.

If she hadn't drawn a map, I would never have found her home in the foothills of the Blue Ridge Mountains. We talked in her work area—a large, uncluttered, efficient-looking room that also housed all her many editions and numerous awards. A few years ago she received the Grand Master Award, Mystery Writers of America, for Lifetime Achievement. In 1989 she received two more such awards, the Agatha from Malice Domestic, and another from Romance Writers of America. Her earlier mysteries for young readers received two Edgar awards from the Mystery Writers of America.

*   *   *

THE "A" in my name stands for Ayame, which is the Japanese word for iris. How do I have a Japanese name? well, that's part of a romatic story, a family romance. My father and mother had gone to school together in Cleveland, Ohio, and they were the typical high school sweethearts who would eventually marry. That is, until one of those lover's quarrels intervened and they stopped speaking to each other.

Then an actor-playwright with his own company of players came to town. My mother married the actor and went off to appear on the stage herself in England and the Scandinavian countries. Well, it was not a happy marriage because the actor was pretty much of a drinker, and years

Phyllis A. Whitney

later he died of alcoholism. In the meantime, my father, who was nursing a broken heart, had gone out to the Orient, which he had always wanted to see. When he somehow heard that my mother's husband had died, he sent her the fare from London to Yokohama, Japan—boat fare, of course—to come there and marry him. He said, "Take it or leave it." So she came, and I was born in Yokohama in 1903. Perhaps that's one of the reasons why I always have some romance in my suspense stories.

Until I was fifteen, I lived in Japan, China, and the Philippines. As far as the different lifestyles in those areas go, my great desire was to see America. Riding in rickshaws, the foods, languages, and customs were things I just accepted as they existed there—it was an everyday thing. With racial tensions, it was not so much between the whites and the Japanese as it was that both races were down on the Eurasians. They were the ones who suffered. My mother was always against prejudice, and she planted that trait in me. When we left Yokohama, we went to Manila. I was about seven then and was enrolled in the American school there. An interesting sidelight—some of the Americans who went to that school the same time I did now live in California. They have a little club there; one member who read my books wrote to me about it, and that's enabled me to keep in touch with some of the girls I remembered. Our family lived in Manila for about seven years.

My father had been in the shipping business in Japan, but he and my mother wanted to start a hotel, so when we went to Manila, they did open and run a hotel. It wasn't a success, and later he went to work for a Manila hotel, and finally to a Hankow, China, hotel. There were no schools in Hankow so I went to a missionary school in Kuling, high up in the mountains of China. There were no automobile roads and we went up in sedan chairs. We were carried up a very steep path, and I can still remember swinging out over gorges as we went around the sharp curves. All in all, though, it was a wonderful experience. One of the missionary teachers gave us very good assignments and she liked what I wrote—that acclaim went to my head and I've been writing ever since.

My father died in Hankow, and my mother and I went to America. We had no money, and she took a job as housekeeper for the grandmother of a family we knew in Yokohama. After that we went to San Antonio, where my mother died, and I went to live with an aunt in Chicago. During those years I thought I was going to be a dancer. I danced quite a lot and even taught dancing in San Antonio. However, in high school in Chicago my thoughts turned back to writing because I realized I would never be a professional dancer. Also, I couldn't resist making up stories and putting them down on paper. My thoughts were not focused on being famous and rich—all I wanted was to sell *one* story.

One thing about beginning writers, and that included me—we all start stories and then can't finish them. It's easy to begin but it's hard work to finish a story. Eventually, though, I learned something about my craft and began to sell my writing. After high school I went to work in the Chicago Public Library—no money, no college! At the end of one summer there, however, I was told, "It's doubtful you will ever make a good librarian. Many times it's been difficult to *find* books you've put away." My head was just too full of stories. They did suggest that I get a job in the book section of a department store, and that proved to be good experience. I used to see huge piles of books come in from some famous author and I'd think, oh, how wonderful to be the author with all those books. Now *I* have piles of books.

As far as getting a better focus on writing because of working in bookstores, I have to say *everything* gives you a focus. Anything is grist for the writer's mill, any experience. The manager of the book department was very unpleasant, and years later I put her in my second book, I got even with her for the way she treated me! I don't usually use real people in my stories, but it was good therapy to get my feelings on paper.

After a few years of writing, I sold my first story to the *Chicago Daily News*—their magazine section. I got a check for thirty-five dollars, it was great—I slept that night with the check under my pillow. Then I started to write for the Sunday school papers and sold a few more stories. I tried writing for the "slick" magazines in the early years—*Ladies' Home Journal*, *The Saturday Evening Post*, and so on. I wasn't good enough, and the stories all came right back. Finally, I discovered the pulp paper magazines, the love story category—*Love Story*, *All Story*, *Thrilling Love*, etc. I wrote some three hundred stories and about one hundred sold, while the rest went into the wastebasket because they weren't any good. I did sell one story to *Weird Tales*, which was actually a more literary magazine than the others. I was still learning, and I really wasn't a short story writer.

All this short story writing took years of effort while I was still working in bookstores and libraries. As soon as I came home from work, I wrote evenings, weekends, whenever I could. I wasn't a very good housekeeper; I never did care about things like that. My husband at that time didn't want me to write, and that didn't make for a very successful marriage. We had gone to high school together; he sat behind me in geometry class. Eventually, though, after twenty years we did divorce. We probably married too young, and when people grow in different directions, it's difficult to stay together.

I didn't have a short story mentality, and I wasn't happy about what I was doing. I thought I'd like to try a book, but I knew better than to try to write an adult novel. I felt I'd be lost there, so I tried writing a book for teenagers. We were in the later years of the depression, and I wrote about kids who found a way to make some money in those times. The book was called *A Place for Ann*. After three rejections it was accepted by Houghton Mifflin. It was fun writing for teenagers, although I discovered that it took skill to write for that market. When I wrote stories for the Sunday school papers, I used memories from my life in the Orient. The love story magazines, however, never wanted locales that were out of this country—they've learned a lot since then. Basically, you always use what you know, or you find out. You don't have to write about what you know, but if you don't know, then find out.

My first adult novel in 1943 was called *Red Is for Murder.* It earned about eight hundred dollars. There were good reviews but it didn't sell. So I thought crime doesn't pay *enough,* which is the slogan of Mystery Writers of America. I decided not to write more adult books, and I didn't until about a dozen years later when *The Quicksilver Pool* was published. However, *Red Is for Murder* was reissued some twenty years later when my name became known. It was published in paperback as *The Red Carnelian,* and it's been earning money ever since—about thirty-five thousand dollars. That isn't much compared with my other books. But, for *that* book! It's still in print, and another publisher has just brought out a new edition of it. From eight hundred dollars to thirty-five thousand dollars—that's not bad!

The Quicksilver Pool was a period novel set on Staten Island during the Civil War. When I tried to sell it to two of my juvenile book publishers, they turned it down. I like to think that they were sorry later. I did sell it to Appleton, Century, Crofts—a publisher long gone. From that point on I did two books a year—one juvenile, one adult. Then I began writing juvenile mysteries regularly. My earlier juvenile books related to careers and job stories for teenagers. With the mysteries, however, I dropped down to the ten-to-twelve-year-olds, and those are still in print. They're coming back in new paperbacks shortly.

We had a wonderful writer's organization in Chicago, the Chicago Fiction Guild. Every young writer should belong to a group like this. At one time, I invited a scientist who had written a fascinating biography to speak to our group. We became friends after that and because of his interest in young writers, he helped some of us. When one of my early books was published, he saw to it that I had an author's party at Marshall Field's. Unknown writers don't have parties like that, but he had tipped off the book buyer and she gave me a party. "O.E.," as we called the author, sent in people from his office to buy the books so I would be supported.

Later, when the *Chicago Sun* was looking for a children's book editor, he suggested that I apply. I felt I had no background or education, and they would never take me. He said, "I've spoken to the book editor. Just go in and see him." I went in timidly and was given three books to take home and review. The editor was trying others as well. I took home my three books, and although I had never written reviews before, I was a fiction writer and I knew how to interest a reader. I apparently caught my editor's attention and became children's book editor for the *Chicago Sun*. I wrote for the paper for three or four years before I moved to New York. Out of New York, I also reviewed children's books for the *Philadelphia Inquirer*—for about a year.

While I was working for the *Sun* in Chicago, I was sent to New York twice a year to call on all the children's book editors. Fortunately, they seemed to like me, and I was able to write sound reviews. This experience was good for me in many ways. It was also a wonderful adventure, going to the big city twice a year as representative of the *Chicago Sun*. It was still wartime and on one of those trips to New York, I went into the dining car for dinner. A man came in from the opposite end of the car and the waiter put us at the same table. One of those happy accidents—four years later we were married! After that it became complicated, since my daughter later married one of *his* sons. At least we could share the same grandchildren.

Being a children's book reviewer helped me in my own writing since I enjoyed reading all those books the publishers sent me. My daughter grew up with wonderful books around her—literally, since they were in piles everywhere.

My own writing was greatly enhanced by a teacher of writing whom I met in Chicago. Frederic Nelson Litten had published many books for boys, and he taught juvenile writing at Northwestern University. Mr. Litten held seminars once a week for beginning writers who were selling and needed more knowledge of their craft. I learned a great deal about the techniques of writing. Later, under Mr. Litten, I taught juvenile writing for a year at Northwestern. In New York, I applied to New York University and taught a night class in juvenile writing. Over the years I've written three books on writing.

It often takes a long time to earn one's living by writing. In New York, I reviewed books, acted as a reader for a publisher, taught writing classes—did everything I could to bring in enough money to support my writing. I had written eight novels, none of which had gone into paperback because the editors claimed that nobody would read those books. Finally, one editor who noticed how much his mother enjoyed *Rebecca* started to wonder if there were any other books in that genre. He found my novel called *Thunder Heights* and published it in paper very cautiously. He called it a gothic, the first of a series of gothics he planned. The book sold well, and a number of paperback publishers started to bid for my books. This was in the 1950s and was only the beginning for me.

I kept records for a long time which listed the income from jobs other than writing and the income from published writing. When the latter finally overcame the former, I could stop all other activity and concentrate solely on writing. It's important never to give up. I took the rejections for years, but I knew I had to tell stories, and I hoped that I would learn to tell better stories. One other thing I learned was how to take criticism! It's necessary to take criticism with your *mind* and not with your emotions.

I had to learn the hard way about criticism. I wanted to write about race relations in a Chicago suburb. When *Willow Hill* was written, I gave it to my writing teacher, and he told me that I was on a soapbox. Well, I just fell apart, like any beginner, but I pulled myself together and wrote the whole book over. In doing *Willow Hill* over, I let the characters feel the emotions, and I told the story through the characters. That book is still in print, on and off. It won first place in a contest and sold more copies than any juvenile book I've done.

In the adult field, I write mystery and suspense, but not detective stories. I do a lot of research for my novels and a great deal of travel. Often I've used the same setting for both an adult novel and a book for young readers. People like to read about places and ideas that are somewhat out of the ordinary and enable them to travel in their imagination. Mystery stories lend themselves to complicated plots and suspense situations that keep the reader involved and, also, entertained. I don't want to write something "more profound" in the sense that it's difficult to understand. At the same time, I want to continue writing suspense themes that explore contemporary issues—even the New Age things that are so provocative today.

I am fortunate in that I happen to write something that is popular with the readers. I like to write the kind of book that I like to read. I don't think some readers have been upset because I have written recently about parapsychology and the psychic. I hope that most of my readers are willing to be open.

In *Singing Stones,* I went to Waynesboro, here in Virginia, to a man who regresses people into past lives. I wrote this into the book just as it happened, except that I added a few plot details to move the story along. No doubt, I'll find out eventually whether reincarnation is an actuality. I did this for my characters and my story. *Rainbow in the Mist* is another example. It has a psychic character, a woman who could foresee terrible events that were going to take place. In my new book, *Woman Without a Past,* there will be some aspects of channeling, and in my next book there will be a healer. What is also interesting is that in my own home area in the foothills of Virginia's Blue Ridge Mountains, there are psychics, healers, channelers. This has been a whole new world for me—an exciting one.

Tomorrow, I will send my new book, *Woman Without a Past,* off to my agent. Right now my head is full of the next one. We've just been on a trip to Virginia's Northern Neck, which I had never known about. It is a strip of Virginia between the Papahanock River and the Potomac, with a toe in the Chesapeake. Out in the bay is Tangier Island, which will be fascinating to write about. There are about eight hundred inhabitants, all of English descent, and they still speak Elizabethan English. It's not like anything else in America. A new book is exciting to explore, and when someone asks if I have any hobbies, I can only say mine is visiting and researching new areas as backgrounds for my books.

I enjoy writing each day, and there's no thought of retirement. Of course, sitting at the typewriter each day means I have to exercise, watch my diet, and maintain a sensible schedule. I grew up in the Philippines and I was sick much of the time. Even in my twenties I always seemed to have ailments, and there were several operations. Although I wasn't in good health, I always worked, but it was a struggle. Then one day when I was in my fifties, I heard Carlton Frederick's voice on the radio and he was describing *my* symptoms. Hypoglycemia was not a popular ailment at the time and nobody had ever told me what was wrong, but as soon as I got off sugar and coffee and started on a different diet, the fatigue and depression were gone. I decided this was something I wanted to know more about, and I began a study of nutrition. Now I take many vitamins and food supplements, by way of prevention. I can't be as strong and vigorous as I might have been if I had learned all this when I was young. Basically, I have *vitality.* I don't have physical strength, but I can summon vitality to do what I want.

Of course, I have a zest for living—we all need that. I remember an interviewer asking me where I got my enthusiasm. I suppose my genes have played a part. At the same time, a writer must be capable of being as excited as a child and not lose that child's wonder of every new thing that comes along. If we can be excited, we can stay young. First we need to do something new and different. Then we get interested and the excitement comes. For a writer, there are endless subjects to investigate and write about.

This holds true for the nonwriter as well. Be interested, get excited. The whole world is out there to keep you interested and keep your spirit young.

September 16, 1990

EPILOGUE

PHYLLIS WHITNEY'S concluding words say it all: "Be interested, get excited. The whole world is out there to keep you interested and keep your spirit young."

They are more than just words, they are meaningful goals for all of us to achieve—at any age! Yes, advancing age does have the tendency to slow us down physically and gradually rob us of our once-joyous strengths. Our previously normal, but strenuous, activities tend to lessen, and limiting disabilities may often occur. But none of these are mandatory signals for anyone to quit on life! Or to bow to the well-meaning social pressures around you that automatically label you as old, dependent, passive, and so on.

All the participants in this book have retained their "vitality," the power to keep on living with mental and/or physical vigor. Age has nothing to do with this *energy of interests*. One has only to peruse any weekly newsmagazine or schedule of television programming to fully realize Whitney's words—"the whole world is out there to keep you interested." It is almost impossible to believe that among this overabundance one would not find something to stimulate one's interest. Consider . . . people, crime, politics, world affairs, behavior, health, the environment, sports, cinema, music, opera, design, television, theater, art, books, viewpoints, careers, hobbies, business, international relations, and on and on. It seems inexhaustible. If all that blows your mind, try looking to your immediate surroundings—the same type of subjects and interests are all around you, *localized* to your own vicinity.

But *you* have to actively participate. It matters not if the involvement is physical or solely mental—just don't quit on life. Don't for a moment think this relates only to those who have entered the magic octogenarian circle. On the contrary, there are many who haven't even achieved a senior status who have already retreated from living life.

308

Plus a very large group who have prematurely wilted and succumbed to that popular, blared-about, thoroughly overworked "this is the age of youth" syndrome. Of course, youth will have its turn . . . but make sure you keep your own space and plenty of running-around room.

Give a thought to some of the words you have just read: "Never give up, just hang in there." "If you lose interest, you yourself are lost!" "[Getting] older doesn't hurt . . . you start to think better." "What you get out of life is what you put in."

Not too long ago, the Associated Press reported that Gian Carlo Menotti, the Pulitzer Prize–winning musical impresario, had been hospitalized for exhaustion. A few months later Menotti, who was busily preparing two future arts festivals, commented on that episode. "My doctor told me I had an incurable disease—I'm eighty years old." He continued, "Now instead of two glasses of wine, I drink one, and I go to bed at 1:00 A.M. instead of 2:00 A.M.—but I still have two festivals to do."

Yes, you do slow down a bit at eightysomething. But there's no doubt that Spoleto, Italy, and Charlestown, South Carolina, will once again enjoy Menotti's summer festivals.

All in all, there's been a commonality of thoughts expressed by those who have been interviewed, and others who have activated themselves into their eighties. *Whatever* your age, if you want to continue to savor life—as tough as it may be—be curious, interested, and, above all, involved!